D1233093

17.50
A15709

The Atlantic World of Robert G. Albion

The Atlantic World of Robert G. Albion

Edited by BENJAMIN W. LABAREE

With Chapters by William A. Baker, Harold L. Burstyn, John H. Kemble, Benjamin W. Labaree, Archibald R. Lewis, Clark G. Reynolds, Jeffrey J. Safford, and Edward W. Sloan, III, and a Bibliography of the Works of Robert G. Albion by Joan Bentinck-Smith. Drawings by William A. Baker

Wesleyan University Press
Middletown, Connecticut

Copyright ©1975 by Wesleyan University

Frontispiece: Mystic Seaport Photo, by Mary Anne Stets

Library of Congress Cataloging in Publication Data

Main entry under title:

The Atlantic world of Robert G. Albion.

Festschrift for R. G. Albion.
"The writings of Robert G. Albion": p.
Includes index.
CONTENTS: Kemble, J. H. Maritime history in the age of Albion.—Lewis, A. R. The medieval background of American Atlantic maritime development.—Baker, W. A. Fishing under sail in the North Atlantic. [etc.]

1. Atlantic Ocean—Navigation—History—Addresses, essays, lectures. 2. Shipping—Atlantic Ocean—History—Addresses, essays, lectures. 3. Naval history—Addresses, essays, lectures. 4. Albion, Robert Greenhalgh, 1896- I. Albion, Robert Greenhalgh, 1896- II. Labaree, Benjamin Woods. III. Baker, William A.
VK18.A8 909′.09′6308 75-14329
ISBN 0-8195-4085-4

Manufactured in the United States of America

First edition

Contents

Preface

THE YEAR 1975 closes half a century since the publication in 1926 of Robert Greenhalgh Albion's classic study of the English navy's timber problem, *Forests and Sea Power*. To mark the occasion and to express our respect and affection for its author, several of his colleagues and former students offer this collection of essays. It is characteristic of the field that none of us is exclusively a maritime historian. Like Bob Albion himself, we began our respective careers with other specializations and have come to the subject of maritime history as an act of love rather than of duty. In keeping with this theme, we have written broadly based interpretative essays rather than more specialized articles. We have chosen as our common subject the Atlantic Ocean, primarily because that sea has engaged the attention of Bob himself throughout his long career. Furthermore, only the Atlantic among the world's oceans could bring together a medievalist, a naval architect, one colonial American historian and several of the national period, a historian of science, and a naval historian—to honor a man who made his own start as a scholar of English history. While recognizing the inevitable heterogeneity of any cooperatively written work, we hope that our common theme has given cohesiveness to the Atlantic world of Robert G. Albion.

New Year's Day
1975

BENJAMIN W. LABAREE
Editor

The Atlantic World of Robert G. Albion

CHAPTER ONE

Maritime History in the Age of Albion

WIDESPREAD INTEREST in maritime history developed with remarkable speed in the United States during the years immediately after World War I. This has continued to grow since then, forming a period in the history of concern for affairs of the sea both mercantile and naval which contrasts sharply with the previous years. There has been great expansion in scholarly research and writing on many aspects of the subject, courses in maritime and naval history have been established at the collegiate and graduate levels, and maritime museums both afloat and ashore have proliferated. As the days of the square-riggers faded into the past and travel by sea became less frequent except in pleasure cruise ships, general interest in the field grew apace. As has happened repeatedly before, the disappearance or threatened disappearance of a reality aroused nostalgia and a sometimes desperate effort to hold onto a past which seemed to be slipping away.

In this era of burgeoning maritime studies of all kinds, Robert Greenhalgh Albion has played an active and useful role in many ways. His research and writing have touched significantly on more facets of the American marine experience than those of any other man of his day, he has pioneered the teaching of maritime history to both undergraduate and graduate students, and he has given aid and wise counsel to many rising centers of marine research such as libraries and museums. It is the purpose of this essay to examine at some length these developments in the scholarly approach to maritime subjects, with special reference to Albion's part in them.

The years before 1920 were certainly not years in which the

American seagoing past was wholly neglected. The shelves of libraries bear witness to the work of many writers in the field. Naval history was more attractive than mercantile marine history, however, and one finds more books on the Revolution, the War of 1812, and the Civil War, as well as memoirs and biographies of naval figures, than works on other parts of the maritime spectrum. True, there were basic works like those of Arthur H. Clark, Alexander Starbuck, and J. H. Morrison, and perhaps the best general history of the American merchant marine yet written, that of W. L. Marvin, appeared in 1902; but important histories which have stood the test of time were few. While the reminiscences and surviving papers of American sailors from this period form an invaluable source of material for subsequent scholars, the paucity of truly historical writing on American maritime history prior to 1920 is notable. No professionally trained scholar wrote much mercantile marine history in these years, and there was not much more of this sort of scholarship directed to naval history either.

There was no formal instruction in maritime history available except for some attention to naval history at the United States Naval Academy and at the Naval War College. Naval and mercantile marine history were not wholly neglected in courses in United States history in colleges and universities or in general historical works, but the subject was not central in instruction or writing.

The only real maritime museum in the United States prior to 1930 was the Peabody Museum of Salem, and this was just emerging from a long phase when anthropology and natural history were emphasized over the maritime past which had been so central to the early work of the East India Marine Society. Other museums had marine rooms or displays of individual models or pictures, but none of them centered on the broad subject. The only old ship which had aroused wide support for her preservation was U.S.S. *Constitution,* and although there were enthusiasts who regretted the destruction of *Glory of the Seas* or the deterioration of U.S.S. *Constellation,* U.S.S. *Hartford,* and the yacht *America,* little or nothing was done about their preservation, let alone any proper restoration.

At this point, when commercial sailing vessels were becoming virtually things of the past and Americans were losing touch with many aspects of marine life, interest in maritime history and the preservation of manuscripts, books, ships, and marine artifacts began to grow. Two events seem to have ushered in the new era. One was the publication in 1921 of *The Maritime History of Massachusetts, 1783-1860* by Samuel Eliot Morison, and the other was the inauguration of publications by the Marine Research Society, Salem, in 1922.

In the latter year, Robert Greenhalgh Albion (born Malden, Massachusetts, 1896), was appointed Instructor in History at Princeton University. He had taken his B.A. at Bowdoin College in 1918, had moved to Harvard University for graduate study, and had been awarded the M.A. in 1920. In 1922 he was midway through studies leading to the Ph.D., which he received in 1924. At the suggestion of Professor Wilbur Cortez Abbott, Albion had selected as a dissertation topic the timber problem in the Royal Navy. It combined his long-standing interest in maritime affairs, stemming from a boyhood spent on the shores of Casco Bay, and his love of the out-of-doors. The completed dissertation was published in 1926 under the title *Forests and Sea Power: The Timber Problem of the Royal Navy, 1652-1862* by Harvard University Press in the Harvard Economic Studies series.

Albion's subsequent career as scholar, teacher, stimulator, and adviser over the next half-century touched at almost every point the growing field of maritime studies in the United States. His own writing and publication in maritime history represented a broader range of approaches to the field than that of any of his contemporaries. Books ranged from the dissertation already mentioned to *The Rise of New York Port, 1815-1860* (1939); its by-product *Square-Riggers on Schedule: The New York Sailing Packets to England, France, and the Cotton Ports* (1938); the history of the Farrell Line entitled *Seaports South of Sahara: The Achievements of an American Steamship Service* (1959); the broad study of the American merchant marine in periods of international conflict, *Sea Lanes in Wartime: The American Experience, 1775-1942* (with J. B. Pope, 1942), which was later carried on to 1945 in a 1968 edition; and a series of studies of American naval policy and administration, the most important of which were *Forrestal and the Navy* (with Robert H. Connery and J. B. Pope, 1962) and the still unpublished *Makers of Naval Policy, 1798-1947*. A host of articles in the *Dictionary of American Biography,* chiefly on figures connected with the merchant marine and the Navy, represented wide research in periodical sources and served to familiarize Albion with materials which he would use in his subsequent writings. A perusal of the bibliography of Albion's works at the conclusion of this volume will further illustrate the breadth of his coverage of American maritime history. Of all his books, *The Rise of New York Port* is, in Albion's own opinion, his best work. Many of those interested in the field will regret that he did not carry out his original intent to make this the second volume of a trilogy on the subject, with another book on the colonial period and a third on the years after 1860.

Albion's method involved the wide study of both manuscript and printed sources. He fully appreciated the importance of newspapers and periodicals as foundations for mercantile marine history, and he developed an uncanny ability to get to the heart of source materials in rapid fashion, extracting their essence without a laborious sifting of every line of them. It was his practice to collect notes, work up an outline, and write a first draft, which he then handed over to his wife, Jennie Barnes Pope, who "turned it into English," as he is wont to say. Thus he was entirely responsible for the research and the organization of materials, but the final text included Mrs. Albion's finishing touch, which was frequently recognized on the title page; or if not there, in the author's preface. This collaboration extended from the doctoral dissertation through *New England and the Sea* (with William A. Baker and Benjamin W. Labaree, 1972).

These many approaches to aspects of maritime history on the part of Albion represent in microcosm the research and writing in the entire field as it went on in the United States as a whole. It was a period when scholarship and writing were products of a great variety of persons. In contrast with most other fields of history, the maritime field has attracted the non-professionally trained fully as much as the professionals. Excellent scholarship has come from men who are not teachers by profession or holders of advanced degrees in the field of history. One needs only to consider the work of such men as William A. Baker, Marion V. Brewington, Howard I. Chapelle, William Bell Clark, Carl C. Cutler, Harold Huycke, James Duncan Phillips, and Donald Ringwald to recognize that standards of accuracy and thoroughness as well as breadth of vision have been exemplified by them as well as or better than by the products of graduate schools.

The years since 1922 have witnessed an enormously greater production of writing in maritime history than those before. An examination of the shelves of any first-rate collection in the field reveals that aside from sources themselves—logs, journals, memoirs, official reports, business papers, and the like—there are relatively few books published in maritime history in the United States before 1922 which have not been superseded. Furthermore, a host of topics which had not been studied at all in the earlier period have received attention during the years since 1922. Most of the books in the field worthy of listing in such a bibliography as that prepared by Albion in 1951 and repeatedly revised and enlarged since have come from the press since Albion's own first work was published.

To attempt to analyze the field as to topics which have already received adequate attention and those which demand investigation is quite beyond the scope of this essay. It is probably true to say that there is no aspect of maritime history which does not warrant further study. It is fairly clear that naval history has received more attention than that of the merchant service, and that the clippers have attracted more students than the "Hog Islanders." Still there is room for research and scholarly writing in every phase of the subject, although whether the publishers would agree and would cooperate by issuing more and more books on the same topics is perhaps questionable.

In 1966 a symposium on untapped sources and research opportunities in American maritime history was held at Mystic, Connecticut, and its proceedings were published the next year. A scrutiny of the papers read and the discussions which followed clearly reveals the wealth of material which has appeared in print, and even more the challenges which remain for further work.

The United States Government has been a major contributor to the published sources of maritime history and has also provided increasingly rich collections of materials for research in the Library of Congress, the National Archives, and the Navy Department. In the publication field, the Navy began in 1894 to issue the *Official Records of the Union and Confederate Navies in the War of the Rebellion,* which eventually ran to thirty-one volumes. Then in 1935 the first volume of a series of documents on naval operations in the Quasi-War with France appeared; and after this series was completed in seven volumes, another on the Barbary Wars, also seven volumes in extent, was published. An even more ambitious series on the American Revolution began to come out in 1964.

The private sector has also been active in publishing, albeit with collections of less size than the Navy series. The Marine Research Society, which was closely allied with the Peabody Museum of Salem, published in the 1920's a number of handsome volumes largely centered on the sailing ship era. A number of publishers have undertaken to bring out books on maritime history in one or another series, and in 1970 the American Maritime Library was inaugurated, designed to publish significant new works in the field. Mystic Seaport and Wesleyan University Press were joint sponsors of the series, and Albion was one of its authors.

The appearance of the *American Neptune,* a quarterly journal of maritime history, in 1941, marked the growing scholarly interest in the field. With editorial headquarters and logistical support from the Peabody Museum of Salem, the *Neptune* over the years has published a distinguished series of articles and reviews. Albion was on its original Editorial Advisory Board, and he has remained a member of that body. Between 1952 and 1958 he contributed regularly to the *Neptune* quarterly bibliographical articles, titled "Recent Writings in Maritime History."

The *American Neptune* was not the first or the only journal devoted to American maritime history or important aspects thereof. The pioneer of our period was the *Rhode Island Mariner* which appeared in 1927, a publication of the Rhode Island Ship Model Society. In 1929 it became the *Mariner* with the Ship Model Society, New York, as copublisher, and it continued to bring out scholarly articles which were not beamed at the ship-model builder alone until 1936. *Steamboat Bill,* the quarterly journal of the Steamship Historical Society of America, began publication in 1939; the Great Lakes Historical Society inaugurated its quarterly, *Inland Seas,* in 1945; and the Puget Sound Marine Historical Society, the Marine Historical Association, the San Francisco Maritime Museum, and other organizations have issued journals and occasional publications.

Despite the large number of nonprofessionals in maritime scholarship and publication, there has been a growing number of men with traditional academic training in the field. James Baughman, Kenneth Haviland, George W. Hilton, J. G. B. Hutchins, Robert E. Johnson, John Kemble, Benjamin W. Labaree, John Lyman, Arthur Marder, James Merrill, Elting E. Morison, E. B. Potter, and Clark Reynolds are but a handful of the names among the many which might be cited who have carried out research and writing in maritime history. A survey of the record indicates that between 1922 and 1970 there were some seven hundred doctoral dissertations written in the United States which dealt with aspects of mercantile marine or naval history. The larger part of these were done in the years after World War II. By contrast, about fifty such dissertations were written before 1922. Thus it is readily apparent that the writing and publication of maritime history has been a lively field in the United States since World War I, and there is no indication that interest in it is diminishing.

The increased study and writing of maritime history in the United States was accompanied by the inauguration of instruction in the field at the collegiate and graduate levels. Courses in strictly naval history had been part of the curriculum of the United States Naval Academy at Annapolis, and more serious and advanced studies were important features of the course at the United States Naval War College at Newport since 1886. The series of epoch-making volumes on British and American naval history by Captain A. T. Mahan, USN, were first presented as lectures there. With the advent of the Naval ROTC program following World War I, a certain amount of naval history was included in its curriculum. At no time, however, was there instruction in the broad field of maritime history including both its mercantile and its naval aspects until Albion began to offer such courses at Princeton University. After joining its faculty in 1922 as an Instructor, Albion taught "precepts" or small discussion groups from the large general lecture courses until the year 1926-1927, when he offered his first independent course, one in military history, which was designed as an adjunct to the ROTC and was open only to seniors in that program. This course he continued to offer until 1935.

Albion's first graduate course at Princeton was one on the expansion of Europe in the seventeenth and eighteenth centuries, which was first given in 1926-1927 and continued thereafter. This theme ran close to his research interest in maritime history and offered the opportunity to direct graduate students in work of a maritime character. A second graduate course, this one on the economic history of Europe and the United States (1760-1860), appeared in 1927-1928, and was continued with only the change that "England" was substituted for "Europe" in 1929-1930. The descriptive notes in the Princeton catalogue stated that particular attention would be paid to the commercial history of the period and that problems of immigration would be considered. Again it is apparent that maritime history was being approached in the subject matter of this instruction.

At the undergraduate level, Albion's courses at Princeton were chiefly in English history with some general European history, and a course on the expansion of Europe was introduced in 1942-1943. In 1936-1937, however, a new course in The Maritime and Economic Development of Modern England appeared in the catalogue listings. It was described as a study of English activity on the seas and overseas, taking into account commercial, naval, and imperial development as well as the industrial and financial background of maritime growth. This course was numbered History 310 and was offered annually until 1941, when the title was changed to "Modern Maritime History." The number was not altered, and apparently the change was made without formal faculty approval since it was deemed to be merely one of detail. The course was now described as before, with the word "English" omitted, and with a further statement that particular emphasis was to be placed on British, American, and German maritime development. This course continued to be offered one term each year during Albion's remaining years at Princeton, with only the change of number to History 309 and of title to "Naval and Maritime History" in 1946-1947. The course, which came to be generally known as "Boats," was immensely popular among Princeton undergraduates. Albion's remarkable ability to convey his enthusiasm for the subject to others had full play in his lively lectures in this, the first broadly conceived course in maritime history to be offered in the United States.

In the academic year 1948-1949, Albion was Visiting Lecturer in Oceanic History and Affairs at Harvard University, and during that year he resigned his Princeton professorship and was appointed Gardiner Professor of Oceanic History and Affairs at Harvard, a chair which he occupied until he achieved emeritus status in 1963. At Harvard his undergraduate course was first titled "Oceanic History and Affairs," later changed to "Maritime and Naval History and Affairs." The name "Boats" was popularly applied to it as at Princeton. The first term carried from 1415 to 1860, and the second from 1860 to the present. The course description emphasized its concern with movements such as the expansion of Europe, commercial and naval developments, methods of seafaring, economic and naval rivalries, and especially the British and American aspects of these subjects. Albion also regularly taught a one-term graduate seminar on maritime and naval history and a graduate conference course on the expansion of Europe. For a short while, Samuel Eliot Morison also offered a course on the naval history of the United States, so that the total instruction available in maritime history in all its aspects was far and away more extensive and distinguished at Harvard than at any other institution. With Albion's retirement, his successor in the Gardiner Chair, Professor John H. Parry, did not continue to offer the general undergraduate course, but turned more to his own special field of Spanish maritime expansion and colonial history.

Instruction in maritime history throughout the United States has tended to reflect the interests of individual faculty members rather than the settled determination of institutions or history departments within them to offer such courses. The Naval Academy at Annapolis has continued to offer naval history and to offer it on an increasingly broadly conceived scale. At the Naval War College, history has waxed and waned in emphasis depending on the enthusiasm of presidents and deans. Naval ROTC's have offered naval history consistently. Beyond these instances, however, it would not appear that maritime history or any of its components was part of a fixed curriculum. Over the years since World War II, maritime history has been taught in a variety of colleges and universities where faculty members with an interest in the field have persuaded department chairmen or curriculum committees to approve such courses. They have existed or are still taught at the University of Alabama, Carleton College, the University of Delaware, the University of Connecticut, Christopher

Newport College, Emory University, the University of Maine, the University of Massachusetts, Pomona College, Rensselaer Polytechnic Institute, Rice University, Skidmore College, Trinity College, Western Washington State College, Williams College, and Yale University. No complete census of such courses exists, and they have doubtless been offered in other institutions as well.

The only regular instruction in strictly American maritime history has been given by the Frank C. Munson Institute of American Maritime History under the aegis of Mystic Seaport, in Connecticut. Conceived by Edouard A. Stackpole and planned mainly by Albion, the Institute was generously endowed by Cora Mallory Munson and further supported by gifts from her brother, Philip C. Mallory. Since 1955 it has offered a graduate course each summer covering the history of the American merchant marine, as well as an advanced research seminar in this field. Its faculty has been led by Albion with assistance from one or two resident instructors each year and from a good many visiting lecturers. During the academic year, groups of undergraduates from Trinity College and from Williams College have come to Mystic Seaport for extended periods of study in American maritime history.

Despite these varied and interesting developments in the teaching of maritime history in the years since Albion began a regular course in the subject at Princeton, and despite the longer tradition of naval history at Service institutions, it cannot be said that teaching in the field has kept pace with scholarship, writing, and publication. Perhaps this merely further emphasizes the extent to which maritime history is studied and written outside academic institutions. The regular establishment of the field in academic curricula is yet to come.

The most spectacular aspect of the enthusiasm for marine historical studies since the early 1920's has been the rise and proliferation of marine museums. At the outset, as noted earlier, the Peabody Museum of Salem had an important maritime collection, part of which was displayed in its impressive marine room. There was a fine collection of models at the Smithsonian Institution, the Naval Academy had an impressive museum, and many museums throughout the country displayed anything from a painting or a ship model or so to full rooms of such exhibits. The first of a series of major new departures was the founding in 1930 of the Mariners Museum at Newport News, Virginia. Archer M. Huntington, then president of the Newport News Shipbuilding and Dry Dock Co., was responsible for the establishment of the museum, and for many years it was closely related to the shipyard. With relatively ample funds at its disposal in the early years, the museum staff proceeded to gather by purchase or by gift an impressive collection of ship models, paintings, lithographs, marine artifacts, and books; it also brought together a number of historically important small watercraft. Although somewhat isolated from major cities and therefore not serving as much as a center of research as might have been hoped, the museum has assembled in catholic fashion the most extensive nautical collection in the United States, and its library is doubtless the best of any wholly devoted to maritime affairs.

In 1941 the Peabody Museum of Salem undertook a major program of reconstruction and reorganization which eliminated some of the institution's previous exhibits and placed greater emphasis on its marine collections. The allocation of more space to these exhibits and the expansion of its library and research collections of maritime materials has enhanced the standing of the Peabody Museum as one of the half-dozen major marine museums in the United States.

In 1929 Edward E. Bradley, Carl C. Cutler, and Charles K. Stillman organized the Marine Historical Association at Mystic. Pooling their own collections as a beginning, they established a museum on the east bank of the Mystic River where the Greenman Shipyard had once been. After the deaths of Bradley and Stillman, Cutler valiantly carried on alone. His courageous acquisition of the last surviving nineteenth-century whaler, the bark *Charles W. Morgan,* in 1941 brought wide attention to the museum. It underwent major expansion in the early 1950's, and under the name Mystic Seaport became a highly popular tourist attraction. Mystic's exhibits afloat and ashore began to be matched in scholarly resources with the construction of the G. W. Blunt White Library in the early 1960's and major additions to its collections of books and manuscripts.

Of the over thirty other marine museums with important shoreside exhibitions and collections, there are various major types. Some are primarily devoted to the particular regions in which they are located. Outstanding among these along the Atlantic coast are the Penobscot Marine Museum at Searsport, Maine; the Bath Marine Museum; the Marine Museum at Fall River; the South Street Seaport Museum at New York; the Philadelphia Maritime Museum; and the Chesapeake Bay Maritime Museum at St. Michaels, Maryland. In the Great Lakes region are the Great Lakes Historical Society Museum at Vermillion, Ohio; the Dossin Great Lakes Museum at Detroit; the Mackinac Maritime Park; the Manitowoc Marine Museum; and the Thousand Islands Museum at Clayton, New York. At Marietta, Ohio, is the outstanding Ohio River Museum. Along the Pacific Coast are the maritime wing of the Seattle Museum of History and Industry, the Columbia River Maritime Museum at Astoria, the San Francisco Maritime Museum, the Allen Knight Maritime Museum at Monterey, and the Cabrillo Beach Marine Museum at San Pedro. These institutions vary greatly in size, and although their emphasis is usually on local marine history, some have important holdings which range widely.

Three collections come to mind which are primarily centered upon ship models although there is hardly a museum which does not have at least a few. The Hall of the American Merchant Marine in the National Museum of History and Technology, Washington, D.C., contains an outstanding collection of models of historically important vessels, and the Francis Russell Hart Nautical Museum at the Massachusetts Institute of Technology is strong in its model collection as well as in materials to support study of naval construction. Finally, one might mention the splendid model room at the Boston Museum of Fine Arts.

In the Washington area there are four important naval museums, namely the Navy Memorial Museum at the Washington Navy Yard, the Truxtun-Decatur Naval Museum of the Naval Historical Foundation, the naval section of the Armed Forces Hall at the National Museum of History and Technology, and the United States Naval Academy Museum at Annapolis. Most navy yards and naval stations maintain museums of sorts. Outstanding among them are the Portsmouth Naval Shipyard Museum at Portsmouth, Virginia, and the Submarine Force Library and Museum at Groton, Connecticut.

There are at least four important museums devoted to the

history of American whaling. The largest of these is the Whaling Museum at New Bedford, Massachusetts. Less known but of high quality, and especially notable for its worldwide coverage of whaling, is the Kendall Whaling Museum at Sharon, Massachusetts. There are also whaling museums at Nantucket, Massachusetts, and at Cold Spring Harbor and Sag Harbor, New York.

Most of these museums have come into existence since 1920, and all have experienced major growth since then. In large measure they represent the dedicated interest of a few enthusiastic collectors and supporters who have realized the importance of preserving remnants from the past. Some are more devoted to the attraction of tourists than others, and scholars will sometimes find them baffling in their helter-skelter of all that is old or curious. In the main, however, they represent highly significant collections and offer potential if not actual resources of major historical value.

An aspect of the major museum development has been the enormous enthusiasm for the preservation of old ships. There is much that is attractive about the notion of floating museums, of the use of vessels, hopefully of historical importance, as adjuncts to shoreside marine historical institutions or as museums in themselves. Their attractions to visitors are highly regarded although the stamina of the American tourist to visit an endless succession of old ships may be overemphasized. At the beginning of the 1920's, as has already been noted, only the frigate *Constitution* was consciously being "preserved" for display purposes, although of course there were in existence many old ships which had potentials in this direction. By the mid-1970's there were at least fifty old vessels open to visitors in connection with museums, serving as floating restaurants, or in service carrying passengers but with major emphasis in their "billing" on age and historical interest.

Ships afloat represent not only really old vessels but also modern reconstructions. These range from *Susan Constant, Goodspeed,* and *Discovery* at Jamestown Festival Park in Virginia to William A. Baker's excellent, scholarly reconstruction of *Mayflower* at Plymouth, Massachusetts; H.M.S. *Bounty* built for use in a moving picture and moored at St. Petersburg, Florida; and a "replica" of an eighteenth-century British frigate, H.M.S. *Rose,* at Newport, Rhode Island. Restored nineteenth-century merchantmen include the whaling bark *Charles W. Morgan* at Mystic

Seaport; three British-built square-riggers, *Star of India* at San Diego, *Balclutha* at San Francisco, and *Falls of Clyde* at Honolulu; and the schooner *C. A. Thayer* at San Francisco. Among naval vessels are the frigates *Constitution* at Boston and *Constellation* at Baltimore; the cruiser *Olympia,* Dewey's flagship at Manila Bay, now moored at Philadelphia; the battleships *Texas* at San Jacinto, *Alabama* at Mobile, *Massachusetts* at Fall River, and *North Carolina* at Wilmington; as well as at least four World War II submarines. Grand Banks fishing schooners are represented by *L. A. Dunton* at Mystic Seaport and *Sherman Zwicker* at Boothbay Harbor, Maine. The Northwest Seaport at Seattle and South Street Seaport at New York both have small navies of old vessels awaiting restoration. In addition to *C. A. Thayer,* the San Francisco State Maritime Historic Park has a coastwise steam schooner, a San Francisco Bay ferry boat, an oceangoing steam tug, and a scow schooner. The Ohio Historical Society's towboat *W. P. Snyder, Jr.* is moored at Marietta. There are at least half a dozen old steamboats which have some claim to be "historic" which are plying the lakes and rivers of the United States.

The list could go on and on. The enthusiasm for the preservation of old ships seems inexhaustible, and one can only hope that this does not represent such a wide dispersal of energy that even the best will not eventually be saved. Maritime historians have been on the edges of many of these efforts at preservation, and such historically trained and alert naval architects as William A. Baker and Howard I. Chapelle have been at the center of activity in some instances, but more than a few of these manifestations of interest in preserving large and expensive maritime artifacts have been largely in the hands of amateurs or "public relations experts."

A glance back over the years since 1920 reveals a remarkable growth of interest in various aspects of maritime history on the part of scholars and the general public. Unprecedented numbers of individuals have worked and produced, and their manuscripts, books, pamphlets, and periodical articles fill many shelves which were empty or nonexistent at the beginning of the period. Library and manuscript resources for the study of all sides of the subject have been notably expanded and enriched. Undergraduate instruction in maritime and naval history has been introduced and has flourished, albeit fitfully. The proliferation of maritime museums and old ships "preserved" reflects wide and growing public interest.

In every one of these phases of the study, publication, and promotion of maritime history in the United States, Robert Greenhalgh Albion has played an important part. His infectious enthusiasm, his popularity as a classroom teacher, his generous encouragement of graduate students and fellow scholars, his energy and ingenuity in research and writing, have placed him in a central and commanding position in the whole study and appreciation of the history of the sea in his generation.

JOHN H. KEMBLE

CHAPTER TWO

The Medieval Background of American Atlantic Maritime Development

THE ATLANTIC MARITIME development which represents such an important feature of the New World during early modern times did not appear suddenly as the result of the activities of Western European colonists who arrived in the New World after 1492, but was the product of a European Atlantic civilization which had deep roots in the medieval past. Indeed, even colonization itself over long maritime routes was not a new phenomenon, since it had begun as early as the eighth and ninth centuries of our era when the Irish and the Scandinavians began to establish the first Western European overseas colonies in Iceland and Greenland. Later on, during the Crusading period of the High Middle Ages, other overseas colonies were established by the Italians, Spanish, French, Belgians, Danes, Swedes, and Germans in portions of the Byzantine and Islamic worlds and along the eastern shores of the Baltic. And finally, beginning about 1250, for some two centuries before Columbus sailed west, maritime-minded Spanish and Portuguese had proceeded into the Atlantic to settle the Madeiras, the Azores, the Cape Verde Islands, and the Canaries and to set up trading posts along the coasts of West Africa. Such activities in the Mediterranean, the northern seas of Europe, and the Atlantic over a period of more than half a millennium reveal to us a maritime-minded Western European medieval civilization as advanced as that found in any other part of the world. Let us examine the nature of this civilization which was exported across the Atlantic with the first waves of colonists.

We might best begin by noting that, prior to the last years of the fifteenth century, Western Europe's maritime activities took place in a part of the world which provided an extremely varied set of geographical and climatic conditions which duplicated *in advance* most of those which were found later in the Americas. These varied from the tundras and arctic coastlines of northern Norway and Iceland, so similar to conditions along the northern shores of North America or the Patagonian coast and the Falkland Islands, through a coniferous belt of forest stretching from Scotland, central Scandinavia, and the Baltic as far east as northern Russia, much like that which existed in Canada and New England. South of these belts in Europe lay a series of rolling fertile plains whose forest cover was largely deciduous and which closely resembled in terrain and climate those found in the Middle Atlantic colonies of British and Dutch North America. And finally, along Mediterranean shores and in southern Atlantic Spain and Portugal as well as in the offshore islands of the South Atlantic, there prevailed a semitropical climate and vegetation not unlike that which was encountered later in the southern colonies of North America, in the Caribbean, and along the coasts of Brazil. Even the great tablelands of northern Mexico and the North American West and the pampases of Argentina, Uruguay, and southern Brazil had earlier Old World counterparts in the dry *mesetas* of the Iberian peninsula, the fertile grasslands of Hungary, or the steppes of South Russia, with which medieval Western Europeans had long been acquainted.

The natural resources of this medieval European nexus were also quite similar to those which were to be exploited later on in the New World. The cod, haddock, herring, and shellfish which were so abundant in the waters off New England, Nova Scotia, and the Grand Banks of Newfoundland were familiar to fishermen who for centuries had caught cod off Iceland and the Lofoten Islands or who had exploited the herring and other fisheries of the North Sea and the Baltic. And the same whales which were to help develop the maritime enterprise of New Englanders had long been hunted along the coasts of Spain, the British Isles, Scandinavia, and Iceland, just as the pursuit of the walrus and various varieties of seals and sea birds had their prototypes in similar medieval activities in European Arctic and non-Arctic waters.

In general, it is also true that the same fur-bearing animals which had long been exploited for the warmth of their skins in the

Old World, like the bear, the fox, the beaver, the marten, the sable, and the squirrel, prepared Europeans for the fur harvest North America was to provide, just as Old World deer, reindeer, and elk prepared them to make use of the meat and skins similar animals were to furnish them in the Americas. Even the buffalo had a European bison relative which still roamed the forests and clearings of Poland and Lithuania.

Equally important is the fact that during their medieval centuries Western European maritime peoples had learned to make use of a variety of deciduous and coniferous trees to furnish them the timber and naval stores which were essential in building the ships they used, and these supplies were similar to those found in even greater abundance in the Americas. Such timber resources for centuries had been exploited in forest areas of Scandinavia, the Baltic, the British Isles, and along the coasts of Spain, Portugal, Italy, the Balkans, and Asia Minor. And one should add to timber an extensive exploitation of Old World mineral wealth from iron, copper, lead, silver, and other mines, though by the later Middle Ages most of Europe's indigenous gold had been exhausted and supplies of this metal had to be imported from outside sources.

It is true that by the time of the arrival of the white man the New World's aboriginal population had developed fewer varieties of domestic animals than were to be found in medieval Europe, and that these and the plants which they cultivated differed considerably from those of the Old World. Nevertheless, raising the alpaca or the turkey or growing maize, potatoes, yams, manioc, tomatoes, beans, squash, cacao, and tobacco presented few problems to European colonists accustomed to animal husbandry or to making use of a variety of their own grains, root crops, or fruits. Their agricultural skills and practices were to prove quite easy to adapt to New World conditions and the plants and animals they found there.

Equally important for us is an understanding of Western Europe's long experience in dealing with and often dominating a variety of human resources—a process which was still going on at the close of the Middle Ages. Part of this experience consisted in a pattern of controlling relatively primitive tribal peoples like the Lapps, Wends, Balts, and Finns of northern Europe, the Irish and the Scot Highlanders of the Celtic fringe of Britain, or those African blacks or Guanches of the Canaries whom the Portuguese and

Figure 1. Mediterranean Trader, c. 1300

Spaniards encountered along the shores of West Africa. Equally important, however, as a prelude to their later American experience was a pattern of domination of more highly sophisticated populations of non-Western Europeans, such as the inhabitants of the Byzantine Empire, the Moors of Spain and Sicily, or the Moslems of the Near East. Such experience prepared Europeans for the Incas, the Chibchas, the Mayas, and the Aztecs as well as for the Araucanians, the Caribs, the Arawaks, the Iroquois, the Eskimos, and the Algonquin tribes of North America.

With these important generalities in mind, let us turn our attention in more detail to some specifics of the maritime experience of Western Europe in medieval times. And here we need to emphasize that this took place in three quite different European environments in each of which certain special maritime traditions developed over a long period of time. First was the Mediterranean; then a northern-seas area consisting of the Irish Sea, the English Channel, the North Sea, and the Baltic; and finally the Atlantic Ocean proper.

In the Mediterranean, drawing upon a long-standing maritime tradition and a variety of craft common to Byzantine and Moslem shores which went back to Phoenician, Greek, and Roman prototypes, early in the Middle Ages Western Europeans began to make use of two kinds of ships which were specially adapted to these waters—the oared galley and a group of heavier, more cumbersome transport and cargo sailing vessels (Figure 1). Both types were carvel-built, carried more than one mast, and were generally lateen-rigged and equipped with steering oars.

In the Baltic and the North Sea, however, quite different types of ships developed during these same centuries. The best known were the so-called Viking *longships* which had appeared by the ninth century A.D. and are known to us in detail from examples furnished us by the famous Gokstad ship and by the remains of a number of others revealed to us by underwater archeology. Such ships were oared, flat-bottomed, clinker-built vessels with a single mast amidships, and made use of a single large square sail and steering oars. An especially large type of longship, known as the *drekkar* or dragon ship, began to be built in Scandinavian and North Sea waters by the tenth century and was used by monarchs and sea-kings of the period in naval operations. As late as the 1080's, the vessels depicted in the Bayeux tapestry as those used by William the Conqueror for his invasion of England represent a kind of longship.

In addition to such oared warships, there were a number of quite different clinker-built vessels which by the eleventh century were used extensively in these waters for both transport and trade. One was the Scandinavian *knorr* (Figure 2), much like the longship in general design, but sturdier, broader in the beam, and less

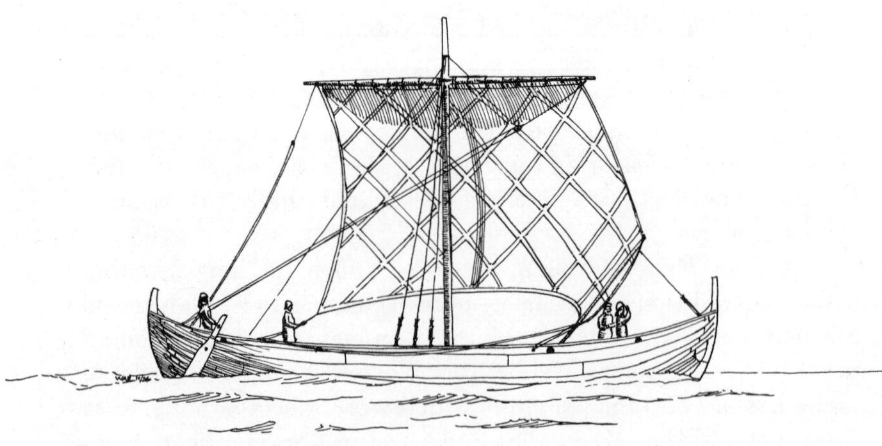

Figure 2. Knorr

flat-bottomed than the former. It did not carry oars, except those used in steering, and made use of a single mast which carried a square sail. Two others were the *cog* (Figure 3) and the *hulk,* both of which seem to have originated along Frisian or Flemish shores by the year 800 and which were flat-bottomed craft with a single mast and square sail. The hulk differed from the cog in being banana-shaped, though in other respects it was quite similar to it. And finally we have still a fourth type of North Sea sailing ship, the *keel* (Figure 4), a coaster about which we know little as far as design is concerned.

Last of all, there was still a third and separate maritime tradition which we must regard as an Atlantic one. In Ireland and Celtic Britain this tradition, which went back to Neolithic times, resulted in the building of skin boats or *curraghs* (Figure 5), in which as early as the seventh or eighth century mariners ventured to Iceland and beyond. And certainly we must consider the knorr, already mentioned, as an Atlantic craft, for it was used by ninth- and tenth-century Scandinavians to travel the ocean as far west as Iceland, Greenland, and the North American continent. To these two vessels, however, we need to add a third called the *barca*

Figure 3. Cog, c. 1350

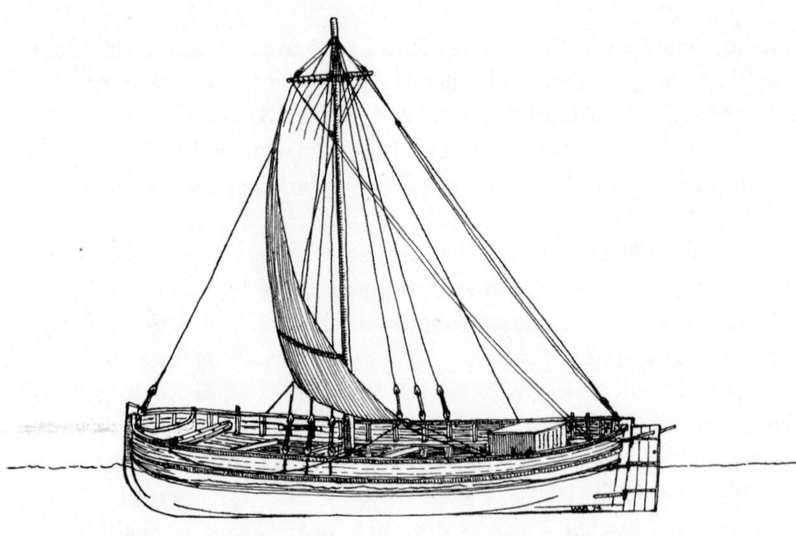

Figure 4. Keel

(Figure 6) or barge, a ship which had been developed along the western coast of France by the early Middle Ages. It seems to have been a single-masted, flat-bottomed craft, which was perhaps carvel-built and which may have been derived from those Atlantic ships which Caesar found the Venetii employing along the shores of Brittany some centuries earlier.

By the twelfth and thirteenth centuries of our era, the ships which have been mentioned above had developed and changed in a number of respects. The only exception to this statement concerns the knorr, which remained unchanged and continued to be used by the Scandinavians in the North Atlantic. Both the cog and the hulk, however, grew in size and by the year 1200 had begun to be fitted with a large stern rudder in place of steering oars and to have large castles constructed on bow and stern to give them greater protection from pirates and other enemies afloat. The size of both the keel and the barca also seems to have increased as they began to be used to transport cargoes of coal and wine on long voyages along European Atlantic shores.

During these same years a certain mingling of design took place among Mediterranean and northern ship types. Cogs with their square sails and stern rudders began to appear in the

Mediterranean and affected ship design there. And Mediterranean galleys from Genoa, Venice, Pisa, and Catalonia soon after 1250 began to sail out into the Atlantic past Cádiz and Lisbon on their way to and from Southampton and Bruges. At the same time special northern oared war galleys, which owed something to Mediterranean practices, began to be built in the dockyards of thirteenth- and fourteenth-century Britain and in the new French royal arsenal of Rouen.

By the last century of the Middle Ages, this development and mingling of ship designs from the three separate regions of maritime Europe ended up with the creation of two *new* major Atlantic ships, the *carrack* and the *caravel* (Figure 7), both of which were better adapted to oceanic travel than any of their predecessors. The design of the carrack was basically that of the hulk or cog, with a stern rudder and high permanent fore and aft castles. If seems, however, to have borrowed from either Mediterranean craft or the barca a carvel system of construction of its planking, and from the former multiple masts carrying more than

Figure 5. Skin-covered Wicker Boat — "Used by the Wild Irish," 1670, after Capt. Phillips

one sail. All of this made it the Atlantic sailing ship par excellence. The caravel, which may originally have been designed by Atlantic-based Moors of Spain and Morocco, was also perfected soon after 1400. It was a slender, carvel-built vessel, lateen-rigged with a stern rudder and several masts, and was especially adapted for sailing along African coasts. Incidentally, during this same century both the carrack and the caravel began to be armed with cannon, which made them formidable opponents on the sea. To them the future of Atlantic navigation in the New World was to belong, rather than to the galley, the cog, or the hulk, which could not safely venture into stormy distant waters.

Matching this progress in ship design and construction during the Middle Ages was a remarkable development in the techniques of navigation. In northern European waters it would appear that the pioneers in this regard were the Scandinavians, who by the ninth century not only used sun and stars as a basis for celestial navigation but also had learned to use sunstones and lodestones when the skies were overcast. Their knowledge of such techniques made possible latitude sailing directly across the Atlantic from Norway to Iceland or Greenland as early as the year 1000, although they still were unable to compute their longitude during

Figure 6. Barca

Figure 7. Portuguese Caravela *Redonda,* 1533, after "Livro das Armadas"

such voyages. By the twelfth century these same Scandinavians had also come to develop manuals of sailing directions which made possible long voyages past Ushant in Brittany, Cape Finisterre in Galicia, and other Iberian ports into the Mediterranean. Once there, we know northern Europeans had available other sets of sailing directions, perhaps of Arab origin, which covered the entire Mediterranean and during the late twelfth century facilitated the voyages of northern crusading fleets to the coasts of Syria and Egypt.

In this same century the compass had been developed in northern European waters and is first mentioned in a treatise dating from the year 1187 by an Englishman, Alexander Neckham. It was in the Middle Sea, however, that the compass developed in a significant way, for here, starting about 1250, it revolutionized navigation, as Italian and Catalan sailors began to use a boxed form of it in direct voyages out of sight of land to various ports and began to construct *portolan charts* for the entire Mediterranean and Black Sea area of the world. As their galleys began to sail on regular schedules north to England and Flanders in the late thirteenth and early fourteenth centuries, they carried with them their compasses and their portolan charts and combined them with pre-existing northern European manuals of sailing directions to produce the well-known Sea Rutters of Atlantic Europe, which continued to be used until relatively modern times.

As portolan charts, compasses, and sailing directions become perfected and more complex in character, so too did the art of cartography, whose long history cannot be fully covered here. Suffice it to say that by the thirteenth and fourteenth centuries there had appeared in Italy and Catalonia a number of talented mapmakers, whose masterpiece was probably the famous Catalan Map of 1375. This map not only gave a relatively true graphic picture of the coastlines of the Mediterranean, Black Sea, and northern Europe but also included a relatively accurate representation of the wider world, including most Atlantic offshore islands, the coast of West Africa, and the Indian Ocean, Southeast Asia, and China as well.

By the fifteenth century European cartography continued to improve, and this art was no longer confined to Southern Europe. A series of maps made by Fra Mauro and other cartographers between 1460 and 1490 show that Western Europeans were aware that Africa could be circumnavigated and that the islands of the East Indies presented an extremely complex pattern of geography. By this time both fifteenth-century maps and the writings of Toscanelli also show us that Europeans had begun to conceive of the entire Old World as an area surrounded by oceans, and that one could reach the Far East by sailing west, an effort incidentally which is recorded to have first been attempted in 1291 by the Genoese Vivaldi brothers, some two centuries before Columbus sailed west on the same mission. Also it is worth noting that during the fifteenth century Europeans had learned from direct contact with Indian and Indonesian mariners that they could navigate south of the Equator, using the Southern Cross in place of the North Star. In short, before 1492 medieval Western Europeans had perfected those advanced cartographic and navigational skills and knowledge which had prepared them to exploit successfully the maritime resources of the New World, and they now possessed adequate ships and marine technology to dominate not only the Atlantic but the wider world.

It would be a mistake, however, to concentrate our attention exclusively upon the way Europe in medieval times developed better ships and navigational skills which assured the success of an American Atlantic maritime tradition. We should not overlook certain other Old World developments of an institutional sort which were equally vital in making possible a healthy New World maritime civilization. I refer to a number of institutions which could be and were transplanted to the Americas from Europe and which formed an indispensable base for their subsequent maritime civilization. These institutions were the mission, the seigneury, the village, the family farm, the ranch, the plantation, the mine, and the commercial town. The mission, that remarkable institution which was derived from medieval monasticism and which was used with such success by the Franciscans, the Dominicans, and the Jesuits to Christianize, control, and civilize a considerable native population in regions as diverse as French Canada and parts of Portuguese and Spanish America, was only indirectly and peripherally connected with the maritime civilization of the New World and need concern us little here.

The other institutions had a greater basic importance. The medieval seigneury was first introduced overseas in the Canaries, and when Cortez was granted estates in Mexico, they were organized in this fashion. Other seigneuries followed on the heels of these; and especially later on, when a modified form of this institution known as the *encomienda* became a principal method used to organize the lives and labor of much of the settled native population of Spanish America, they provided much of the production which ultimately found its way to shipping which served the New World's needs. Nor were the Spanish the only ones who made use of a form of medieval seigneury, for so too did the Portuguese in Brazil, the French along the St. Lawrence, the Dutch in their Hudson River valley patroonships, and the British, though with scant success, in the Carolinas. Even proprietary colonies like William Penn's Pennsylvania and Maryland and Georgia were a form—imperfect, it is true—of the medieval seigneury.

The village, which generally coincided with the parish, was still another institution which was transported across the seas by European colonists to what was to be the hub of British American maritime development, colonial New England, where it became the New England town with its common and other village institutions writ large in history. In a somewhat different form the village and/or parish was introduced by the French into Acadia and Louisiana as an institution controlling the lives of settlers. Only in New England, however, did it directly affect maritime development.

Quite different was the detached family farm, which also had Old World prototypes in the British Isles and Germany and which assumed the dominant role in the agricultural production of the British Middle Colonies of North America and along frontiers where it was planted by Scotch-Irish and other pioneers who pressed west. It produced the surplus wheat, cattle, and other foodstuffs that formed much of the cargoes which left American ports for distant markets.

Equally important was the ranch, which proved to be an institution closely associated with Iberian New World colonization. The cattle ranch had begun during the thirteenth century in the dry plains of southern Spain and Portugal where the full panoply of cowboys, branding irons, and regular roundups of semiwild cattle made its appearance several centuries before Columbus. In this same general area large-scale raising of sheep also developed, as well as that great annual trek of flocks from north to south which was controlled by the *Mesta* throughout Spain and which produced the prized Castilian wool of the later Middle Ages. Both types of animal husbandry were introduced into ranches which were established in the plains areas of North, Central, and South America by the Spanish and Portuguese in the sixteenth century and soon were widely extended, making possible flocks and herds which produced wool, hides, and meat on a scale that dwarfed anything the Old World had known. The production from New World ranches resulted in cargoes that helped immensely to stimulate the maritime enterprise of the Americas in the Atlantic.

Even more vital was the plantation, which also had a long history of development in the Old World. This method of agriculture, employing a large work force on extensive holdings, first appeared in twelfth-century Syria, where European crusading families established there found Arab sugar plantations. In the course of the thirteenth and fourteenth centuries, other plantations were established throughout the Mediterranean and especially in Crete, Cyprus, Sicily, and southern Spain and Portugal. At the same time it became clear that the most efficient plantation labor force consisted of slaves, and the Genoese in particular soon specialized in this traffic and procured for plantation owners the Islamic, Greek, and other Near Eastern slaves which they needed. During the fifteenth century the Portuguese, who had important Genoese colonies of merchants in their principal seaports, discovered a new source of such servile labor—the blacks from the African coasts they began to exploit. They were carried back to the Portuguese Algarve and used there as plantation labor and then introduced along with the sugar plantation itself into the Madeiras and other offshore islands. Thus, when they and the Spanish colonized the tropical shores of the West Indies, the Caribbean, and Brazil, they transferred both the plantation system and the black slaves they were already procuring from West Africa into these new overseas areas.

Soon thereafter it was discovered that certain other tropical crops were just as adapted as was sugar to a plantation system using slave labor. First, plantations began to be used to cultivate tobacco and cotton, and then somewhat later rice, indigo, and coffee. A great plantation belt developed from the Chesapeake Bay area to Rio de Janeiro as a characteristic form of agriculture in tropical and semitropical areas of the New World, and millions of unfortunate blacks began to make the miserable Middle Passage across the Atlantic from Africa on their way to bondage. The transportation of both these slaves and the crops their labor made possible was an important basis of the prosperity of the maritime peoples of the Americas and of Europe during the next few centuries.

The mine, however, had quite a different origin as a medieval institution. It emerged in its final capitalistic form in a number of areas of Europe such as Britain, Sweden, France, and the Iberian peninsula, but especially in Germany and the Balkans where families like the Welsers and Fuggers became the bonanza kings of the fifteenth century as they invested in silver, gold, and copper mining ventures. Their close connections with the Hapsburgs made it easy for them to transfer their activities to Spain when Charles V became the ruler there soon after 1500, where they were particularly concerned with the Rio Tinto mines. Then, when Spanish *conquistadores* discovered the great mineral wealth of New Spain and Peru, it was only natural the Fuggers and their compatriots should transfer their mining expertise and technical skills to the New World, especially to the great silver mountain of Potosí. In the colonies, however, and especially in Peru, an ominous development took place in the way mines were run. This consisted in the use of impressed Indian labor, under a *mita* system, not dissimilar to the *encomienda,* to provide the work force needed to bring ores to the surface from the pits. Thus a form of the medieval seigneury was grafted onto the mine to form a New World institution with servile overtones—one which helped produce first the silver and then the gold and other metals which formed the most valuable cargoes which the Americas sent to Europe. And this servile system of operating mines in Bolivia, for instance, has lasted right down to the present day.

Finally, Western Europe created the commercial town as early as the eleventh century—an institution which was the most important one of all for the maritime civilization of the New World, since it was here that overseas maritime commerce quite naturally tended to center its activities. Medieval towns differed considerably from one another in a number of ways and especially as regards the extent of the freedom, economic and political, which they allowed the merchants and artisans who formed the majority of their population. Thus many Italian and German towns were fully independent city-states, while those of the Iberian peninsula, France, Britain, the Netherlands, and Scandinavia enjoyed a more limited freedom, depending upon their charters. And the same thing was true of the New World urban centers which quickly arose and which were modeled in many ways upon those already in existence in Europe. But wherever towns appeared, they formed vital centers of commerce and maritime life, whether we are referring to a Santo Domingo, a Havana, a Pernambuco, a Vera Cruz, a New Orleans, a Charleston, a New York, a Boston, or a Quebec, all of which reproduced across the ocean features like those found in Genoa, Seville, London, Bristol, Rouen, Dublin, Ghent, Hamburg, and Bremen and which were just as important as these latter in the maritime trade they helped to stimulate.

Turning from a consideration of the institutions vital to a healthy New World maritime establishment which medieval Europe created and which were exported overseas, let us consider something else—the Old World's long experience in gathering, shipping, and distributing bulk cargoes over distant sea routes. This was especially important because it was not until relatively late in the nineteenth century that the Americas became industrialized enough to ship many goods which were anything but natural commodities especially adapted to sea transport in bulk. The products of this sort with which medieval Europe had had a long experience were wheat and flour, timber and naval stores, wool and hides, wine, furs, fish and salt, and a variety of minerals, including coal, all of which had become important cargoes on the sea by the twelfth and thirteenth centuries.

Wheat, for instance, was shipped extensively throughout the Mediterranean, especially that originating in Sicily and southern Italy, North Africa, and south Russia, which reached Constantinople and a number of Catalan and northern Italian ports and cities which could not feed themselves using local grain supplies. In northern Europe initially, the British Isles were a major source of wheat and flour which was sent to Scandinavia, Gascony, and the continent in considerable amounts. By the later Middle Ages, however, it was Baltic grain which pre-empted the export markets in this commodity throughout northern Europe. Our second category of bulk exports, timber and naval stores, for centuries figured as an important element in Mediterranean trade, as did wheat, especially that of the Black Sea, Asia Minor, and Balkan shores in the eastern Mediterranean and that of the Iberian peninsula, Italy, and Morocco in the west. In northern Europe, however, by the late Middle Ages, timber and naval stores from Scandinavia and the Baltic had come almost to monopolize the export market for such commodities, a situation that continued relatively unchanged into the more modern period.

In the Mediterranean, wool and hides originating in the Iberian peninsula and especially North Africa were shipped in bulk to textile and commercial centers in Italy and Catalonia, while in northern and Atlantic Europe it was the wool clip of England which initially largely met the needs of the cloth towns of Flanders and the continent. After 1300, however, fine Castilian merino wool, produced by the *Mesta,* replaced English wool as an important export along European Atlantic routes, even though some areas like Ireland and Iceland continued an important trade in hides and sheepskins. As for wine, it was always an important bulk cargo which was shipped throughout the Mediterranean, and this continued to be true until the close of the Middle Ages. In the north, however, a more complex situation prevailed. By the thirteenth century, although Rhineland and Moselle wines shipped north figured in maritime commerce, it was the growth of the wine trade of Gascony which was especially spectacular, so much so that by the early fourteenth century a fleet of about a thousand large vessels existed which specialized in transporting this wine each year to the British Isles and other continental markets. Soon thereafter, however, the Gascon wine trade declined and was replaced in importance, first by that of Andalusia and Portugal and then by that of Madeira and other Atlantic islands into which wine had been introduced in the course of the fifteenth century. Wine by 1492, then, had become an Atlantic maritime commodity of immense importance along European sea routes.

Matching wine as a bulk export was fish. In the Mediterranean and along southern Spanish and Portuguese shores, the tuna and the sardine challenged the enterprise of large fishing fleets, and the fish they caught were already being packed in olive oil for shipment to distant markets by sea. In northern European waters the herring of the North Sea and Baltic and the cod of Iceland and Norway played a similar role and were responsible for a considerable share of the maritime trade of the Hansa, the British Isles, Iceland, the Netherlands, and the Atlantic shores of France and northern Spain. Since the processing of these northern fish demanded large amounts of salt, it resulted in a considerable exploitation of Europe's salt resources also. In the Mediterranean this did not change things, since the older salt pans of Venice, Languedoc, and the Balearics continued their production as before. In northern and Atlantic Europe, however, after 1300 this demand for salt stimulated production at Borneuf in Brittany and along Portuguese shores, which was so efficient that it seems to have eliminated long-established producers at places like Droitwich in Britain or Luneville in German Saxony. Thus new sources of salt distributed widely by sea in Europe prepared the Americas for similar salt which was to be exploited in the Dry Tortugas and other localities in the New World.

Last of all, we need to note the development of an important bulk commerce in furs and minerals of various sorts. Furs need concern us little, since by the late Middle Ages they tended to be produced mainly in northern Scandinavia or in Baltic and Russian regions, from which they were shipped to a number of Western European ports and markets. The story of the shipping of minerals by sea is again a more complex one. By the fourteenth and fifteenth centuries a number of ports specialized in large-scale sea transport of mineral materials. Dubrovnik owed much of its prosperity to its shipment of copper, while Italian mariners transported alum from mines in Italy and the Near East as far north as Britain and the Low Countries. Spanish Basque ports and some Scandinavian centers exported considerable bar iron, while copper, which came from great mines in Sweden, figured in the maritime trade of the Baltic, just as that from Rio Tinto reached distant ports along maritime routes. So too did coal from Newcastle and tin from Cornwall, which were both widely distributed by sea.

What is important about all this, however, lies not in the specific bulk materials we have been discussing, but in the patterns of trade which developed to handle them. This explains why it was so easy to fit bulk commodities from the New World into a network of Atlantic and European trade—not only the timber, wheat, fish, and furs of North America, or the silver which the mines of Mexico and Peru produced as cargoes for Spanish plate fleets or the gold from eighteenth-century Minas Gerais, the salt from the Caribbean, or hides from La Plata—but much more as well. I refer, of course, to the sugar of Brazil, the West Indies, and Louisiana; the tobacco of Maryland, Virginia, and Latin America; the rice and indigo of the Carolinas; the coffee of Brazil and Central America; and the cotton of the gulf states—all handled expeditiously and profitably in the period after 1500 because their transportation and distribution over long maritime routes presented no special new problem.

The heritage of medieval Europe which the Americas were to draw on, however, concerned much more than the handling of a variety of bulk cargoes over long maritime distances. It also was represented by a complex series of business techniques and arrangements which facilitated maritime activities of all sorts. As early as the time of the Vikings, we know that these Scandinavians arranged that the profits of their raids be divided among ships' crews and leaders on the basis of percentages or shares, a system which we find again among the Genoese and Pisan privateers of the eleventh century and later on as they raided Moslem ports and shipping. This same practice of working on shares was employed by European fishing folk and those who pursued the whale in ocean waters and was passed on as a practice to New World fishermen and whalers.

Equally important was the development of various forms of business partnerships among those engaged in long-distance maritime commerce. Those employed by the Genoese, Venetians, Catalans, and Provençals during the twelfth and thirteenth centuries have been most thoroughly examined by scholars, but it is worth noting that the partnership also was extensively used during this same period in Scandinavia, Britain, the Netherlands, and Germany. In the Mediterranean such partnerships became more elaborate as time went on, giving rise first to the *commenda* and finally to various kinds of marine joint-stock and insurance business arrangements. By the fourteenth century perhaps the most famous of these was the well-known Genoese *Mahone,* which not only controlled an extensive commerce overseas but served as a kind of colonial government. During the fifteenth century a similar arrangement controlled by the stockholders of the Bank of St. George of Genoa was able for decades to dominate and govern a series of Black Sea ports and the trade of much of this region.

Out of these and other business arrangements, we find that there developed not only a number of remarkable maritime trading enterprises like the Hanseatic League but also later joint-stock companies which had governing powers overseas, like the Dutch West India Company, the French West India Company, the Royal African Company, and the Hudson's Bay Company—all of which had a vital influence upon New World maritime development. Even the settlement and development of Newfoundland by a chartered company and the similar granting of charters to the Virginia, Plymouth, and Massachusetts Bay Companies would have been impossible if medieval Europeans had not had a long experience with such methods of pooling their efforts in regard to maritime colonial enterprise.

Finally, we must comment briefly upon the fact that medieval Europeans had managed to develop a number of business techniques or instruments which helped to stimulate maritime activities. Some of these, like bills of exchange and various types of marine credit arrangements and insurance, were well known by the twelfth or thirteenth centuries. Others, such as double-entry bookkeeping and the use of Arabic numerals in accounts, became common somewhat later on. Still others, like merchant manuals of which the most famous is that written by Pegolotti, and the advanced banking practices found especially among the Italians and Catalans, remind us of how much the later maritime practices of the Americas owed to the business traditions of medieval Europe.

Turning now from business arrangements, we must examine the way in which during the Middle Ages governments came to function and what effect such activities had upon American Atlantic maritime development—a subject which we can only sketch here. First of all, in this regard we need to note the importance attached to the issuing and circulation of regular gold and silver coins which facilitated trade, whether we are referring to the gold *ducat* or *florin*, or important silver coinages like the *sterling* of Britain and the silver pennies of the Netherlands, Germany, and Spain. Such coinage helped the commerce of the New World as it accompanied European mariners and colonists to the Americas and returned to them in the form of a useful trade medium some of the bullion they had been shipping back to the Old World since 1500.

But more important was a long process of developing colonial overseas government during Europe's medieval centuries. The overseas *podestàs* and governors of Venice and Genoa, especially in places like Constantinople, Crete, and Cyprus, were the ancestors of the viceroys and captains-general who governed Spain's and Portugal's empires in the Americas, just as the *baillis* and *sénéchals* of medieval France were the direct precursors of the French governors and intendants of Canada, Louisiana, and the West Indies. And it was the viceroys of medieval Ireland and Gascony who were the ancestors of Britain's eighteenth-century royal governors of her colonies in the Americas and Africa.

Still other medieval practices and governing arrangements had a direct effect upon New World maritime development. One was the habit of making use of organized fleets for warlike purposes. In the Mediterranean, Venice, the Kingdom of Two Sicilies, Genoa, and Pisa seem to have had the first organized navies, though others were developed soon thereafter by Aragon, France, and Dalmatian cities. In the north, Scandinavia and Britain were precocious in developing organized naval establishments, and it was not until much later that the Hansa, France, Castile, and Portugal followed suit. At any rate, long before 1500 every portion of medieval Europe which engaged in maritime activities was accustomed to the use of navies, and such practices became part of the maritime traditions of the New World without any exception. Two aspects of this warlike naval activity which developed in Europe are of special interest—convoys and piracy or privateering. The Atlantic convoy system of the Spanish and Portuguese in the sixteenth century and later went back to a medieval tradition which developed out of Venetian, Genoese, and Catalan convoys in the Mediterranean and those fleets of Mediterranean galleys sent out into the Atlantic on their way to Britain or Flanders. It also was influenced by similar convoy systems set up by English kings as early as the thirteenth century to protect the wine fleets of Gascony, or those which the Hansa established at about the same time in the North Sea and Baltic.

Piracy and privateering, so much a feature of activity along North American or Caribbean shores, also had a medieval European background in centuries of naval warfare of this sort in the Mediterranean. Or we must view it as in part a result of that old duel between French mariners of Atlantic shores and their English maritime brethren on the other side of the Channel, which was such a feature of the period of the Hundred Years' War and later. And much of the maritime law used in the New World was also in no small measure developed out of such hostilities.

Last of all, we need to emphasize the structure of a longstanding medieval mercantilism upon the sea which influenced and set the pattern for such systems as the Council of the Indies in Spain and the sixteenth- , seventeenth- , and eighteenth-century mercantilist systems of Portugal, France, England, and Holland. Perhaps Venice developed the earliest and most complete system of medieval mercantilism, although the honors may rather go to the Norman Kingdom of the Two Sicilies. But if so, the latters' Pisan, Genoese, southern French, and Catalan rivals soon followed suit and copied them. In northern Europe both Britain and the Hansa experimented with maritime mercantilistic practices also at a relatively early date. By the fifteenth century all of Europe did so, as in Portugal, Castile and Aragon, France, Britain, and the Netherlands mercantilism had become a way of life leading to those colonial systems which were to be established in the New World and which governed, directed, and controlled much of its activities upon the sea.

We must sum up then. The Atlantic maritime development of the Americas was the direct heir of Europe's previous medieval experience in a variety of ways so all-pervading that it is impossible to imagine it taking place without this experience. Western Europeans, over a span of centuries, had managed to gain a knowledge of varied terrains, climates, and natural and human resources quite similar to those they encountered in the New World and had learned also how to make use of them to the best advantage. Their long, slow development of specialized oceanic ships of various types and of advanced navigational techniques made possible operations in distant American waters with a minimum of difficulty. A number of institutions which Europe had developed, such as the mission, the seigneury, the village, the family farm, the ranch, the plantation, the mine, the commercial town, could be and were easily exported overseas to form an underpinning of much of the New World's maritime activity.

Western Europe's experience in organizing a large-scale system of bulk commodity transport and distribution laid the groundwork for an even more extensive system of this sort in the Americas, just as her financial arrangements—trading or fishing on shares, the partnership, the joint-stock company, and the chartered company—and mechanisms like bills of exchange and loan instruments, made possible an easy use of such practices in the New World. And finally a pattern of coinage, colonial administration, navies, convoys, and piracy as well as the entire gamut of mercantilism had been worked out in Europe long before Columbus sailed west. In short, the maritime history of the New World shows it was quite simply the direct child of medieval Europe.

ARCHIBALD R. LEWIS

CHAPTER THREE

Fishing Under Sail in the North Atlantic

> That leave might be given to hang up the representation of a cod-fish in the room where the House sit, as a memorial to the importance of the cod-fishing to the welfare of the Commonwealth, as had been usual formerly.

So MOVED AND PASSED at Boston on 17 March 1784 by the House of Representatives of the General Court of the Commonwealth of Massachusetts. At that time the Commonwealth included both the native and adopted home sites of Robert Greenhalgh Albion, for Maine did not achieve statehood until 1820.

The above motion serves to recall to modern readers that codfishing led to the earliest exploitations of the coasts of Maine and Massachusetts as well as the short intervening coast of New Hampshire. Although the codfishery has been studied from many points of view there has been no attempt, to the best of this writer's knowledge, to note the changes through the years in the vessels employed both in Old England, the home country of the first colonists, and in New England. This brief survey will start with the common background and trace the divergence to the end of sail-propelled fishing vessels.

Because of the high price and scarcity of meat and poultry and the requirements of the Roman church that called for eating no meat on numerous days of fast or abstinence, averaging perhaps three a week, the fisheries were important in medieval Europe and England. The consumption of fish, principally herring and cod, was enormous. It is said that the first market in London had fifty-four stalls of which thirty-six were for fish. Throughout the period from the thirteenth to the sixteenth centuries, fishmongers, if not the fishermen, were counted among the wealthy. Fair-sized fishing fleets were active, but until 1384 their catches were landed fresh. In that year Willem Beukelzoon of Biervliet in the Netherlands was said to have invented the process of salting herring down in barrels. For a time the Dutch had a monopoly of the herring market and prospered. The salting process, also applicable to the cod, made distant fishing voyages possible. Another method of preserving cod was by drying in the sun, a procedure started in the Scandinavian countries. After splitting and cleaning, the tails of two fish were tied together and they were slung over stakes or stocks—hence the name stockfish—until they were as hard as boards. The cod was the ideal fish for either method of preservation.

Hand-line fishing for cod off the shores of Old England may date from man's earliest memories. Special vessels for the cod-fishery date at least from the fourteenth century, the type employed probably being adapted from that used by the fishermen of the Low Countries. The type name *dogger* is said to have been derived from the Dutch phrase *ten dogge varen*—to go to the codfishing—and there is an obvious connection with the famous North Sea fishing ground, the Dogger Bank.

The cod moves in schools of varying size, being governed by the absence or presence of food, the spawning instinct, and the water temperature. Because the movements of the cod are unpredictable, English fishermen quite early had to look farther afield than the coasts of England. In 1754 it was written that during the reign of Edward I [1272-1307] Dunwich on the east coast of England was sending out a fleet of 20 ships annually to the fishing grounds in the North Sea and off Iceland. Icelandic records of 1337 refer to English "doggerers," and there are various fourteenth-century English records indicating the use of doggers. King's Lynn had an Iceland Company which sent out its first vessels in 1412; fishermen from other east-coast ports went to Iceland in the years following. As in modern times there were problems about foreign fishermen in Icelandic waters but in 1490 a treaty with Denmark gave English fishermen the right, on the payment of customs and under license, to fish off Iceland. In 1528 the Iceland fishing fleet

Figure 1. Two-masted Fishing Vessel, c. 1480, after W.A.

from east-coast English ports reportedly numbered 149 vessels.

Definite material pertaining to these early doggers is scarce, but prior to the introduction of the three-masted rig about the middle of the fifteenth century there was little to distinguish a seagoing fishing vessel from an ordinary small trader. No painting or drawing of an English fishing boat by an English artist is known before the seventeenth century, but the fifteenth-century Flemish master "W.A." [or W. plus a key symbol], in a series of nine engravings of vessels, left a portrait of a typical fisherman of his day, say about 1480. Figure 1 is a tubby two-master whose barrels immediately suggest a fishing craft. In medieval times, however, the single-masted rig predominated; hence it has been suggested that a single-master with twin turrets aft in the same series might also be a fishing vessel. The two-master has no forecastle and the space under her half-deck aft appears to be entirely open. The twin turrets aft may be lanterns, as lights were necessary in fishing fleets at night. The purpose of the crutch between the turrets is unknown; a similar crutch on a merchant vessel supports a lowered lateen yard. Herring drifters of later eras lowered their mainmasts while riding to their nets, but the mainmast of the vessel shown in Figure 1 does not seem to be of the lowering type. The two-master's rig with its large mainsail and small foresail was used widely in later years. The presence of a bowsprit is good evidence that both sails could be carried when beating to windward, as it served as a lead for the fore bowlines.

It is possible that on long voyages independent of shore stations some codfishers tried drying part of their catch at sea. In this connection it has been suggested that the four curved members, half-hoops, over the main deck were stocks over which the fish were slung. On the other hand, this vessel may have been employed in the herring fishery, in which case these half-hoops could have been used for drying the nets. In spite of her chubby appearance this two-master was quite likely capable of sailing seventy miles a day that was the average in her time on a passage from the east coast of England to Iceland.

The voyages of the Cabots, John and his son Sebastian, to the coast of North America in 1497-1498, and those of an Anglo-Azorean syndicate during the first few years of the sixteenth century, were supported by the merchants of Bristol, primarily to discover new fishing grounds. Once the new banks were found, however, the English were slow to fish off Newfoundland, and it apparently took reports of the successes of French and Portuguese fishermen to stir them to action. The French probably were the first European codfishers in North American waters; they were fishing off Newfoundland at least as early as 1504 and some may have done so even before the Cabot voyages. By 1506 enough Portuguese were fishing in North American waters to cause King Manuel to order that they pay a 10 per cent tax on their catches.

It is not necessary here to recount the growth of the Newfoundland fisheries as the details are available from many sources. It is sufficient to say that fishermen from the continental European countries outnumbered those from England for the first three-quarters of the sixteenth century, but by 1575 the English were in charge of the fishing at the various Newfoundland ports. This state of affairs was attributed to their experience in the Icelandic fishery and their stronger vessels.

Although several species of fish suitable for curing abounded in the waters off Newfoundland, fishing there in the sixteenth century meant only one thing, the taking of the cod. There were two methods of preserving the fish caught. Because they had good supplies of salt, the French and Portuguese, particularly when fishing on the offshore banks, used the "wet" or "green" method. The cleaned fish were heavily salted, packed in casks, and taken home where the final drying was done. The French often made two "wet" trips a year, setting out on the first in January or February and returning in April or May; they returned from the second trip in October. The English, who had relatively little salt, followed the Icelandic or "dry" method of curing their catches near where they were taken and transporting the dried fish home or directly to markets in the south of Europe. After cleaning, the fish was lightly salted and laid to dry on *flakes,* beds of boughs. From about 1560 on the master of the first vessel in each Newfoundland port was the "admiral" of that port. He had first choice of a beach site for his wharf and flakes, and he set out and enforced the rules under which other fishermen operated for that season. Newfoundland became England's first colony in 1583.

The vessels employed by the English in the Newfoundland fishery came mostly from ports in the west of England, and there was probably some exciting sailing as well as a few unpleasant incidents in the race to be admiral. As in the case of the earlier vessels employed in the Icelandic fishery, little is known about the sixteenth-century Newfoundland codfishers. We can assume, however, that the English fishermen would have employed the same type of deep-sea fishing vessel that they were then using off Iceland; but, of course, we do not really know what they were. During the second half of the century these vessels were said to have measured from forty to fifty tons and to have carried crews of twenty, eight of whom did the curing on shore while the others fished. The fishermen handled their lines from upright barrels hung over the vessel's rail or went out in open small boats usually called *shallops*.

Of the 149 vessels that went to Iceland in 1528, 10 were listed as *crayers* from ports on the River Colne; "crayer" was a variation of the word "carrier." The average crayer of that time was a small square-rigged vessel measuring between fifty and sixty tons. A drawing of the port of Calais made around 1545 shows a fleet of about a dozen of what are thought to be crayers employed in fishing. One of these is shown in Figure 2. She carries a three-masted rig, but the only sails that are certain are the fore and main courses and a lateen mizzen whose mast is stepped well aft. While the bowsprit may have served only as a lead for the fore bowlines, it is likely that a spritsail was set under it. Although some of the rigging details are questionable, a main topsail probably was set flying from the deck. Hull details are meager. The vessel has a square stern and there are two heavy wales in addition to the gunwale. Her superstructures are a small forecastle of the medieval form which overhangs the stem and a half-deck from the mainmast to the stern.

For characteristics of fishing vessels of the latter part of the sixteenth century we can first take a look at the type, the *buss*, employed in the other great fishery, that for herring in the North Sea. The herring were caught in a long drifting net supported by buoys along one edge so that it hung vertically in the sea; when fishing, the buss rode at the leeward end of her net as she might

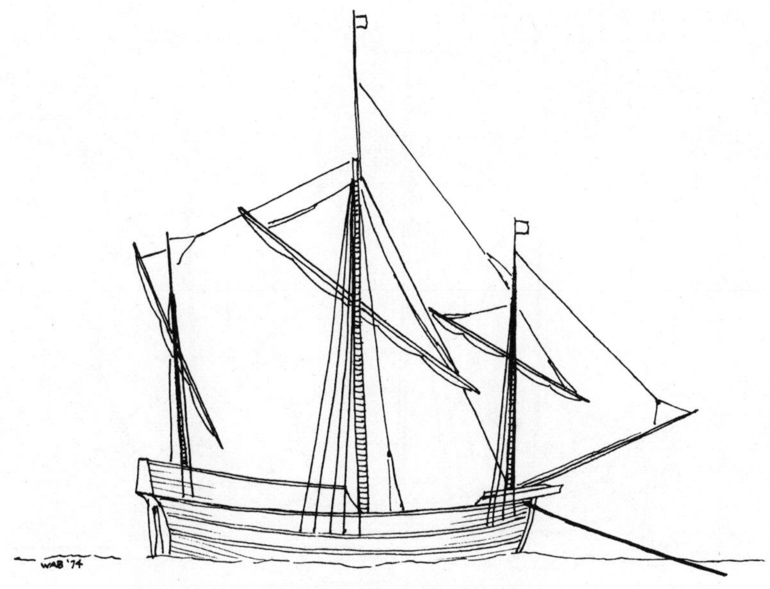

Figure 2. Fishing Vessel at Calais, c. 1545

ride to a sea anchor. The basic features of a buss are shown in Figure 3. The hull of this buss, a substantial craft measuring about fifty-five tons, was essentially doubled-ended; she had a short poop but no forecastle or head structure. The typical buss had three masts, but only the mainmast carried a topsail which usually was set flying from the deck. In place of a bowsprit to which the bowlines of the foresail could be led, the buss carried the so-called "spar bowline" or *vargord* to support the weather leech of the foresail when beating to windward. The buss usually set a small square mizzen sail which served to keep the vessel's head to the wind while she was riding to her net with both the fore and main masts lowered onto a crutch aft. For sailing to and from the fishing grounds a lateen sail replaced the square mizzen. A Dutch drawing of the period shows a similar vessel fishing for cod with a two-hook hand line and a long line which will be described later.

In the absence of definite pictorial evidence, we may imagine that the Newfoundland codfisher of the late sixteenth century, the forty-to-fifty tonner mentioned above, was a cross between

Figure 3. Herring Buss, c. 1585

Figures 2 and 3. To battle the Western Ocean en route from the west of England to Newfoundland she had a stout hull, probably with a square transom. For better sailing qualities she would have had a bowsprit instead of a vargord. Considering that an English fishing vessel was expected to carry home a substantial cargo of dried fish and that the curing of the fish was done on shore, there is no reason to expect her to differ much from a typical small cargo vessel.

As the English fishing fleet overflowed from the Newfoundland harbors down the coast of Nova Scotia and eventually to the coast of the present State of Maine, there are more and more references to the shallops previously mentioned. They became the primary fishing craft operating from shore stations on the offshore islands where the fish were cured. The large vessels became little more than freighters, bringing the shallops and their crews to the North American coast and taking them and the dried catches home to England. In a sense, the fishermen were the first European settlers in New England, for a number wintered over at the fishing stations during the early years of the seventeenth century before the Pilgrims established the first permanent colony at Plymouth.

Perhaps the best-known shallop in American history is that which the Pilgrims brought with them in some sort of cut-down condition on board the *Mayflower* in 1620. Not only was this shallop cut down but she was further damaged during the storms that the *Mayflower* encountered and by the passengers who slept in her during the Atlantic crossing. After the *Mayflower* anchored in what is now Provincetown Harbor at the tip of Cape Cod, carpenters worked sixteen or seventeen days to make the shallop usable. While some of the Pilgrims set off in her to explore Massachusetts Bay, others of the company were searching out suitable trees and cutting timber for another shallop. Shown in Figure 4 is a modern reproduction, designed by the writer, representing the Pilgrim shallop; it has been exhibited since 1957 at Plymouth, Massachusetts, by Plimoth Plantation, Incorporated. She is thirty-three feet and three inches long over all with a breadth of nine feet two inches and depth amidships of three feet and three inches. With her leeboards and simple rig of staysail and sprit main, she looks strange to modern eyes, but such craft were common in the seventeenth century. Modern yachtsmen have found to

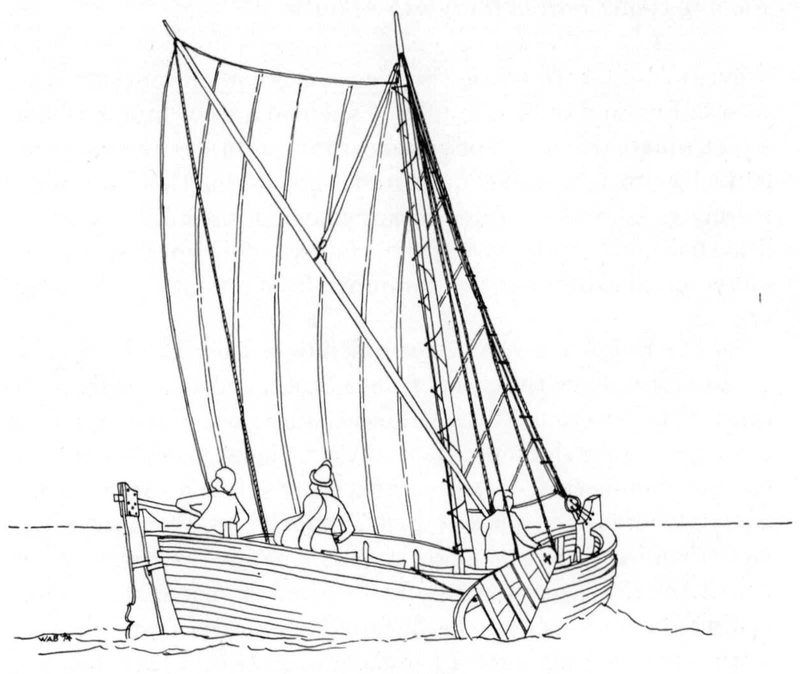

Figure 4. Pilgrim Shallop, c. 1620

their consternation that this shallop is often more than a match for their fiberglass flyers.

Another early New England shallop was that built by the shipwrights of the ill-fated Popham colony established at the mouth of the Kennebec River in 1607. This shallop was constructed before the well-known thirty-ton pinnace *Virginia*, and there is evidence that two more shallops may have been completed before the colonists abandoned the site and returned to England in the late summer of 1608.

When, in the spring of 1630, John Winthrop and about four hundred colonists sailed west across the Atlantic eventually to settle on the shores of what is now the harbor of Boston, Massachusetts, the company included six shipwrights. The five ships of the fleet that brought the new settlers carried for the building of vessels such supplies as pitch, tar, rosin, oakum, old ropes for oakum, nails, cordage, and sailcloth. The six shipwrights were instructed to build as soon as possible three shallops which, when completed, were to be sent out to fish. At least one larger vessel had been constructed in Massachusetts before Winthrop's arrival, hence it is quite probable that other fishing groups along the New England coast constructed shallops of native timber in the years between 1607 and 1629.

The majority of the early English fishermen along the coast of New England came from the west of England. The communities they established, unlike those settled by seekers for religious freedom, were intended solely as fishing ports. The one now called Marblehead was founded by fishermen from Cornwall and the Channel Islands; one of its early names was Foy, a good phonetic spelling of Fowey, a well-known town in Cornwall. In the early seventeenth century and at least as late as the fourth decade of the eighteenth century the fishermen of Cornwall, those of the Channel Islands, and those of Brittany, with whom the Cornishmen had close racial and cultural ties, employed double-ended fishing boats similar to that shown in Figure 5. A map of New England that has been dated about 1680 shows two fleets of small vessels that can be nothing but fishing shallops of the same type. Anchored between the Isles of Shoals and Cape Ann are four boats riding to the prevailing southwesterly wind. Further north are four more under sail heading into the coast between Cape Elizabeth and Wood Island off the mouth of the Saco River. Shallops so rigged were the primary New England fishing craft to perhaps 1670, and a few probably were still employed in the fisheries as late as the mid-eighteenth century.

Although they used the same type of boat in England and North America, the Cornish fishermen at home were concerned mainly with catching the pilchard—in an early stage this fish is the sardine of commerce—while at first the cod was the only fish thought worth taking from the waters of the New World. By the 1660's New England fishermen were catching and curing hake, haddock, and pollack as well. Their cured catch was divided into two grades, merchantable and refuse. The former were sound, full-grown, and well-cured fish "clear like a Lanthorn horn and without spots"; refuse fish were "salt burnt, spotted, rotten, and carelessly ordered." Merchantable fish were bought by Massachusetts merchants who shipped them to ports in France, Portugal, and Spain; the same merchants sent the refuse fish to the Caribbean islands.

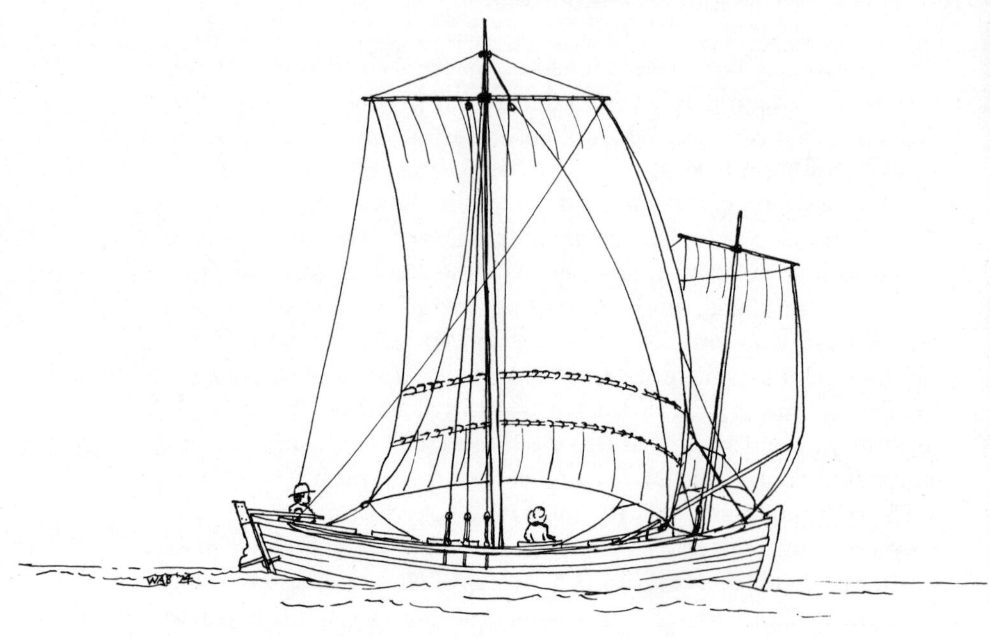

Figure 5. Square-rigged Shallop, c. 1660

At first entirely open, the typical New England fishing shallop was, by the last quarter of the seventeenth century, full sheathed on the inside and partially decked. There was a cuddy forward to shelter the crew, and although small and cramped, it had a fireplace for cooking and to provide some heat. Also decked over were the fish holds between the "rooms," open spaces bounded by transverse bulkheads in which the crew stood while fishing. Water could slop into the rooms but the bulkheads restricted its flow fore and aft. Covers were sometimes fitted to these rooms when a shallop was not actively engaged in fishing. Shallops ranged in size from about twenty-five to forty-five feet in length over all, from about six to ten feet in breadth, and from about two and one-half to four feet in minimum depth. For the standard New England codfishery the average shallop had a crew of four—a master, a midship man, and a foremast man who went to sea, while the fourth man remained on shore to dry the catch and cook the main meals for the entire crew. The largest shallops may have had more than four men in their crews.

As the New England fishermen pursued the cod farther afield, they needed vessels more seaworthy than the shallops, and during the second half of the seventeenth century we find a growing number of references to *ketches*. The typical ketch was a strongly built, beamy, fully decked, round-sterned vessel. Ketches ranged in size from about twelve to seventy tons burden, but those measuring over forty tons were rare. That they were employed in considerable numbers is shown by the fact that in 1677, when the Indians were trying to drive the English from the coast of Maine, twenty ketches from Salem were captured by the first of August. In 1697 there were sixty fishing ketches belonging to Salem alone.

Although the ketch rig has been described as that of a ship without a foremast, this definition applied mainly to the naval

Figure 6. Ketch, c. 1670

bomb ketch; it would have been absurd on a twelve-ton fisherman. There are reasons for believing that the smallest ketches may have carried the simple single-masted rig of the shallop shown in Figure 4; in the slightly larger sizes a lateen mizzen was added. Still larger ketches that did have square rigs probably looked like Figure 6, which is based on a sailing reproduction designed by the writer in 1969 for the South Carolina Tricentennial Commission. The rig of this vessel differs from the ship-without-a-foremast concept in that, unlike the usual ship proportions, her square mainsail is relatively deep and narrow and her topsail is quite small.

Meanwhile, what of the fishing vessels of Old England? Through the seventeenth century the deep-sea fishing vessels seem to have continued to be three-masters with square sails, but the evidence is confusing as the majority of the century's marine artists were Dutch. When looking at paintings of fishing vessels in English waters, we do not know whether they are English vessels whose builders may have followed Dutch examples or typical Dutch vessels with which the artists were familiar. The early decades of the eighteenth century, however, saw the introduction of a herring buss with two masts and a bowsprit (Figure 7), a type that could have been employed in the codfishery as well.

For fishing off the southeast coast of England, transom-sterned, open boats carrying a single mast and square sail are known to have been employed in the 1570's. About a century later there is evidence for the use of similarly rigged double-enders off the west coast. The two-masted, square-rigged double-enders of Cornwall have been mentioned earlier. It is known that the Dutch employed larger decked vessels carrying this rig during the seventeenth century and it is likely that the English did too. These would have been the then up-to-date versions of the "W.A." 1480 engraving. The British artist Richard Wright (1735-1775) showed just such a vessel, with leeboards, in his painting "The Fishery," which can be dated between 1760 and 1773; this craft may have been a visiting Dutchman.

It is said that all catches of cod were salted until about the beginning of the eighteenth century, when wells were introduced in English vessels which allowed the cod, along with ling and halibut, to be brought to port, kept for a long period, and sold alive.

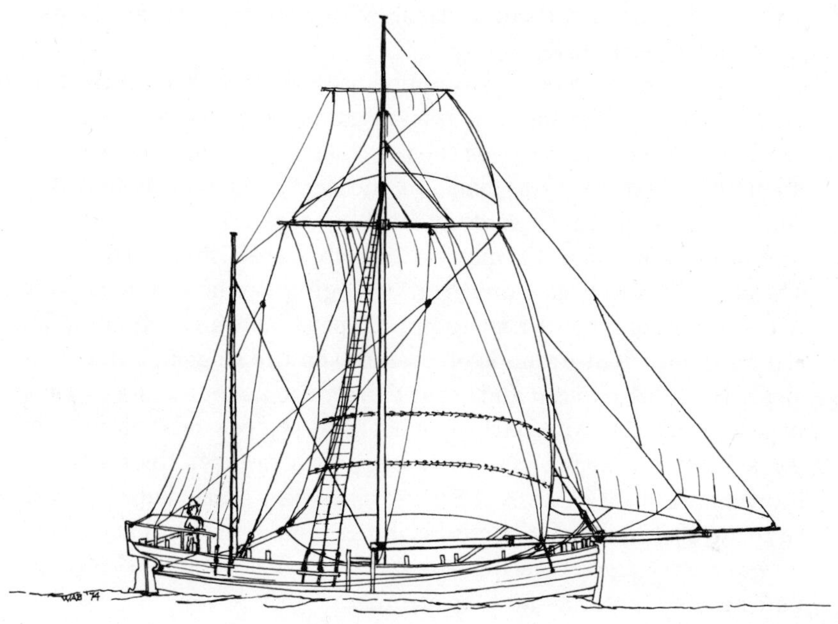

Figure 7. English Herring Buss, c. 1750

The first wells seem to have been no more than tanks in a vessel's hold which could be filled with water through a pipe. Soon, however, the wells were bulkheaded sections free flooding from the sea through a number of small holes bored through the vessel's bottom planking. As in other matters marine, the Dutch had led the way; similar wells are in wrecks from the early seventeenth century that have been found in the new polders reclaimed from the Zuider Zee during the 1960's.

In spite of this means of providing fresh fish, the average Englishman tasted little for a considerable number of years. Until the end of the eighteenth century a large proportion of the fish caught by the English was cured and sold in the countries of southern Europe. The poorer classes in England considered fish a fancy food, and it is true that the first catch of the year of certain species brought high prices from the wealthy of London. It was not until land transport improved early in the nineteenth century that inland Englishmen began to enjoy fresh fish. The development of the railroads completely changed the marketing of fish;

ports having good rail connections with London grew at the expense of those that did not.

For years London was supplied with fresh fish by a fleet of vessels whose home port was Barking, a town on the north side of the Thames. To modern eyes the town seems far from the sea, but its fishing history dates back to the early fourteenth century. During the eighteenth century Barking was the home port of a number of fine *smacks,* many of which were fitted with wells. These smacks served a dual role, bringing catches from distant fleets, an employment that required speed, as well as fishing for cod on the ancient grounds off Iceland, on the Dogger Bank, and elsewhere. The live cod and other fish for the London market were usually landed by the Barking smacks at Gravesend, where they were kept in floating chests. Enough fish to meet the daily requirements of the market at Billingsgate were carried up the river in the wells of *hatch boats,* clinker-built double-enders that carried a two-masted rig consisting of a staysail, a loose-footed standing-gaff mainsail, and a small sprit mizzen.

Early in the eighteenth century the Barking smacks had what today would be called a cutter rig—one mast carrying a boomless long-gaff mainsail, staysail, jib, and two square sails—a course and a topsail—as shown in Figure 8. Late in the century the mainsail, although still loose-footed, had a boom that extended a considerable distance over the stern and the square sails had been abandoned. During the Napoleonic Wars, when fishing was disrupted, many smacks were employed successfully in the Mediterranean fruit trade, where also speed was essential; some never returned to fishing. At Barking in 1820-1830 there were two classes of cutter-rigged smacks, new and old, the division being at the age of sixty years.

The use of the trawl net, a great net shaped like a flattened bag and dragged along the sea bottom, is said to have originated with the Barking fishermen, although those from Brixham in Devon have usually claimed the honor. Barking men are known to have employed the trawl net at least as early as 1750, but a form of trawling was known in English waters back in 1622. A small type of drag net was in use in 1377.

Although hand-lining for cod was common around 1760, the Barking smacks were long-lining in the autumn and winter sea-

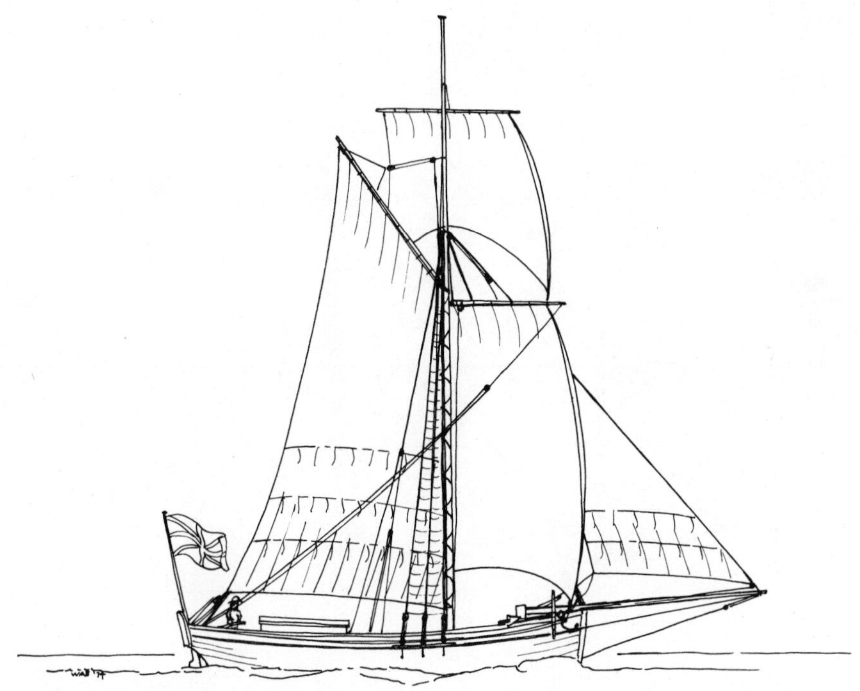

Figure 8. Barking Smack, c. 1750

sons and trawling the remainder of the year. Long-lining, as the term implies, involved a long line to which were secured shorter lines, called snoods, each having a baited hook attached. Although details of the earlier long-lining practices have been lost, during the mid-nineteenth century British fishing smacks carried 180 such lines each 40 fathoms long and fitted with 26 snoods. This number of lines when fastened end to end made a total length of a bit over eight statute miles and 4680 baited hooks were out. Lines ranging from ten to twelve miles in length with from 9000 to 12,000 hooks were used in later years. At about half-tide the eight miles of line were paid out as the smack sailed as free as possible across the tide so that the snoods would stream clear of the main line. A small anchor with a marker buoy held the beginning of the line and another anchor was put down at each forty-fathom length to steady the line. When all the line was out, the smack hove to until the tide was nearly slack, and then the process of taking in the catch began. Pulling up the leeward end of the line, the smack

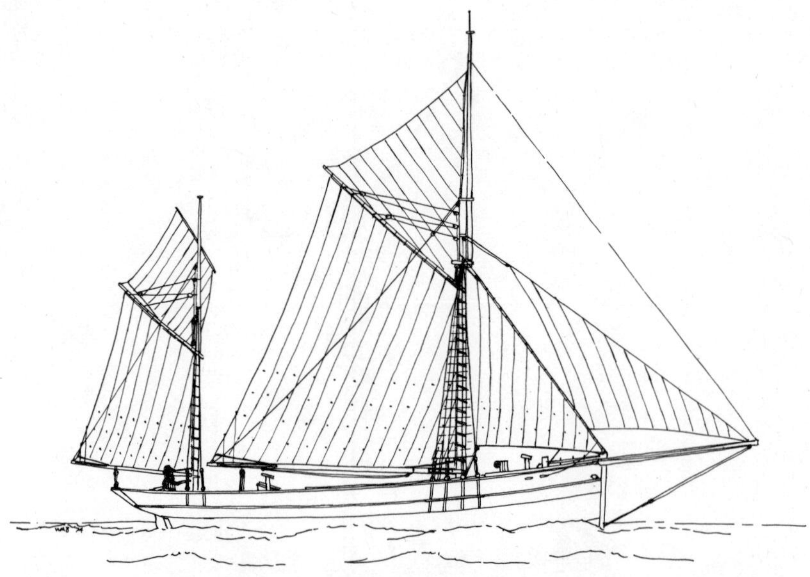

Figure 9. English Ketch-rigged Cod Smack, c. 1880, after March

made short tacks along its course as it was hauled on board. The best fish went into the well and were carried to port alive while the others were salted and packed in ice.

By the mid-nineteenth century the Thames had become so polluted that it was no longer possible to keep fish alive in the floating chests at Gravesend and Barking, and other fishermen began to land their catches at ports on the east coast of England north of the Thames. Eventually, because of a far-sighted railway policy, Great Grimsby at the north of the Humber became England's greatest fishing port. There were changes in the fishing vessels too. The cutter-rigged smacks gradually increased in size until the mid-1860's, when it became apparent that they had reached the limit in handiness. Their long booms were definite hazards when reefing was required; hence there was a shift to the ketch rig as shown in Figure 9. The month of November 1877 marked the beginning of the end of trawling under sail, for during the first week of that month a steam paddle tug was first employed to tow a trawl. Her owner was derided for wasting his money, but the venture was profitable, and after the tug's second successful trip other tug owners rushed to follow his example. The year 1881 saw the construction of the first specially designed, steam-propelled trawler, the *Zodiac,* launched at Hull.

Far to the north the Shetland Islanders had for centuries fished off-shore for cod, ling, and hake in open boats whose basic features were established in the days of the Vikings. This is not surprising, for from the late ninth century to 1469 the Shetlands were Norwegian territory. These open boats were fine-lined, lightly built double-enders, low amidships with high ends. They were similar to the small boats found with the Gokstad ship, dated about A.D. 900, and their sisters are still being constructed along the west coast of Norway. Timber supplies on the islands were meager; hence houses and boats were imported from Norway as bundles of prefabricated and numbered pieces. From 1807 to 1814, because of an English blockade of Norway, the Shetlanders were forced to build boats of timber from other sources, but the fishermen did not consider them as good as those from Norway. After the lifting of the blockade the importation of boats was resumed and continued until about 1860.

The Shetland fishermen employed two sizes of boat, a four-oared and six-oared, known respectively as the *fourern* and the *sixern.* There are occasional references, even as early as 1640, to eight-oared boats, enlarged sixerns, which were used primarily for transporting goods and fish to and from outlying fishing stations. A large sixern of the mid-nineteenth century might have measured as much as thirty-seven feet in length over all, with a breadth of ten feet and a depth of three feet amidships. Such a craft had more depth but less sheer than the earlier boats. The construction of the fourerns and sixerns followed typical Norse practice, with clinker planking and widely spaced ribs which were connected to the keel only through the garboard strakes. Both sizes had a single mast stepped a little forward of the mid-length, and originally the sail was square. The fourern's sail remained practically that to the end, while the sixern's became a dipping lug having four rows of reef points. A typical sixern is shown in Figure 10.

In such entirely open boats Shetland fishermen ventured far

offshore, as far as thirty-five to forty miles in the sixerns. When the wind was foul they would usually row the entire distance rather than working to windward under sail. The fish were taken on long lines similar to those described earlier; in 1812 a sixern carried forty lines each fifty fathoms long with about fifteen hooks. It is obvious that the employment of open boats for offshore fishing practically invited losses of men and vessels. In July 1833 the loss of 105 men and thirty-one boats in a heavy gale led to the building of a few half-decked boats, but because of their increased weight they were not adopted by the Shetland fishermen. Yearly losses of men and boats continued. Improved types of fishing boats appeared during the 1860's, but there were still large numbers of fourerns and sixerns. A heavy gale of 20 July 1881, during which 58 men and 10 boats were lost, was the final blow to these ancient types. Their replacements were fully decked double-enders which carried a two-masted lug rig.

Returning to the western shores of the Atlantic, a reputed American invention of the early eighteenth century, the *schooner,*

Figure 10. Shetland Sixern, after Tudor

quickly replaced the ketches previously mentioned and in time came to be the standard rig of medium- and large-sized American fishing vessels. By tradition the first schooner was built about 1713 by Captain Andrew Robinson at Gloucester, Massachusetts, but the account of her launching was not written down until several years after the event. We do not know, of course, the details of the rig of this first schooner. By the modern definition it could have been quite simple—two masts, the second being of the same height as or slightly taller than the first, and three sails, fore-and-aft gaff sails of about equal size on each mast and one triangular headsail.

Prior to the advent of the schooner, two-masted, fore-and-aft rigged boats without headsails were employed widely in American waters for inshore fishing and other purposes. A few examples of this rig even persisted into the early twentieth century. One of the common late-seventeenth-century boat types carried two short-gaff sails, both loose-footed though the main had a boom; for lack of a better name this type was known simply as a *two-mast boat.* The *Bermudas boat* was also well known along the Atlantic coast of North America; she carried two loose-footed boomless triangular sails that were laced to well-raked masts. Both rigs were used in the Netherlands before 1650. Who first added a triangular headsail to a two-mast boat to create what we recognize as the schooner rig probably never will be known. It is equally unlikely that we will ever know what he called it. Whatever the name, the schooner rig was not new in 1713. An example of an early schooner rig in England might be dated about 1690, while Dutch versions range back to the middle of the seventeenth century.

Regardless of the origin and age of the rig, the type-name "schooner" was new in the second decade of the eighteenth century. An early written use of the word—then spelled "scooner"—was in the Boston port records for May 1716. Gloucester town records mention the loss of a new fishing "scooner" in August of the same year. The new name and the vessel it represented found favor with American fishermen, and within a decade of its reputed invention it had replaced the ketch in the New England fishing fleet.

The rapid shift from the ketch to the schooner cannot easily be explained. It is unlikely, however, that there was a great burst of ketch-scrapping and schooner-building. The shift may have been little more than a slight rerigging of the existing ketches, a small increase in the height of the second mast and the area of its sail, along with the construction of some new schooners. If it be accepted that ketch hulls were basically double-ended, as indicated by Massachusetts vessel registers, such a rigging change implies that the history of the *pinky schooner,* so popular in the nineteenth century, started about 1713.

While details of their hulls and rigs are lacking, three early schooners employed in fishing out of Small Point Harbor, Maine, in 1718 were quite small; two measured about ten tons while the third was an eight-ton vessel. The ten-tonners would have been about thirty-five feet long on deck, no bigger than many modern cruising yachts. Some of the earliest American pictorial representations of schooners are in the 1722 view of Boston by William Burgis. One of these, outward bound, is shown in Figure 11.

Along with the two-masted vessels mentioned above, *sloops*—presumably single-masted, fore-and-aft-rigged vessels—were also employed in the New England fisheries at the end of the seventeenth and the beginning of the eighteenth century. During the ten-year period ending in 1713 more than thirty sloops were built at Gloucester. Four sloops with a total of eighteen men on board were lost in 1716 along with the "scooner" previously

Figure 11. Schooner, c. 1722, after Burgis

mentioned. It has been said, however, that for a number of years after 1713 it was common to apply the term "sloop" to all vessels carrying gaff sails. To add to the confusion, the English until about 1750 reportedly called a small open schooner a "shallop" and a large decked one a "sloop."

Until the 1760's we have little definite information about American fishing vessels. Shallops were still in use during the 1720's, for there are references to shallops and schooners fishing together off Nova Scotia, but all of these shallops may not have carried the two-masted square rig of the seventeenth century. Some may have carried a two-masted, fore-and-aft rig and may have been no more than a decked version of the two-mast boat. Pictorial representations of small vessels during these years are few and far between, and even from those available we cannot tell whether they were employed for deep-water voyages, coasting, or fishing.

The year 1741 was a prosperous one for the codfisheries of New England. In that year Massachusetts, which then included the present State of Maine, had not less than 400 fishing vessels, "besides an equal number of ketches, shallops, and undecked boats," according to Lorenzo Sabine's 1853 report on the fisheries. The average size of the fishing vessels was fifty tons and Marblehead alone owned 160; Gloucester at the same time reportedly sent seventy schooners to the Grand Banks. The term "vessel" is confusing, but we can assume that it meant "schooner," and at this date the large schooners had square sterns while it is probable that the majority of the small schooners had pink sterns.

The various European wars of the mid-eighteenth century that turned French privateers loose against New England's fishing fleet and merchant ships created a demand for fast sailing vessels. One answer was the so-called Marblehead schooner, which was known all along the Atlantic coast of North America. Some Marblehead schooners captured by the French were sent to sea again as privateers. Even as late as 1799 the type was considered in the same class with two other well-known fast-sailing types, the Bermuda sloop and the Virginia pilot boat. At present, plans are known to exist for only two schooners of the Marblehead type. One plan shows a full-lined vessel obviously intended for a cargo carrier. The other plan is a design drawing for a fine-lined schooner for naval service in the West Indies. The form of the average fisherman may have been between these two examples.

Although plans are not available, there do exist from the 1760's a number of building contracts for square-sterned fishing schooners that measured about fifty-five tons. They averaged about forty-five feet long on the keel, sixteen and one-half feet in breadth, and seven and one-half feet in depth. One contract of 1763 provided that the builder of the hull supply the masts, booms, and bowsprit while the owner furnished the gaffs, the standing rigging consisting of single shrouds for each mast and a jib stay, and the running rigging which required fourteen blocks. This schooner carried only three sails—mainsail, foresail, and jib. While the larger schooners that sailed to the West Indies and in the coasting trade often carried square sails, it is unlikely that the smaller fishing schooners ever did.

For the inshore codfisheries in the 1760's New England fishermen were using more substantial two-mast boats than earlier in the century. These craft were at least partially decked, with a prominent cuddy forward that would have been fitted with berths and a fireplace. The foresail was still boomless, but the gaffs had grown in length as shown in Figure 12. Considering the small sizes of some of the mid-eighteenth-century schooners—a craft of ten tons in one case and "something under 20 Feet Keel" in

Figure 12. Two-mast Boats, c. 1770, after Remick

another—the continued existence of these relatively large gaff-rigged two-mast boats without headsails may seem surprising today. We might assume that the natural action would be to add a bowsprit and set a jib forward, but in fact these two-mast boats were quite satisfactory for the services in which they were employed.

New England's fishermen were badly affected by the Revolutionary War, and their lot did not improve materially until the establishment of the Federal Government in 1789. On 4 July of that year the Congress granted a bounty of five cents per quintal of dried fish or barrel of pickled fish exported, and on 9 February 1792 further federal support was provided. A payment ranging from one to two and a half dollars per ton depending on size was granted to vessels employed in the codfisheries for at least four months a year. Under these bounties the few old schooners that had survived the war resumed fishing on the Grand Banks of Newfoundland. In general the fishermen could not afford new vessels of the size needed for the Banks fisheries, so they concentrated on the inshore

Figure 13. Chebacco Boat, c. 1800

fisheries in which they could use smaller vessels—the local ledges, the coast of Maine, and even to the Bay of Chaleur and the Labrador coast where fishing rights had been obtained. By 1808 the Bay and Labrador fisheries provided about three-quarters of the dried fish exported from Massachusetts, which then still included the present State of Maine; less than one-quarter came from the Grand Banks, which required larger vessels and more expensive gear.

The craft developed for these inshore fisheries were known widely as *Chebacco boats*—so named for the locality in which large numbers were built, the Chebacco parish of Ipswich, Massachusetts, which became the Town of Essex in 1819. The basic Chebacco boat was a sharp-sterned vessel ranging in size from twelve to twenty-five tons burden, which carried a two-masted fore-and-aft rig without headsails. Her low bulwarks or rails were carried aft where they met behind the head of the rudder. No one knows just when the bulwarks were given the sharp kick-up at their junctions that made them serviceable as a support for the main boom as well as a seat-of-ease for the crew. Forward, the bulwarks often were stopped clear of the prominent stem that served as a mooring bitt. Although the pink-sterned Chebacco boat was the most common, a typical one being shown by Figure 13, there was a somewhat smaller square-sterned version known as a *dogbody,* a designation whose origin is lost in time.

A simpler description of both forms of the Chebacco boat might be that they were the then favored developments of the old two-mast boat. Their construction was not limited to the Chebacco parish or to Cape Ann from which so many sailed; they were built all along the New England coast eastward from Cape Cod and into the Maritime Provinces of Canada. Inevitably both types grew in size until their simple rig became heavier and harder to work; eventually the larger sizes were superseded by schooner-rigged vessels of the same basic forms.

Figure 14, based on a detail of a painting attributed to M. F. Corné, shows a large American schooner employed in fishing on the offshore banks at the end of the eighteenth century. We do not know, of course, whether she was old or new at the time. This vessel was probably quite similar to the Banks schooners of the

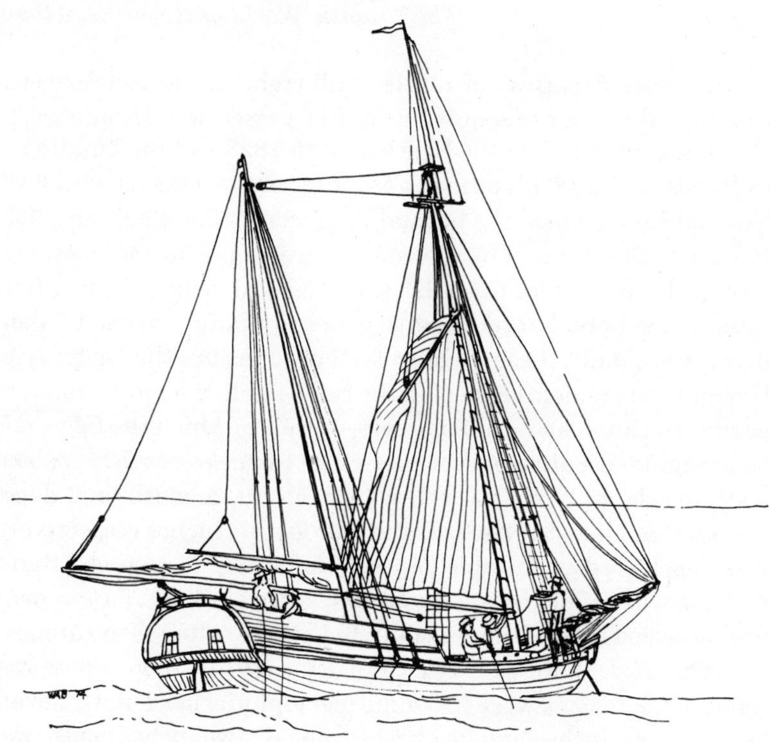

Figure 14. Fishing Schooner, c. 1800, after Corné

1760's, and indeed the type changed but little during the first two decades of the nineteenth century. The most prominent feature of this schooner is her high quarterdeck, which extended from her stern to a little forward of her mainmast. It is said that up to about 1820 all the crew was berthed under the quarterdeck and that the traditional forcastle space below the main deck forward was used for stowage of gear. Because of their fancied resemblance to a shoe or perhaps because of the winter occupation of many Marblehead fisherman—shoemaking—schooners of this type were sometimes called "heel-tappers."

Jefferson's Embargo and the War of 1812 were disastrous to the New England fisheries, and after the war there was another but shorter period when Chebacco boats were common. By a treaty of 1818 the United States retained fishing rights along certain shores of Newfoundland and for an indefinite distance north along the Labrador coast; elsewhere in British North America she gave up the shore fisheries but retained all rights to the sea fisheries. This had the effect of requiring stouter vessels for offshore work.

The completion of the Erie Canal in 1825 and the building of railroads in the 1830's opened good interior markets for salt, pickled, and smoked fish, the normal products of New England's fishing fleet. The growth of the coastal cities and towns, however, provided a market for fresh fish that the local inshore fishing fleet could not supply. Larger vessels, generally called "market fishermen," were built; these could go farther to sea but the longer trips brought the problem of keeping the catch fresh. We saw the answer earlier in Dutch and English craft—a well in which the fish could be brought back alive. A schooner-rigged *smack* or *well-boat* about sixty feet long, having a well whose length, breadth, and depth were sixteen feet, twelve feet, and four feet six inches respectively, was considered of suitable capacity for a trip to Georges Bank. Fishing was said to have started on Georges in 1831; for a considerable period most of the vessels fishing there salted their catches.

The *Glide,* built at Essex, Massachusetts, in 1836, whose registered dimensions were fifty nine feet eight inches length, seventeen feet two inches breadth, and seven feet two inches depth, was typical of the period. She was a full-ended vessel with the old type of double-transom stern. By her time the high quarterdeck was only about nine to twelve inches above the main deck; there was no cabin trunk but a large companionway led to the space below where eight men were berthed. Four men could be berthed in the forecastle below the main deck forward of the well. The *bankers,* the salt-fishermen of the period, were essentially of the same size, form, and arrangement without the well.

During the 1840's the feasibility of using ice to preserve fish was recognized, and because of the perishable nature of both ice and cargo there was a demand for vessels faster than the smacks and bankers. The Essex-built *Romp* of 1847 was reputedly the first sharp-lined schooner built for the New England fisheries; yet she was by no means as sharp as the Boston pilot boats of her day. Unfortunately no record of her form has been preserved. Following her there developed two types of faster schooners, the *file bottom* or *sharpshooter* and the *clipper* schooner. The term "file-bottom" was a good description of the roughly triangular-shaped hull sections below the water. There are so few builders' models

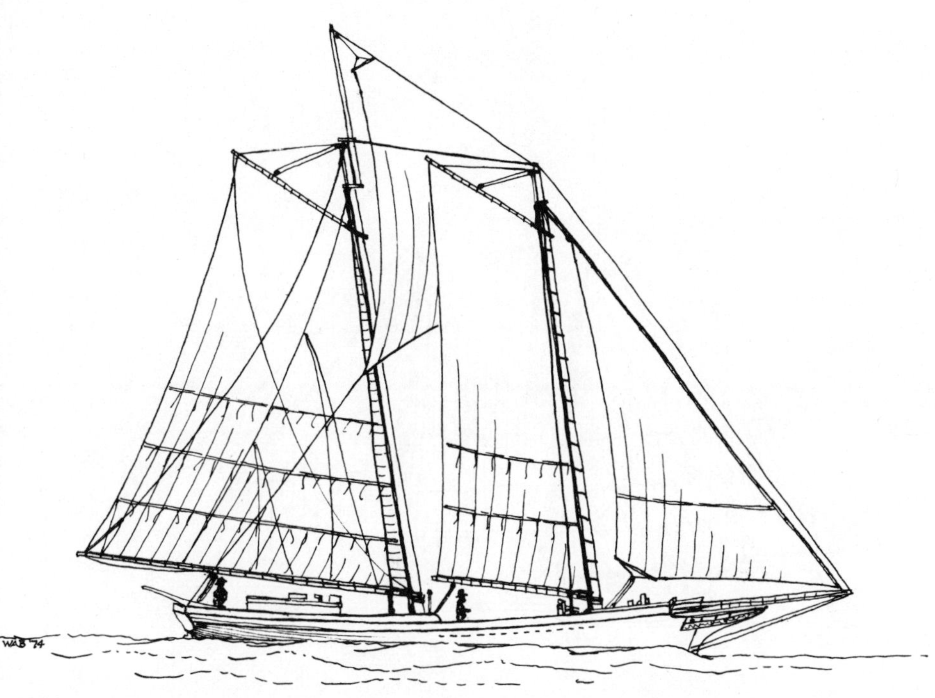

Figure 15. Sharpshooter, c. 1853, after Chapelle

definitely identified as sharpshooters that it is practically impossible now to write a description of this type that might not also serve to describe an early clipper schooner. In addition, there were several variations depending on the primary use.

All schooner development at Gloucester was influenced by the available depths of water in that port's slips, twelve feet being generally the maximum with ten feet being common. In general, the clipper schooner was larger than the sharpshooter, but because of the draft limitation the hulls were shoaler in proportion. Comparing the profiles of the two types, the clipper had less drag to her keel and less rise of floor amidships. While outboard profiles and sail plans tell little about a vessel's form or her capabilities under sail, Figures 15 and 16 show respectively a sharpshooter and a clipper of the 1850's.

The Civil War had somewhat the same effect on the New England fishing fleet as had the earlier wars. When schooner construction was revived, the new craft had essentially the same

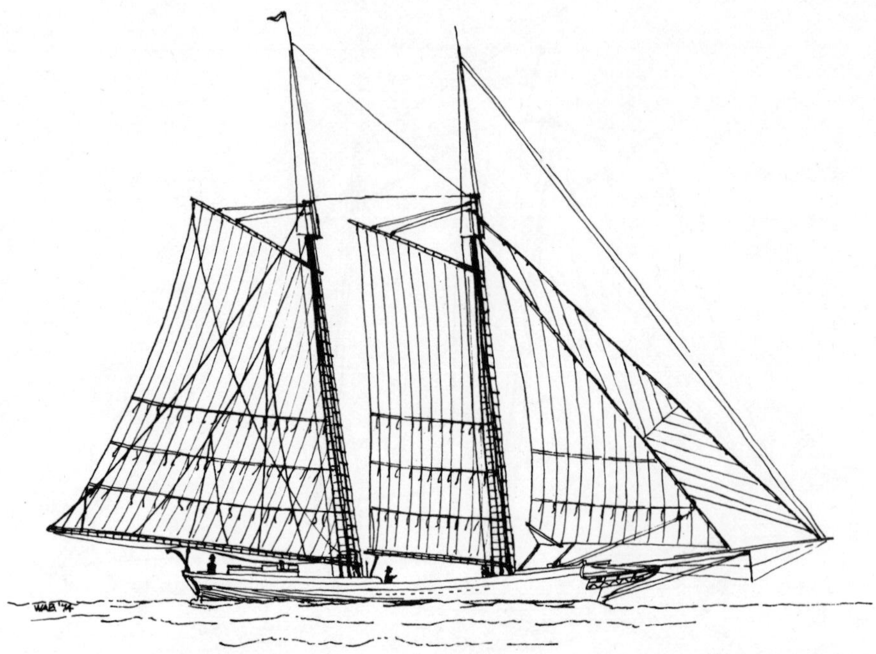

Figure 16. Clipper Schooner, c. 1860, after Chapelle

dimensions and proportions as those built before the war except that the majority were of the clipper type. A postwar clipper schooner had low freeboard with a relatively straight sheer line, a straight keel with moderate drag, a moderate rise of floor with hard bilge, a long sharp bow, and a long run showing some straightness in the buttocks. Clipper schooners had great stability initially and up to the angle at which the deck edge went under; beyond this they capsized or swamped. Up to this point, however, they were very fast, but they lacked the power to carry sail in a gale and were not very weatherly nor safe in clawing off a lee shore. Great losses of men and schooners during the 1870's—the worst year was 1879, when 249 men and 29 schooners were lost—led to growing criticism of the clipper schooner, which, however, proud owners and masters of handsome schooners were loath to accept. Losses of men and schooners continued into the 1880's.

Beginning in 1882 Captain Joseph W. Collins, a successful fisherman who was then a member of the United States Fish

Commission, conducted a long campaign to replace the clipper-type schooner, which he compared unfavorably with the old pinkies. He also claimed that the English North Sea fishing cutters were safer than the clippers, thus adding fuel to the then current yachting controversy over the shallow-draft American sloop versus the deep-draft English cutter. Captain Collins and others who joined his cause argued that fishing schooners should have deeper hulls with sufficient deadrise in their midsections that they would be able to right themselves when heeled even beyond the deck edge. Further, transoms should be narrower with softer quarters, rigs should be lighter, and ballast along with the fish and ice in the hold should be secured against shifting in the event of a knockdown. Many of the desired qualities were stated by an unknown writer who apparently was a competent designer and shipbuilder, perhaps Dennison J. Lawlor of Chelsea, Massachusetts.

From the 1850's to the 1880's clipper schooners grew considerably in length and breadth, but because of the slip restrictions at Gloucester, then the major fishing port, the depth remained about the same, which aggravated the stability problem. The earlier clippers ranged from sixty to sixty-eight feet in length, seventeen to eighteen feet in breadth , and seven to eight feet in depth. At the beginning of the 1880's the lengths ranged from eighty-five to ninety-five feet and the breadths from twenty-one to twenty-five feet.

In his campaign for better schooners Captain Collins gathered plans from several designers and builders, including Lawlor who in 1884 designed and built the *Roulette,* the forerunner of the deeper and more wholesome schooners that Collins proposed. Although owned in Philadelphia, the *Roulette* usually fished out of Boston, which had no draft restrictions; she was fast and more weatherly than any schooner then fishing. The Fish Commission sponsored the construction of a research schooner, the *Grampus,* which was launched at Noank, Connecticut, in March 1886. Captain Collins should receive due credit for proposing improved schooners, but Lawlor actually designed the hull and rig of the *Grampus.* Three other deeper-than-normal schooners were constructed by Essex builders at about the same time, but because of the draft restriction at Gloucester there was no great rush to build others until the *Roulette* and *Grampus* had proved themselves. In addition to the deeper hull, the *Grampus* introduced a number of other features. The heavy head structure was eliminated and she was given a plumb pilot-boat stem. Compared to the standard clipper schooner, her foremast was shorter, the jumbo jib was discarded in favor of a fore staysail and jib, she had iron wire standing rigging, and her blocks were strapped with iron.

The *Carrie E. Phillips* (Figure 17), launched in 1887, was the first fishing schooner from the board of Edward Burgess, who had designed three *America*'s Cup defenders. She was credited with many "firsts," several of which had already appeared on the *Grampus*. The *Phillips,* however, was an extreme vessel for her day, and because of the reputation of her designer she was more influential than the *Grampus* in the move toward deeper-draft schooners.

The first of the new-type schooners whose features were copied widely were two near sisters designed by Burgess and launched in 1889 by the same builder, the *Fredonia* at Essex and the *Nellie Dixon* at East Boston. The former served as a yacht for about a year

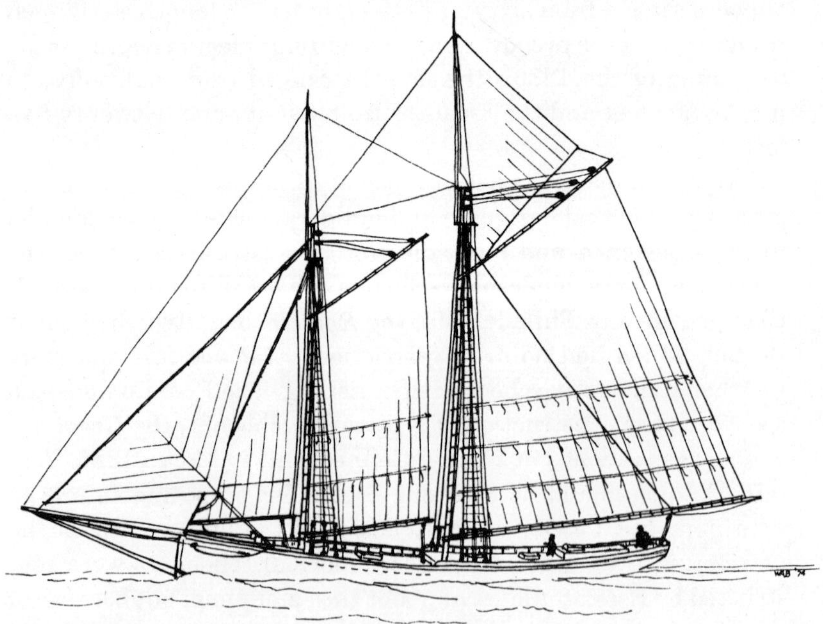

Figure 17. *Carrie E. Phillips,* 1887

before going fishing, while the latter was employed as a fisherman right after her completion. The midsections of these schooners showed a hollow garboard, a steep straight rise of floor, a hard bilge, and considerable tumble home of the topsides. There was a deep rockered keel below the rabbet line. In these schooners Burgess reverted to the old clipper bow profile above water but cut away the forefoot. No exact duplicates of these schooners were built, but their general features were used by other designers and builders for both large and small vessels. They can still be seen in the Friendship sloop, which in recent years has been revived by yachtsmen. In spite of the fact that the *Dixon* went fishing first, the term "*Fredonia* model" was commonly used to describe vessels having the characteristics of these sister schooners. The new deeper schooners often grounded out at low tide in Gloucester's shallow slips, sometimes damaging their hulls, hence the shift to the new type resulted in a decline of the Gloucester fishing fleet and an expansion of Boston's.

On 12 November 1891 an unusual vessel sailed on a fishing trip from Gloucester. She was the Essex-built *Resolute,* for all practical purposes a typical English fishing ketch, which was intended to introduce the English practice of beam trawling to American waters. After four poor trips the beam trawl was abandoned, and following two fresh and salt fish trips to the eastward, the ketch rig was abandoned too. In the late months of 1892 the *Resolute* was rerigged as a schooner. Beam trawling was not practiced successfully in New England waters until 1905, when the steam-propelled trawler *Spray,* built at Quincy, Massachusetts, went into service. She was followed by four more in 1910-1911, and a second group of four were built in 1912-1913.

The term *trawling* is somewhat confusing in the American codfishery, as it originally meant what the English called "long-lining," described earlier. Vessels engaged in this form of codfishing carried from six to twelve two-man dories which were about fifteen feet long on the bottom. Each dory was outfitted with from four to six "tubs-o'-trawl," each of which had one three-hundred-fathom long ground line that carried three hundred hooks. This method of taking cod was said to have first been used in the American codfishery in 1845. Curiously, hand-lining from dories was also said to have started about the middle of the nineteenth century; previously all cod had been taken by hand-lines dropped over the side of the fishing vessel. It was found that hand-lining from dories enabled a vessel to fill her hold faster, as the practice spread the fishing over a larger area of the sea bottom. In this method of fishing there was only one man to a dory; he handled a double-hooked line over each side of his craft.

The design of New England fishing schooners launched during the late 1890's and the first decade of the twentieth century was influenced greatly by the work of Thomas F. McManus. Son of a Boston sailmaker, fish broker, and yachtsman, McManus first took up the designing of fishing schooners as a hobby and then gave up his fish business to make it his profession. The first major feature introduced by McManus was a rounded stem profile similar to that then popular on yachts. The early curved-stem schooners bore Indian names, hence the term *Indian-head* was applied to schooners having this type of bow. As Burgess had done on the *Fredonia,* McManus gave most of his Indian-headers relatively

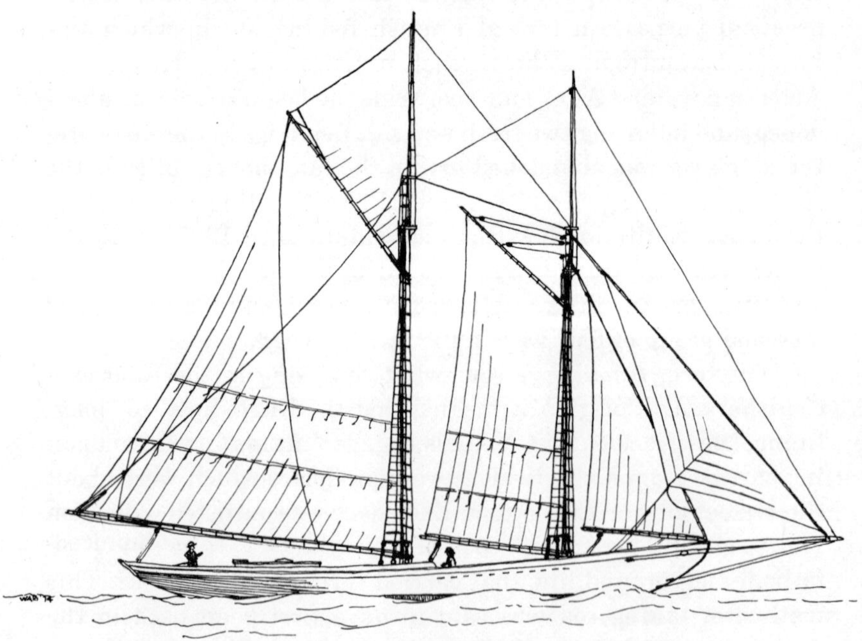

Figure 18. Crowninshield-designed Schooner *Rob Roy,* 1900

deep outside keels that curved for their full length. This made it difficult to set the blocks for hauling out on a marine railway, and there were a number of accidents when the blocks tripped. B. B. Crowninshield, another naval architect of the period, also used the curved stem but gave his schooners a short straight keel having a definite knuckle where it rose to meet the stem. This practice was followed widely for the last of the sailing fishermen and was the standard "fisherman profile" employed for many cruising yachts of the 1920's and 1930's. One of Crowninshield's schooners, the *Rob Roy* (1900), is shown in Figure 18.

During the 1890's some Massachusetts Bay yachtsmen turned to small sailing yachts without bowsprits for knocking about the bay in all kinds of weather—hence the type name *knockabout*. Having in mind the number of men lost from schooner bowsprits, McManus turned out a design for a knockabout (bowspritless) fishing schooner, but considerable time passed before he found someone willing to risk money in such a venture. The first knockabout fishing schooner, the *Helen B. Thomas* (Figure 19), launched at Essex in the spring of 1902, had the appearance of a relatively small schooner whose bow had been stretched out to where the outer end of the bowsprit normally would have been. The early knockabout schooners had two disadvantages—their capacity was small for their over-all length on which builders figured costs, and there was much wasted space forward. Later schooners of the type had relatively short but deep forward overhangs, which led to tall rigs to obtain proper balance.

The New England inshore fisheries were relatively unimportant after the end of the Civil War. They were served by numerous local types of small open craft and by larger decked vessels. Replacing the old pinkies were *schooner boats,* generally under fifty feet in length and in most respects copies of the larger schooners employed in the offshore fisheries. Business conditions in the 1870's ruined many owners of large schooners and few such vessels were built. Knowing that small schooners were not particularly fast sailers, a considerable number of fishermen turned to *sloop boats,* fine vessels that ranged in length from forty to sixty feet. In general appearance the sloop boats were much like the clipper-bowed yachts of the period, but their proportions and form were quite different, the latter being closer to that of the large schooners

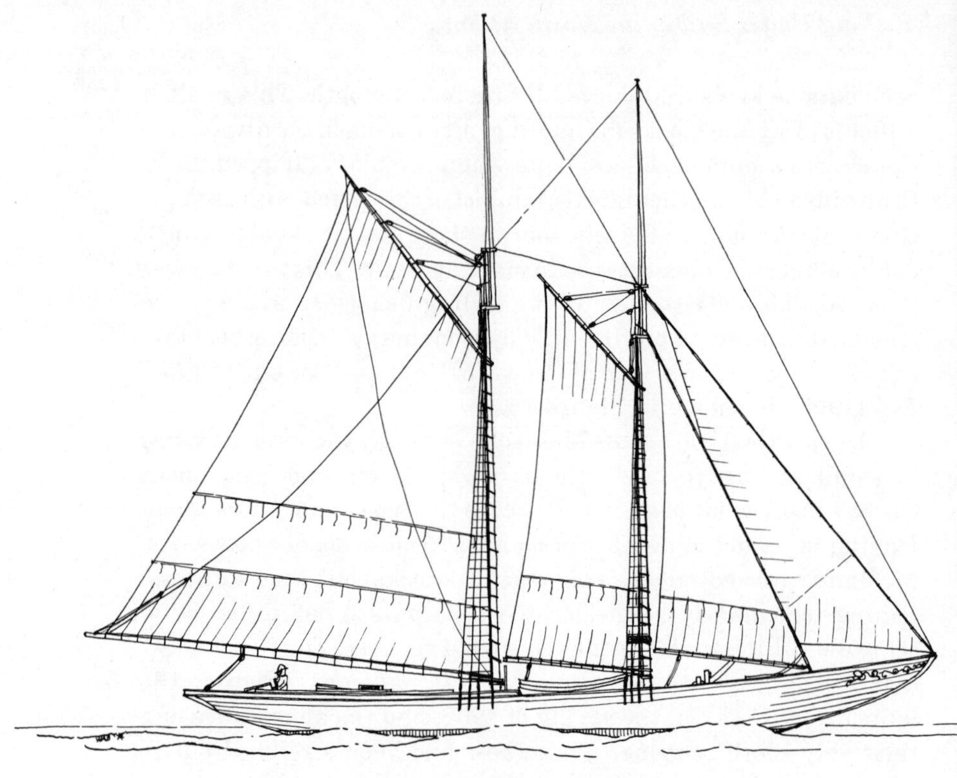

Figure 19. Knockabout Schooner *Helen B. Thomas,* 1902

than to the yachts. Sloop boats were constructed in fair numbers until about 1905, when power boats began to be employed in the fisheries. Most of the sloop boats of the later years were built at Gloucester, usually on speculation during the summer so that a builder could keep his men employed.

The introduction of the gasoline engine as auxiliary power, beginning about 1900, completely changed the character of the New England fishing fleet. There were many mechanical problems in the early days and, as might be expected with gasoline, many fires and explosions, but the advantages of mechanical propulsion were obvious. The early auxiliary schooners were full sail-powered vessels with engines added, a combination that earlier had been proven uneconomical in cargo vessels. Modifications of hull form and a gradual increase of power installed meant the suppression and eventual abandonment of sail. Along with these changes was a shift to net trawling.

Fishing Under Sail in the North Atlantic

The last large fishing vessels carrying full sail-power and no auxiliary engines were built in both Old England and New England in the early 1920's. They disappeared from the fishing grounds before the Second World War, but a few vessels have been preserved here and there so that future generations may know something of codfishing under sail.

William A. Baker

CHAPTER FOUR

Seafaring and the Emergence of American Science

INTRODUCTION[1]

The building of a nation, in the industrial age in which we live, includes the building of a scientific tradition. Though knowledge of the natural universe can, like any commodity, be imported on demand, the search for a new national identity requires that it be produced at home, at least in part. Each new state wishes to prove, by adding to the world's learning, its right to a place among the nations, and so it tries to develop in indigenous institutions an ongoing community of contributors to the expansion of human understanding of the natural world.

In the seventeenth and eighteenth centuries, when modern science began, the dynastic states of Europe had no difficulty in establishing scientific traditions. The weakness of nationalist sentiments made it possible for students of the natural order to migrate from country to country without raising any questions of loyalty to one's homeland, and the structure of European society provided a setting for scientific endeavor as a new form of aristocratic leisure. The sovereign might patronize the new learning as he had the old; if, as in England, he chose to patronize it only in name, a metropolitan community of the leisured could add science to those other delights which competed for their attention and their purses.

The new egalitarian societies of the age of the democratic revolution had no such obvious place for science. France nearly destroyed its scientific institutions during the Revolution: only with the rise to power of Napoleon I were they restored, on a broader base oriented toward supporting the military power of the new nation-state. With a scientific past too glorious to repudiate, France after the Revolution does not provide the prototype of the new nation founding a scientific tradition along with a viable economy, polity, and artistic culture. This role is filled, however, by the other new society begun amid the upheavals of the late eighteenth century—the United States of America. The first to grow to maturity in the age of the nation-state, the American scientific community offers us an example of institution-building repeated in Japan later in the nineteenth century and in a host of developing countries in the twentieth century.

What does the development of an American scientific tradition have to do with maritime commerce in the North Atlantic? Simply this: As the key sector of the American economy in the early Federal period and a vital sector thereafter, the ocean shipping industry provided the economic base on which to develop viable scientific institutions. Beginning with the Coast Survey, founded by President Thomas Jefferson in 1807, three agencies of the American government were established prior to the Civil War to furnish what we now call research and development services to the American fleet. The histories of these agencies—the Coast Survey, the Depot of Charts and Instruments, and the Nautical Almanac Office—are closely intertwined with the history of the American scientific community before the Civil War.

I.

Facing a hostile and untamed environment, with a climate significantly harsher than that of Western Europe whence they came, those who colonized America were drawn to the study of the practical sciences that might furnish the tools for understanding, if not indeed modifying, the world around them. Foremost among the questions they faced were those concerning the sea, for between America and the source of its goods both material and spiritual lay the North Atlantic Ocean. The techniques for bringing ships across the ocean and safely into harbor provided the setting for some of the most important American endeavors in the exact sciences.

Before the Revolution Americans were content that their science be colonial science, dependent upon the great European scientific societies—especially the Royal Society of London—both for new topics and insights and for the approbation so necessary to the lonely seeker into nature's mysteries. The colonial was expected to describe his new environment, to send specimens and data back to Europe where they might be set in proper perspective. Thus Thomas Brattle's observations of comets in the seventeenth century furnished evidence for Newton's theories of the heavens, and the astronomical expeditions from Massachusetts and Pennsylvania contributed to the worldwide effort, directed from Europe, to observe the transits of Venus in 1761 and 1769. Buffon and Linnaeus eagerly seized the specimens of fauna and flora sent them by colonials to be worked into their magisterial systems of the natural world.

This reconnaissance of the New World, a purely empirical endeavor, was at the same time both a means to the definition of a new national identity and a contribution to the data from which new scientific knowledge might be generated in Europe. Not for the colonial was the fashioning of theories; such serious thinking had to be reserved for the European savant, who could never get enough data to theorize about. This arrangement proposed a rational division of scientific labor between the two communities, European and colonial. An exceptional colonial like Benjamin Franklin might make a major theoretical contribution, but the gathering of raw data was the colonial's scientific mission, in his own eyes as well as in those of the Europeans. If he had the talent to make a significant contribution, better that he return to the mother country where he would find greater resources at his disposal and a larger community of his peers.[2]

Following the Revolution, a colonial posture could no longer satisfy, and there came a call for an independent American science, as for independence in every other sphere of human endeavor. The first independent cultural institutions to be developed were learned societies, which provided meetings for the discussion of scientific subjects and periodicals in which to publish contributions. To the American Philosophical Society, founded before the Revolution and reactivated in 1785, was added the American Academy of Arts and Sciences of Boston. But these societies were feeble compared to their European counterparts. Neither Boston nor Philadelphia prior to 1850 provided any significant number of people whose working lives had anything to do with scientific subjects; only an exceptional person like Nathaniel Bowditch used his leisure to master and to contribute to the scientific literature.[3]

However, there was a commercial interest that could be exploited for scientific ends: seaborne trade, the lifeblood of the Republic. Because it formed the key sector of the American economy in the early Federal period, the ocean shipping industry could provide the economic support that an embryonic scientific community needed.[4] There was also a close connection between seafaring and science in the problems of navigation. Nathaniel Bowditch, the most distinguished American scientist active in the years around 1800, had been led from these practical problems into pure mathematics and astronomy.

At the height of prosperity for American shipping, Thomas Jefferson—of all men who have held the Presidency the most cognizant of science and its significance—recognized the link between science and the sea by founding in 1807 the United States Coast Survey, the first scientific agency of the federal government. With Jefferson's guidance, the first head of the Survey was chosen entirely for his scientific competence, without regard for the political problems he was bound to face. Ferdinand Rudolph Hassler, a recent immigrant from Switzerland, had impeccable credentials as a geodesist and a European's conception of the deference owed by society to a man of learning. He was as determined as President Jefferson to survey the coast of the United States according to the soundest principles, those in which he had been trained in the Swiss Federal Survey. But he faced a Congress committed to keeping the machinery of the national government as small as possible and unable to perceive any difference between the scientifically sound surveys of professional geodesists and those of practical men without scientific training. Beginning without suitable instruments or trained assistants, Hassler was delayed in getting into the field until 1816, partly for want of appropriations, partly by the War of 1812. The work had barely begun when in 1818 the Congress removed the Survey from civilian jurisdiction to turn it over to the Navy.[5]

Though the result was a setback for American science, the Congress acted with what was in its own lights a clear sense of priorities. The maintenance in time of peace of a force adequate for defense has always been a problem, and never is it more acute than immediately following a war. The United States Navy came out of the War of 1812 with an officer corps much larger than required to fill all the seagoing billets available. A small shore establishment could absorb only a fraction of the trained officers, whose hope for further cruises—and with them opportunities for promotion—had to be postponed to a distant future. Unlike the modern Navy, the Navy of the nineteenth century provided only half-pay for its officers not at sea. Hence there was always strong pressure, especially just after a war, for the government to find suitable employment for naval officers. What could be more suitable than the survey of the coast? From 1818 to 1832 the civilian Coast Survey was abolished. The Congress had made a decision that the needs of defense should prevail over needs of science. The attempt to harness ocean shipping in support of an American scientific community based in the Coast Survey had failed, at least for the moment.

Science suffered another defeat at the hands of the Congress in the 1820's: the rejection of President John Quincy Adams' plea for a national observatory. Like the survey of the coast, an observatory could lay claim to the support of the shipping community, since navigation is pre-eminently astronomical. But Adams' proposal for an American "lighthouse in the sky" had been derided in the halls of the Congress from the moment of its announcement in his inaugural address, partly from the intense hostility to Adams of the supporters of Andrew Jackson, partly from the general reluctance of the Congress to sponsor national projects. The observatory, chief ambition of the embryo scientific community in the early Federal period, remained unbuilt.[6]

II.

The demand for a national observatory in the United States was part of a worldwide scientific movement. Astronomy from antiquity had been queen of the sciences: the first to develop, the most specialized, the most mathematical, the least accessible to the uninitiated. Astronomy was still queen in Europe, but the completion by Laplace in the *Mécanique céleste* (1799-1825) of the program laid down by Newton in the *Principia* gave to astronomy in the period after 1800 a certain completeness. Theory had been extended as far as existing data could take it, and the time was ripe for the collection of new data: systematically, carefully, precisely.

Astronomy from 1800 to 1850 was involved in the deliberate accumulation of masses of new information. John Herschel, England's foremost scientist, spent years accumulating stellar observations with which to test his father's theories of the universe. To collect data to the required accuracy meant a new order of capital investment. Telescopes, transits, accurate clocks, and substantial buildings to house them: all were required.[7] No clearer indication could be provided of America's coming of age than its dedication to astronomy. No more obvious symbol could be found for America's cultural maturity than the erection of a national astronomical observatory outfitted with the latest and best equipment. Yet once again, when faced with the claims of science upon the public purse, the Congress had given a clear and emphatic no.

On two occasions, first with the Coast Survey, then with the national observatory, the people's representatives had refused to provide the sponsorship necessary to the growth of a scientific tradition. Employment for a number of professional men of science sufficient to form the nucleus of a face-to-face community could therefore not be found in the nation's capital. If such posts were available in Washington, American science could not help but prosper. In their absence, American science had no center, and those few in America who wished to pursue scientific research either stole time from their teaching in schools and colleges scattered all over the country or joined one of the similarly scattered state geological surveys. Face-to-face communication was rarely possible, and only after 1819, when Professor Benjamin Silliman of Yale founded the *American Journal of Science and Arts,* did the scientists in America have a forum of their own.

Lack of communication was one difficulty; the distribution of professional posts among the different fields of science was another. The surveys wholly and the colleges partly required workers in life and earth sciences. Not only were there too few positions for scientists, but those few were mostly in the fields that continued the colonial emphasis on data-collecting. In the slow and halting expansion of American science, the exact sciences, whose pre-eminence was believed to be essential to an autonomous scientific tradition, had failed to gain central place. At a time when professionalization was sweeping over the whole scientific world, American science was in danger of falling far behind.

III.

The shift from amateurs to professionals as the dominant group in the scientific community was the major theme of science in Europe in the 1820's and 1830's. In England the Royal Society became a professional body, no longer dominated by dilettante noblemen. First in Germany, then in England and France, national organizations were established on the widest of bases to bring teachers of science and independent researchers together with the growing body of consumers of science in the industrial community. An effort was made in these organizations, of which the British Association for the Advancement of Science (founded 1831) was the largest, to organize the hitherto disparate activities of scientists into a coherent whole. Science was now taken seriously as a source of national strength and pride as well as a source of techniques to be applied in the workaday world.[8]

Striving to equal if not surpass the nations of Europe, the United States could not long acquiesce in the unwillingness of the Congress to support science in America while it was rapidly expanding in Europe. But the American response was an ambiguous one, involving, in the federal government, military more than civilian scientists. The American beginnings of the kind of education necessary to a professional scientist were at the United States Military Academy under Sylvanus Thayer, superintendent from 1817 to 1833, who based his curriculum on that of the École Polytechnique in France. West Point graduates such as Alexander Dallas Bache were in the vanguard of those who spread sound scientific instruction to American colleges: virtually their only competitors were the self-educated like Joseph Henry.

Though the Army was linked to science through the practice of military engineering and of exploration, the Navy seems to have been more successful in the use of science to keep itself strong. By obtaining Congressional support for peripheral activities largely based on science, the Navy managed to keep its share of the federal government's expenditure virtually constant, the same in peace as in war.[9] There were problems of seafaring for which science might offer solutions, so that an interest in science could be appropriate even for those officers whose sole concern was the fighting fitness of the Navy. In the absence of any other professional employment, a naval career might be the only hope for an embryo scientist, since, in egalitarian America, everyone had to have a career.[10] Until science itself became a profession, military service provided an honorable opportunity for its pursuit.

We have seen how the civilian Coast Survey was strangled at birth by the pressure for peacetime employment for a Navy swollen to meet the demands of war. To be a naval officer in time of peace is a frustrating career, especially in a country whose basic instincts are hostile to the notions from which a professional officer corps must derive sustenance. Only in the South, where the social ideal was that of the gentlemanly *rentier*—living off a plantation if he could afford it, entering one of the traditional professions if he could not—did a naval career offer much hope. During the long years of peace on the ocean which followed the Napoleonic wars, such a career could perhaps offer hope; it could certainly not offer much promise. In the period before the naval reforms of the late 1850's, the Congress kept tight reins on expenditure, and, in the absence of demonstrated need such as a war might provide, was unwilling to weed out the unfit or aged from the upper ranks to insure regular if not rapid promotion. The glacial slowness of promotion led to low morale and the bitterest kind of factionalism. In this poisonous environment, one had to grasp at every straw to pull oneself up the slippery ladder of rank. Since the number of sea billets was extremely limited, after an officer's first cruises he customarily rattled around ashore on half-pay for a number of years, hoping for a command which would carry with it a chance for promotion. Captains could usually choose their junior officers; thus there was constant jockeying and horse-trading for commands and lesser billets. Perhaps the pursuit of science might offer a way out of this slough of despond. For those who could afford to live on half-pay, it offered a way to pass the time during the long periods ashore; for those who could not, it might lead to the kind of employment suitable for a naval officer on half-pay.

Though the civilian Coast Survey had been disbanded in 1818 in the interest of the Navy, the latter only fitfully thereafter attempted to carry out the survey of the coast. By 1828, when the House Committee on Naval Affairs requested an accounting, Secretary of the Navy Southard "characterized the charts produced by those [Navy] surveys as expensive and unsafe, pointed out the inefficiency of such a desultory plan of operations, and recommended a recurrence to the law of 1807."[11] But the Congress showed as little interest in re-establishing the Coast Survey as it had in founding a national observatory.

With federal science foundering, the Navy set up in 1830 its first agency with a remotely scientific purpose: the Depot of Charts and Instruments. Establishing the Depot seems to have resulted more from the need for a shore billet for its first head than from any desire for science in the Navy. As the son of the civilian chief clerk who ran the Navy from 1802 to 1843, Lieutenant Louis M. Goldsborough presumably knew what he was doing when he suggested to Secretary Southard that an office in Washington be set up to stock navigational requisites and to issue them to the fleet. The Navy accepted Goldsborough's recommendation and appointed him to command the Depot, where he remained for two years.[12]

Secretary Southard kept pressing for the re-establishment of the civilian Coast Survey, and in 1832, with the help of the shipping lobby, he finally persuaded the Congress. F. R. Hassler returned to laying out baselines on shore with his civilian assistants, and the survey was extended offshore by the use of naval vessels. Lieutenant Charles Wilkes (who had improved his time ashore between cruises in the 1820's by studying with Hassler) commanded the vessel surveying Narragansett Bay.

From this time on, the revival of the civilian Coast Survey made it a splendid source of tours of sea duty for qualified naval officers. Most of the naval leaders of the Civil War served as lieutenants with the Coast Survey after 1832: Ammen, Craven, Dahlgren, Davis, Du Pont, Jenkins, Lee, and Porter; all these as well as Wilkes saw such service. Of these nine, only Dahlgren, Davis, and Wilkes had any claim to membership in the American scientific community. Thus the pressure of naval interests against a civilian agency proved to be misdirected. From its revival in 1832 until Hassler's death in 1843, the Coast Survey provided few opportunities for professional employment of civilians trained in science. The Survey was small, beginning in 1832 and 1833 with an annual budget of $20,000, and it was forever threatened by a Congress opposed to long-term commitments. Hassler was monumentally inept at politics, he spent most of his time in the field away from Washington, and the slow progress of the actual surveying could only feed Congressional suspicions, especially as the budget increased, reaching $100,000 annually by 1840.

The Depot of Charts and Instruments, on the other hand, flourished, but it was smaller than the Coast Survey and employed no civilians in its early years. When in 1833 Louis Goldsborough left the Depot, he was replaced by Wilkes, fresh from his surveying duty. Wilkes bought himself a house on Capitol Hill and moved the Depot in with himself and his family. He installed a transit instrument in order to rate by the stars the chronometers which his Depot furnished the ships of the Navy. Though hardly the national observatory for which American scientists had hoped, the Depot under Wilkes marked an important beginning in astronomy in the United States. Hitherto private individuals had made astronomical observations: now for the first time an institution had been set up to observe, and the federal government was sponsoring it. In 1836 Lieutenant James M. Gilliss, a naval officer determined to make his mark in astronomy, joined Wilkes at the Depot. Stung by Secretary Southard's remark (made in urging the reactivation of the Coast Survey) that no naval officer was capable of serious scientific work, Gilliss had turned to astronomy and studied at the University of Virginia and then in Paris. His career (of which more below) provides the first example of a scientist making the Navy his professional base.[13]

IV.

Meanwhile, since 1828 the federal government had been considering sending a naval expedition to explore the South Pacific. Pressed by a complex of interests in which the whaling industry was prominent, the Congress in 1836 authorized the expedition's outfitting. Although the primary emphases were "showing the flag" and providing sea duty for surplus naval officers, scientific exploration was one of the aims, and the various scientific societies were asked for advice and civilian personnel. Captain Thomas ap Catesby Jones of Virginia was chosen to command the expedition, and he in turn chose as his astronomer the young Lieutenant Matthew F. Maury, author of a textbook of navigation.[14]

Jones had taken the senior officer's usual prerogative of choosing his juniors, and his choices did not please Secretary of the

Navy Mahlon Dickerson of New Jersey. Dickerson had favored Charles Wilkes for a post in the expedition—a reasonable choice, since Wilkes was the most senior of the officers with scientific training—but Jones would not have him. Wilkes was sent to Europe in 1836 to procure the scientific instruments for the expedition; on his return in 1837 he found Dickerson still feuding with Jones and delaying the expedition's orders.[15] Maury's attempt to obtain the expedition's instruments from Wilkes led to a personal conflict. Late in 1837 Jones, disgusted with his treatment by Dickerson, resigned the command. After virtually every other senior naval officer had turned it down, Charles Wilkes was summoned back to Washington from surveying duty at sea and offered the expedition. The scandal of procrastination was not mitigated by the offer of command to a mere lieutenant; the expedition sailed in 1838 under a cloud. Though not pressed to resign, Maury felt he could not remain with an expedition under Wilkes' command, and the delays had cost Wilkes several of the civilian scientists who were to have accompanied him. Though the observations and collections in natural history and ethnology were in the hands of civilians (of whom James Dwight Dana, Silliman's son-in-law, is the best known), Wilkes insisted that astronomical and geophysical observations be prerogatives of the naval officers, and he terminated the appointment to the Expedition of the one civilian physical scientist, Professor Walter Johnson of the Franklin Institute.[16] Neither the Exploring Expedition itself, which lasted from 1838 to 1842, nor the working up of its results provided a significant opportunity for developing the exact sciences in America.

At the Depot of Charts and Instruments Wilkes was succeeded by Gilliss, who began an ambitious program of astronomical observations designed in part to complement those of Wilkes in the South Pacific. Under Gilliss the Depot rapidly became a surrogate for the missing national observatory at the same time as John Quincy Adams' hope for American astronomy was on its way to fulfillment elsewhere. Where in 1832 there were no public observatories in the United States, by the end of the decade small ones had been established at Williams and Western Reserve Colleges, at Philadelphia High School, and at the Military Academy in West Point.[17] By the time Wilkes returned in 1842, Gilliss' persistent advocacy of astronomy together with the stirrings of nationwide interest had persuaded the Board of Naval Commissioners to recommend to the Congress the construction of a major new observatory building for the Depot of Charts and Instruments. But when the Congress appropriated $25,000 for the new building in August 1842, Gilliss was no longer in charge of the Depot. He had been relieved by Matthew F. Maury.

Not long after he had resigned from the Exploring Expedition, Maury had been injured in a stagecoach accident that left him too crippled to return to sea. During his convalescence he wrote a series of pseudonymous articles on naval reform in which he called for the replacement of the three-man Board of Naval Commissioners by a system of bureaus. In 1842, as the Congress considered the proposed reform, pressure built up once more against Hassler's civilian Coast Survey. The proposal was made that the Navy take over all hydrography in an agency headed by either an officer or a civilian. With so many naval officers underemployed, others as well as Maury "could not tolerate the idea of this job going to a civilian."[18] Yet, in spite of the hostility shown to Hassler in the hearings, the Congress narrowly endorsed the civilian Coast Survey. Maury's interest in hydrography could be pursued only in an existing agency, and in July 1842 he took command of the Depot of Charts and Instruments. He had already begun to reorient the Depot from astronomy to hydrography when the Congress in August passed both the appropriation for the new observatory building and the bill for naval reform. Under the latter the three commissioners gave way to five bureaus; Maury's Depot moved from the Office of the Secretary of the Navy to the new Bureau of Ordinance and Hydrography.[19]

Since Gilliss had initiated the new observatory, he was to supervise its construction, and he went to Europe until March 1843 in quest of ideas and instruments. Soon after his return both Cincinnati, Ohio, and Harvard College began the construction of major new observatories. On their completion and that of the observatory in Washington, Americans would have the institutions with which to contribute to the growing reconnaissance of the heavens.

V.

From astronomy the quest for new and better data was spreading into the other exact sciences, especially those concerned with the planet Earth. In the 1830's attempts were made to obtain coordinated worldwide observations in meteorology, in terrestrial magnetism, and in tides. None of this passion was for data for its own sake; the hope of scientists everywhere was that a five- or ten-year series of such observations would permit the formulation of precise theories. Much of European scientific endeavor in this period was devoted to filling the storehouse of facts about nature in the hope of going beyond the theories summed up so comprehensively in Laplace's *Mécanique céleste*.[20] This vast compendium had been made available to mathematically trained scientists in the copiously annotated and corrected English version of Nathaniel Bowditch, of which publication was completed posthumously in 1839.[21]

A revitalized Coast Survey might join with the new American observatories in contributing to reconnaissance of the celestial and terrestrial environment, yet only if it were under the direction of someone who truly understood the aims of science could a balance be maintained between the theoretical and the practical. When Hassler died late in 1843, the future of the Coast Survey was in question, but an intensive lobbying effort led by Joseph Henry, professor at Princeton and the leading American physicist, secured the job of superintendent for Alexander Dallas Bache. Scion of a prominent Philadelphia family, great-grandson of Benjamin Franklin, grandson and namesake of Alexander Dallas who had been Madison's Secretary of the Treasury, Bache had the political connections and acumen which Hassler so completely lacked. A West Point graduate, he could count on the support of fellow West Pointers, especially Jefferson Davis of Mississippi. To these qualifications for success in the political maelstrom of Washington, Bache added no less impressive scientific qualifications. He had served the University of Pennsylvania as professor of natural philosophy and the city of Philadelphia as school superintendent. Well known in European scientific circles from his extensive travels, he had established in 1840 at Girard College in Philadelphia the first magnetic observatory in the United States.[22]

On taking over the Coast Survey at the end of 1843, Bache energetically expanded its activity. Determined to make his agency the center of science within the federal government, he began building bridges to the scientists in colleges and institutes with joint projects for the precise determination of longitudes. At the same time he placated the Congress by doubling the number of parties at work in the field and by obtaining testimonials to the Coast Survey's accomplishments from shipping and insurance executives.

Though Bache could try to weave the Coast Survey into the permanent fabric of federal agencies, in doing so he ran counter to the intent of the Congress, which was to set up the agency to do a particular job and to disband it when the job was done. Hassler had faced Congressional storms over nothing more vital than the standards to be applied and the relative competence of military men and civilians to carry them out; his ambitions had not gone beyond surveying the coast. To Bache, on the other hand, the survey of the coast was only a means to the end of creating an American scientific tradition firmly based in the federal government. Bache looked on science as a way of understanding the universe; he found himself forced to introduce it almost surreptitiously into American society, with its overwhelming preoccupation with the practical and the lucrative. The past had shown the Congress to be implacably hostile to scientific elitism; Bache's path was bound to be uphill all the way.

In his supremely difficult mission Bache had one important ally, at least potentially: the commercial community, especially those members of it engaged in ocean shipping. From 1815 to 1860 the American merchant marine quadrupled in size. Yet, rapid though its growth was, it did not keep up with the headlong expansion of trade. Imports and exports were almost entirely seaborne, and the American merchant marine was unable to carry more than about 70 per cent. Much domestic trade also went by sea; by law, only American vessels could carry it. More than shipowners and their insurers had a stake in this expansion of American commerce. The entire American economy was becoming more closely tied to an expanding international market, centered on the Atlantic Ocean, in whose dramatic growth before 1860 falling freight rates played a substantial part. In ocean shipping Bache found a burgeoning industry to be harnessed to the cause of science.[23]

The Coast Survey could attract powerful support both economic and political by furnishing what we now call research and development services to maritime commerce, the sector of the economy on which a developing country depended to keep it in touch with civilization. By serving the practical needs of the shipping industry, the scientific community under Bache could earn the wherewithal to pursue its higher goals of broadening human knowledge of the natural world. Ignorance and parsimony could be outflanked by an enlightened leadership that hired for ostensibly practical work only those with training and interest in basic science, providing them maximum opportunity to make fundamental contributions. While these contributions would bring renown in the European-dominated halls of science, the practical work performed at the same time would insure the continued support of the American commercial community and its representatives in the Congress.

VI.

Bache arrived in Washington late in 1843 as the country began to recover from the deflation that had lasted since 1839.[24] Economic expansion could furnish the resources to nourish his hopes for American science. One single obstacle lay in his path: his Coast Survey was not the only agency of the federal government which might furnish "R & D" to the shipping industry. Maury's Depot of Charts and Instruments, though its mission heretofore had been purely naval, was a potential rival in its claims on the seafaring community. Maury had come to Washington, eighteen months before Bache, intending to improve the United States Navy's contributions to the art of navigation. Given the partiality of the Congress to the needs of defense over the needs of science, only if Maury shared or could be brought to share Bache's ultimate goals could the latter be certain of reaching them. If Maury had other aims, there was bound to be fierce rivalry.

At first Maury and Bache cooperated amicably enough. Both were leaders of the National Institute for the Promotion of Science, founded in 1840 "as the hopeful nucleus of scientific life in the nation's capital"[25] and the future repository of the Exploring Expedition's collections. The National Institute reached its zenith in April 1844 when it sponsored the first national congress of scientists. Maury addressed the congress on his investigations of ocean currents; Bache, on the wave of specialization in science spreading from Europe to America. Bache's plea for the professionalization of American science was a harbinger of things to come. The collapse of the National Institute, whose membership was largely amateur, followed shortly after the congress.[26] Its place on the Washington scene was effectively taken by the Smithsonian Institution, established in 1846.

Meanwhile Bache and Maury had had their first difference of opinion. It arose over the Navy's new observatory building, completed in the fall of 1844 under the supervision of Lieutenant James M. Gilliss. The decision of who was to head the observatory raised again all the problems of Congressional support for science. The site on which the observatory had been built was one which George Washington had set aside for a national university, a stillborn project dear to the hearts of the supporters of science.[27] Of the failure of John Quincy Adams' plans for a national observatory we have already spoken, and the Congress had handicapped the legitimate work of the Coast Survey from its revival in 1832 by expressly forbidding it to set up any permanent post for stellar observation. By dint of hard work and careful persuasion, Gilliss had obtained the cherished observatory under the guise of a new building for the Navy's Depot of Charts and Instruments. What was to be the observatory's fate now that its sponsor was no longer at the Depot?

Though there was some support for a civilian head of the new observatory, the scientific community recognized Gilliss' claim, since in his earlier work he had proved himself the equal of any civilian as an astronomer. In addition to planning the observatory's construction, Gilliss had drafted plans for staffing and for the carrying out of astronomical, magnetic, and meteorological observations. Yet, with the legal status of the observatory merely that of a permanent home for the Depot of Charts and Instruments, it was only natural for Secretary of the Navy John Y. Mason, like Maury a Virginian and a strong advocate of naval preparedness, to allow the latter to take over the new building. Thus were the Virginians in general and Maury in particular revenged for Wilkes' takeover of the Exploring Expedition nearly a decade earlier. Now it was Maury's turn to make a scientific name for himself in astronomy. His first step was to take over Gilliss' plans for staffing and operation.

Bache continued to cooperate with Maury in spite of his disappointment over the latter's displacement of Gilliss. The National Observatory, as Maury styled his new building, became the center for Bache's ambitious program to determine precise longitudes by using the telegraph lines spreading rapidly over the country. At Bache's suggestion, Maury hired to work at the Observatory the leader in telegraphic longitude determination, Sears C. Walker, founder of the observatory at the Central High School in Philadelphia. Walker's telegraphic technique, spread throughout Europe as "the American method" of determining longitudes for astronomical purposes, was one of the first scientific contributions from the United States to be given wide recognition in Europe.[28]

VII.

As the institutional structure of American science began to crystallize in the 1840's, the one overriding need seemed to be for a federal agency whose mission was the advancement of science as a whole rather than of one segment. The National Institute had at one time seemed to promise such a central agency, but in spite of its Congressional charter it was not a public body, and its mishandling of the Exploring Expedition's specimens made it suspect in the eyes of scientists. The need remained for a central scientific institution. Finally in 1846, after a decade of Congressional wrangling, the bequest of James Smithson—an Englishman who never set foot in America—became the Smithsonian Institution. To be its first head the leading physicist in America, Joseph Henry, gave up his professorship at Princeton. The legislation establishing the Institution was purposefully vague in order not to antagonize any of the several Congressional factions with their mutually exclusive schemes for a library, a museum, an agricultural experiment station, and so on. Hence all rested on the resourcefulness of the Secretary, and Alexander Dallas Bache as the leading governmental scientist used his considerable powers of persuasion to convince Henry that American science needed him at the Smithsonian. Only with Smithson's bequest in safe hands could American science use it to become the strong, professional community of which Bache had spoken to the National Institute.

With Henry joining Bache in Washington, they could both put into practice a scheme which they long had favored, the development of a national organization of scientists. In the late 1830's Bache had followed Henry to Europe, and both had been impressed by the meetings of the British Association for the Advancement of Science, where British scientists and their foreign visitors gathered annually in August in a different city of the United Kingdom to share the results of their researches with each other and with members of the growing industrial community. One national organization did exist in America, the Association of American Geologists and Naturalists, founded in 1840 by the geologists and broadened to include the naturalists in 1842. In the absence of sufficient jobs in any one place to sustain a group of scientists, the migratory Association permitted at least an annual get-together for the individuals and small groups scattered about the vast American countryside. Its chief drawback, in the eyes of Bache and Henry, united in their dreams for American science, was its emphasis on the empirical life and earth sciences with their concentration on the collecting of data. Bache and Henry hoped for an organization in which the physical sciences and mathematics would not only be welcome but would take the pride of place which should be rightfully theirs.

Accordingly, they were behind the call that went out from the Boston meeting of the Association of American Geologists and Naturalists in 1847 to convene in September 1848 at Philadelphia the first meeting of the American Association for the Advancement of Science. Under the presidency of William C. Redfield, a New York businessman and the leading American meteorologist, this new national organization of scientists was launched. With the Smithsonian Institution as a federal agency for science established at the seat of government, and with professional scientists organized into the American Association for the Advancement of Science, it appeared that the fundamental institutions of American science had been founded.

Yet the Smithsonian could serve only as clearinghouse and publisher for scientific research done elsewhere; the annual meetings of the A.A.A.S could provide only a forum for the exchange of ideas on a more personal level. Essential as both these functions were to the emerging community of American scientists, they presupposed a base of professional employment that was slow to be realized. The Smithsonian and the A.A.A.S. could maintain and disseminate standards; they could not create them. What was necessary was agencies with jobs in which science of the highest kind could be encouraged and promoted.

VIII.

Though the colleges and the surveys increased in numbers and developed stronger scientific interests, the brunt of the effort had to be borne in Washington. Bache's energy and persuasiveness doubled the Coast Survey's budget between 1844 and 1849. Limited both in number and in opportunity for pure science in the full-time posts at his disposal, Bache could nevertheless offer assistance with research to college-based scientists. Professors James Renwick of Columbia, Stephen Alexander of Princeton, Elias Loomis of New York University, Jacob W. Bailey of West Point, Alexis Caswell of Brown, all performed research for Bache in the first five years of his superintendency.[29] For the distinguished newcomer to the American scientific scene, the Swiss icthyologist Louis Agassiz, Bache provided a Coast Survey ship for a summer cruise in 1847, soon after Agassiz's arrival.[30] Commanding the ship was the naval officer in charge of hydrography on the coast of northern New England, Lieutenant Charles Henry Davis, brother-in-law of the Harvard astronomer Benjamin Peirce and himself a Harvard graduate with a background in mathematics. Next to Gilliss, also employed by the Coast Survey after his observatory was given to Maury, Davis was perhaps the outstanding scientist among naval officers.[31]

He was also the founder of the third governmental agency which provided research and development services to the shipping industry: the Nautical Almanac Office. Though part of the Navy, the Almanac Office was linked on its establishment in 1849 to a civilian agency, Bache's Coast Survey, rather than to Maury's National Observatory. Furthermore, the Almanac Office was located at Cambridge, Massachusetts, rather than at the seat of government in Washington. To explain these peculiarities in the founding of the *American Nautical Almanac* we must return to the uneasy association between Bache and Maury as it existed in the early 1840's and follow the gradual sharpening of the differences in their separate answers to the question of what science was to be in the American republic.

Bache stood for science as a profession in its own right and for a scientific community in which the exact sciences would occupy the center of the stage. The scientific tradition he sought to establish in America was based on the standards of elitist Europe rather than on native American egalitarianism. Bache's was the pure science of theoretical understanding rather than the applied science or technology of practical results. For Bache and his close friend Joseph Henry, united in their hatred of quackery as in their respect for pure science, American science could come of age only by superimposing upon the collection of data the higher function of interpreting it by the most sophisticated mathematical techniques.

The self-educated Maury began from different premises. His first step on taking command of the Depot of Charts and Instruments in 1842 had been to move it out of Wilkes' house, in anticipation of the latter's return to Washington. This move unearthed the Navy's large collection of manuscript logs, each recording the details of a naval vessel's voyage. Anxious to improve the Navy's contribution to the art of navigation, Maury began to extract from these logs the details of winds and currents over the ocean. He arranged them by latitude and longitude and combined as many observations as he could find for each five-degree square in order to obtain long-period averages. Where enough information was available, these averages were computed monthly through the year. Maury's data, which he hoped eventually to publish, would permit a sea captain to chart a course which would bring him fair winds and keep him from bucking strong currents.

Maury was the first to apply this technique of obtaining climatological averages, long used on land, to the wind and weather over the ocean. Though a decade behind Major James Rennell in England in the description of surface currents, Maury collected vastly more information. But there was a major difficulty with the climatological approach. Useful though it might be for the navigator, it could not lead to scientific understanding.[32] The averaging process smoothed out the detailed variations which alone could offer insight into the dynamics of the atmosphere and the ocean. Scientific understanding required the study of individual storms and the application to the weather of the principles of physics. Neither of these approaches was likely to furnish quick results to be applied to navigation. While Maury painstakingly extracted from the logs at the Depot the data most immediately useful to navigators, the foundations of the science of meteorology were being laid by others.

Although Maury's main interests remained climatological, he applied the same energy and ambition to astronomy after the new Observatory came into use early in 1845. Assisted by the officers and Navy professors of mathematics assigned him, he began to collect the observations necessary for a Washington star catalogue to complement the catalogues published by the major European observatories. Yet, though apparently a capable observer, Maury was either unwilling or unable to perform the tedious calculations which alone rendered the observations usable. These were either left to his subordinates or not done at all. Maury used his position as director of the Observatory to compel his subordinates to work on the problems he chose and to make himself the senior author of the publications that resulted. Though hardly unknown in European scientific circles, these practices were more representative of the Navy than of science, especially when one considers that Maury's civilian subordinates were more experienced astronomers than he. From Maury's insistence on strict control of the astronomical work of the Observatory grew his second conflict with Bache.

The new planet Neptune was discovered in 1846 as the result of predictions made from theory independently by U. J. J. Leverrier in France and J. C. Adams in England. Astronomers at every observatory in the world rushed to make those additional observations necessary to compute its orbit and to search the published star catalogues for earlier observations.[33] The first to succeed was Sears C. Walker at the United States National Observatory early in 1847, who noted that Neptune had been erroneously classified as a star by Lalande in 1795. With confirmatory observations made by a colleague, Walker began the laborious task of computing Neptune's orbit.

While this task was under way, Walker had a quarrel with Maury, apparently over whether he was to have a mature scientist's right to work on what he pleased. The quarrel led to Walker's resignation; he was immediately hired by the Coast Survey to continue his telegraphic determinations of longitude. His computations of Neptune's orbit were turned over to Joseph Henry at the

Smithsonian for publication, and an abstract was rushed into print in the leading European astronomical journal, Schumacher's *Astronomische Nachrichten*.[34]

Maury's first indication that Walker would publish independently the work on Neptune begun at the Observatory came when he received his copy of the Schumacher journal. He was incensed that his permission had not been obtained and brought the matter to the attention of both his superiors, Commodore Crane and Secretary of the Navy Mason. Both men supported Maury's attempt to obtain an apology from Joseph Henry on the grounds that the Navy's proprietary rights had been violated; but Henry, presumably on the grounds of higher loyalty to the international community of science, refused to admit any wrongdoing.[35] Though he was technically in the right, Maury's action was not likely to endear him to the leaders of the American scientific community.

The conflict between Maury on the one hand and Bache and Henry on the other hand deepened early in the following year, 1848. At the Coast Survey Walker continued his computations on Neptune's orbit, providing the data with which Professor Benjamin Peirce of Harvard could establish the theory of Neptune's motion and in turn benefiting from Peirce's theories to compute a better orbit. Peirce's calculations led him to claim that Leverrier's and Adams' solutions for Neptune had only accidently predicted its location correctly; had the observations they requested been made some years before or after 1846, no planet would have been found where they predicted. Leverrier was offended by Peirce's arguments, which were perhaps overstated, and he defended himself in a letter to Maury which the latter published in the *National Intelligencer*. Peirce replied in the *Intelligencer,* and a narrowly scientific question was thus aired in public at Maury's instigation.[36]

As the discovery of Neptune began to thrill both the scientific and the general public, Maury brought out in 1847 the first fruits of his painstaking analysis of the Navy's neglected logbooks. Beginning with the most heavily traveled ocean, the North Atlantic, Maury embarked on the publication of his famous *Wind and Current Charts*. The first series of these were the Track Charts, on which were plotted the tracks of a number of vessels, giving the month of the voyage and the weather, wind, and currents encountered. On the backs of the charts were printed various explanatory materials.[37] Under Maury's direction the United States Navy was finally making a contribution to the improvement of navigation. With the sailing ships that made up the bulk of the world's fleets totally dependent on the winds for propulsion and anxious to avoid the strong currents which might delay them, the information on the *Wind and Current Charts* could be useful to mariners everywhere. The discovery of gold in California in 1849 put an additional premium on faster sailing passages, and the sleek American clippers vied with each other to set new records for the voyage round Cape Horn. Maury took every opportunity to bring his results to the attention of mariners, and he claimed in the commercial press to have shortened the long sailing routes for those mariners who used his charts.[38]

Bache at the Coast Survey could not have been pleased. He had fought hard to keep his agency independent, out of the hands of the Navy. With his cousin's husband Robert J. Walker his immediate superior as Secretary of the Treasury, Bache had seen his agency flourish in Polk's administration; its appropriation for 1849 was twice that for 1844. The Coast Survey was growing along with the American merchant marine for which it provided services. Now Maury, having snatched the National Observatory away from the dominant group of American scientists led by Bache, was making his agency the Coast Survey's rival in the provision of services to shipping. With the need once more to shrink the naval establishment at the end of the war with Mexico, Bache had reason to be apprehensive of a new bid by the Navy to absorb the Coast Survey and thus strike down the pillar of the embryo American scientific community. Bache survived the first attack: a Congressional investigation in 1848 to show why the Coast Survey should not be transferred to the Navy, but with Walker slated to leave the Treasury as a result of the Whig victory in the election of 1848, a counterattack became necessary.

Countering Maury's attempt to dominate the marine bases of American science was possible for Bache and his friends because, though undoubtedly the best placed, Maury was not the only naval officer with scientific interests. In the scramble for appropriations for nonmilitary activities by naval officers, which led chiefly to a number of expeditions between 1848 and 1855, others might gain the ear of Congress.

IX.

The most important project of the group around Bache became reality when in March 1849 there was slipped into the Naval Appropriation Act passed at the last session of the lame-duck Congress the provision "That a competent officer of the navy, not below the grade of lieutenant, be charged with the duty of preparing the Nautical Almanac for publication."[39] Thus was born the third and last of the federal agencies whose mission was to provide "R & D" for America's expanding maritime commerce. Its first Superintendent, presumably the prime mover behind the new agency, was Lieutenant Charles Henry Davis.

Nautical almanacs provided the basis for accurate celestial navigation, developing in the eighteenth century along with the quadrants and sextants whose observations could be reduced with the aid of the star and sun positions tabulated in the almanac. In the early decades of the nineteenth century American publishers began issuing their own editions of the British nautical almanac prepared for the Royal Navy at the Greenwich Observatory. In the report on John Quincy Adams' original proposal in 1825 for a national observatory, the Chief of Army Engineers had recommended the preparation and publication of an indigenous American almanac, but the Congress' failure to provide an observatory where the necessary work could be done rendered an almanac impossible.[40] American mariners remained dependent on the Royal Navy. Though the mercantile community might not find this situation intolerable, their support even if purely passive would make possible a separate American effort.

Under the Congressional mandate for a Nautical Almanac, Davis brought into operation late in 1849 a new agency, the Nautical Almanac Office.[41] Unlike the Coast Survey, it could expect to be permanent, for a new Almanac would be required each year. Like the Depot of Charts and Instruments (or, as Maury now headed his letters, the "Hydrographical Office and National Observatory") a part of the Navy's shore establishment, the Nautical Almanac Office as a military organization would not be subject to the hostility from the Congress which made Bache's position at the Coast Survey so difficult. Moreover, the tasks required of the Almanac Office's employees in their official duties were closer to fundamental physical science than were those of the Coast Survey. In the Almanac Office all was astronomical observation and calculation; in the Survey, astronomy was overshadowed by surveying in the field, geodetic calculation, and the preparation of charts. In spite of Bache's efforts to stress the scientific side of the Survey's work—tides, terrestrial magnetism, the determination of longitude—the Almanac Office was by the very nature of its duties a better source of scientific employment.

Davis' chief problem in setting up the Almanac Office was his dependence on a major observatory. Forewarned by Bache's earlier difficulties with Maury, Davis looked to the other major observatory on the eastern seaboard: Harvard College. Under the influence of his brother-in-law Benjamin Peirce, Professor of Astronomy, the Harvard College Observatory provided the Nautical Almanac Office with facilities as good as those in Washington.[42] By setting up the Almanac Office in Cambridge, Davis insured that the new agency remained on the side of Bache, Henry, and the other leaders of American science and as far as possible from Matthew Fontaine Maury.

The Almanac Office gained independence of the Depot of Charts and Instruments by setting up in Cambridge; what Cambridge gained was employment for a group of able astronomers large enough to provide a sense of community. One by one leading American astronomers were brought to Cambridge, hired by the Nautical Almanac Office as observers and calculators with the title of professor, and fired by a common zeal to work out solutions to the problems of astronomy for publication in Benjamin Apthorp Gould's newly founded *Astronomical Journal,* the first scientific journal in America devoted to a single speciality.[43] By combining the continuity of support possible for an agency of the Navy with a mission so precise as to require absolutely the employment of the most highly trained specialists, Davis and his successors made the Nautical Almanac Office just the kind of nucleus of an American scientific community that Bache and his friends had long been seeking.

x.

Thus by 1850 three government agencies were extending the fruits of science to the seafarers of America, each competing for support from the Congress. At stake was the future of the American scientific community. Two men sought its leadership, Matthew F. Maury at the Depot and Alexander Dallas Bache at the Survey, each with his own vision of what American science should be. Their rivalry played itself out, in the twelve years between the founding of the Nautical Almanac Office and the outbreak of the Civil War, on land and sea.

The two rivals and their respective allies fought first over their relative shares of a growing federal budget. Though the Congress had not changed its hostility to the spending of public moneys, the increasing receipts of the federal Treasury had somehow to be disbursed. The United States was importing capital from Europe throughout the 1840's and 1850's by buying more abroad than was sold there. With an increasing tariff to protect the growing domestic manufactures, the Treasury's coffers were steadily filling; the proceeds from the sale of public lands helped to swell them. Though neither tariff nor land policy had been designed primarily to increase the government's income, both had that effect. The Congress was thus faced with the question of how to spend the growing income. One possibility was to distribute it to the states, but everyone remembered only too well that the distribution of the federal surplus in 1837 had been followed by panic and deflation. Hence increasing federal expenditure, though distasteful in principle, became necessary in practice.[44]

The chief beneficiaries of the more liberal fiscal policies of the Congress were the Army and the Navy. The period after the Mexican War was one of diversion rather than wholesale retrenchment as both services sent out exploring expeditions and extended the tasks they were prepared to perform for society. Though the necessity to reduce the federal surplus by expenditure meant that claims for science—especially science of the sea, since foreign trade was concentrated, along with financial power, in the great port cities—would be honored, Maury was better placed than Bache to obtain the lion's share. He was part of the Navy, a permanent agency always threatening to take over Bache's avowedly temporary Coast Survey, and his practical results had wide appeal.

After the defeat of Mexico in 1848, the Navy did not retrench as it had after 1815. In the years from 1849 to 1860, its average annual expenditure grew rather than fell.[45] Given the Congress' predisposition to honor the needs of the military, the Navy had only to show a worthwhile purpose to obtain funds. Science, or a reasonable counterfeit, was one such purpose.

Just as it had after 1815, the Navy after the Mexican War attempted to take over the civilian Coast Survey. But 1848 was not 1818, and Bache foiled this initial bid by adroit politicking. The Navy kept the pressure up until 1851, by which time it had found other opportunities in an expansive age. Beginning in 1848, the United States Navy sent seven expeditions to the far corners of the earth in the name of science.[46]

Of these seven, six bore the stamp of the energetic Lieutenant Maury, and none of the six had as its object an important piece of scientific research. Two were seaborne surveying expeditions, respectably scientific, though old-fashioned in an era when Charles Darwin, Joseph Hooker, and T. H. Huxley were doing a different kind of science from the surveying vessels of the Royal Navy.[47] The other expeditions were purely geographical reconnaissance, characteristic of eighteenth-century science and incapable of providing in the mid-nineteenth century the opportunities for physical science so avidly sought by Bache, Henry, and their friends. Furthermore, the basis for eighteenth-century geographical reconnaissance had been territorial expansion,[48] and, of the six naval expeditions he sponsored, those to South America were closest to Maury's heart. For he was a leading Southern thinker at a time when, frustrated by the Compromise of 1850, the slavocracy was seeking new lands outside the United States in which to fulfill its expansionist dreams. Maury persuaded the Navy to send his brother-in-law Lieutenant William Herndon across the Andes and down the Amazon to find the site for a new slave empire.[49]

One naval expedition of this period did represent advanced science, and this was the only one that Maury actively opposed. When in 1847 the request came from German astronomers for measurements of the solar parallax, Lieutenant James M. Gilliss promoted a naval astronomical expedition to Chile. Maury tried unsuccessfully to block Congressional authorization for Gilliss' expedition, which observed in Chile from 1849 to 1852. By coordinating his observations there with others to be made simultaneously at the Naval Observatory in Washington, Gilliss expected to determine the parallax of the sun. On his return to Washington with the Chilean observations, however, he discovered that Maury had failed, either willfully or inadvertently, to make any observations in Washington. Unsuccessful in squashing Gilliss' project before it got started, Maury had managed to sabotage its chief objective.[50]

While his friends and former assistants ranged over the globe, Maury did not remain idle at the Observatory. Astronomical observation, though it continued, was subordinated to climatology. This was the heyday of the sailing ship, thrusting forward in response to the threat of steam. Ocean freight rates fell dramatically after the Mexican War, contributing to a prosperity based in large part on the export of cotton and the import of immigrants.[51] Though the evidence may not support Maury's claim that his charts and sailing directions had much to do with the buoyancy in the shipping industry,[52] he was certainly riding the crest of a wave. The clipper-ship era which followed the discovery of gold in California in 1848 made Maury famous for his recommendations of sailing routes to shorten the voyage around Cape Horn.[53]

His enhanced stature permitted Maury to rival Bache on the latter's home ground: the exploration of the ocean off the coast. The Coast Survey's pioneering investigations of the Gulf Stream, beginning in 1844, led to the first new ideas about the current since Benjamin Franklin's. Maury intruded into this continuing series of researches by the Survey when in 1849 he persuaded the Congress to place at his disposal the research vessels *Taney* and *Dolphin*. Not restricted to coastal waters as was the Survey under Bache, Maury sent his vessels across the North Atlantic to Europe, and the results of their soundings made him a close adviser to the promoter of the transatlantic cable, Cyrus Field.

Faced with Maury's attempt to dominate the Washington scene, Bache looked for support to the growing body of American scientists. To the 1851 meeting of the A.A.A.S. in Albany, Bache, as retiring President, pleaded for his vision of an American scientific community led by an elite of men chosen for their specialized competence. "Our real danger," said Bache, "lies now from a modified charlatanism, which makes merit in one subject an excuse for asking authority in others, or in all, and because it has made real progress in one branch of science, claims to be an arbiter in others." Science, though it might be dependent on the public purse, had to make itself master in its own house. No appeals to incompetent tribunals or "to the general public voice" should be made "from the decision of scientific men or scientific tribunals."[54] Though it might be *for* the people, science could never be of or by them. With the military capturing the largest share of an expanding public revenue, civilian science would be hard put to gain hegemony.

A few months after the Albany meeting the military-civilian conflict came to the fore. Prompted by Captain Henry James of the Royal Engineers, the British government suggested to other governments, among them that of the United States, a cooperative program of uniform meteorological observations all over the inhabited world. Secretary of State Daniel Webster forwarded the suggestion to both the Army and the Navy. In the Navy the request came down the chain of command to Maury. A gifted and energetic organizer, Maury could see immediately that what was wanted to establish this uniform system of observations was an international conference at which the details of the system could be hammered out by representatives of the countries that took part. Furthermore, land observations alone—all that the Royal Engineers had proposed or were authorized to propose—would not suffice. To his superiors Maury suggested an international conference to embrace the meteorology of both land and sea. Authorized by Secretary Webster and by his naval superiors, Maury began in December 1851 to organize an international meeting along the lines he had proposed by writing for support both to foreign governments and to distinguished foreign scientists such as Alexander von Humboldt and François Arago.

Maury's next step was to organize American support for his "Congress of Meteorologists." Here he ran into opposition. Only too aware of Maury's great energy and organizational skill, Bache and Joseph Henry saw his scheme for international observations as a threat to civilian science in America. Insofar as land meteorology was established in the United States, it had been organized by Henry in a network based in the Smithsonian Institution. For

Maury to become the leader in internationalizing the one field of science in which Americans were pre-eminent would mean that he would dominate their efforts in the future. Already, in the eyes of Bache and Henry, Maury had too much power over American science of the sea. Now he was moving to bring land science into his orbit as well. Though his efforts (if not his understanding) entitled him to membership, Maury had been left off the A.A.A.S. Committee on Meteorology. Now Bache and Henry had to thwart his efforts in the international field.

As Bache saw it, the difficulty was that governments, which had a penchant for fostering the military, rather than national scientific associations, were organizing the conference. Maury was able to dominate the American effort since there was no national scientific body in the United States on which the government was obliged to call for advice. But in Britain things were different; the government turned to the Royal Society. In May 1852 Henry wrote Edward Sabine, Secretary (and later President) of the Royal Society, opposing the inclusion of land meteorology in the proposed conference. The Society reported to the British government late in 1852 that a conference on maritime observations alone was one which Britain should support. Sabine, though a Colonel in the Royal Engineers, had been persuaded against Captain James' original proposal.

Maury was willing to settle for the part of the conference agenda of greatest interest to himself, and in June of 1853 he sent, in the name of the United States government, invitations to a conference on weather observations at sea to be held in Brussels in late August. In spite of the energetic advocacy of Lord Wrottesley, a strong supporter of Maury because of the latter's contributions to navigation, the British government still hung back from a commitment to participate. With the British shipping community stimulated by Maury's advocacy as he passed through England on the way to Belgium, the British government finally agreed, just before the conference opened on 23 August, to send delegates.

Except for two men—the President, L. A. J. Quetelet, the Belgian astronomer-statistician and the original advocate of the standardization of observations, and Captain James, Britain's junior delegate—all the participants in the conference were naval officers. Maury succeeded in persuading them to accept for international use a version of the system of observations he had introduced into the United States, and he insured its adoption by offering to send his *Wind and Current Charts* in exchange for any observations sent him by mariners. Flushed with his triumph, the first step in the international organization of meteorology, Maury visited scientific correspondents before returning home. In Germany he saw Baron Alexander von Humboldt, the grand old man of European science, and C. G. Ehrenberg, the pioneering student of deep-sea sediments; in France, U. J. J. Leverrier, director of the Paris Observatory and thus Maury's French counterpart. To them he reported his achievements at Brussels and his hope that the standard system might later spread from sea to land.[55] Maury felt that he had consolidated in Europe the scientific reputation his efforts in America had earned him, yet the pages of the major scientific periodicals of the day gave no notice to the Brussels Conference. Until the data collected by the network Maury had established were turned into significant results, it apparently held no interest for the scientific public in either Europe or America.

XI.

The problem lay in the relationship between science and its applications. The group around Bache and Henry had no objections to stressing the fruitfulness of research for American commerce; to the contrary. What they objected to in Maury was his failure to share their twin beliefs in the primacy of pure knowledge and the hegemony of mathematics. Bache and his followers found these standards in the more advanced science of Europe, and they attempted to embody them in the indigenous scientific institutions of the United States.

"Science is only another expression for the *true* in the Universe,"[56] said the American geologist James Hall in 1856, giving voice to the idea that the pursuit of science was a quest for understanding of the universe and of our place in it, rather than a quest for practical results. Like the theologian, the scientist searched for ultimate answers; unlike the theologian, the scientist developed objective knowledge step by step rather than a whole system of thought.

This search for detailed answers to precise questions that was science led to specialization. As Bache put it, "While a general knowledge of various branches of science is useful in developing even a single branch, it is still certain that subdivision is essential to advancement."[57] With each scientist pursuing ever narrower problems along an ever widening frontier, some ordering principle was required for a scientific community, some basis on which to integrate each individual contribution into a wider whole. Simple empiricism would not suffice; theory was required to interpret observation and experiment. Since the most powerful theories were mathematical, the ordering principle of modern science was mathematics, called by Benjamin Peirce, probably the most distinguished man of science in mid-nineteenth-century America, "the Key of the Sciences; . . . the great master-key, which unlocks every door of knowledge, and without which no discovery—no discovery which deserves the name, which is law and not isolated fact—has been or ever can be made."[58] Though all science need not be mathematical, in the hierarchy of the sciences those branches which could be made mathematical had pride of place, and their practitioners had in the eyes of all scientists a greater claim to speak in the name of science to the wider society.

Maury did not share these principles; indeed, he may not even have understood them. On his return from Brussels he began to compile his earlier writings into one volume, to take to the American public the case for his kind of science. The result was one of the best-selling scientific books of all time: *The Physical Geography of the Sea,* published in 1855. Though poorly received by scientists on both sides of the Atlantic, the book was reprinted many times over the next two decades and translated into six European languages.[59]

Maury had chosen to take his case to a wider audience than the embryo scientific community. The scientists' response was to eliminate him from the ranks of their leaders. Until 1855 he had played a substantial role in the A.A.A.S., delivering one or more papers at each annual meeting and serving on a number of committees. After 1855 he was seen no more at A.A.A.S. meetings; by 1859 he was no longer a member.[60]

The newly organized scientific community in the United States rejected Maury because he failed to reach its standards of insight and objectivity. "He never acquired more than a most superficial understanding of physical processes, or any of the capacity for self-criticism that the scientist must possess."[61] Rather than respond to the criticisms of his theories offered by his contemporaries, Maury repeated his errors and misunderstandings in edition after edition of his *Physical Geography of the Sea*. Further, the book's popularity came from its pious and florid imagery, an offense to the plain language of scientists struggling to free themselves from the predominantly religious culture of their youth. Maury was also working in two areas, astronomy and meteorology, where in the nineteenth century mathematics had to predominate, yet he had neither training in mathematics nor esteem for those who had. Though in his own eyes Maury as a scientist was the equal of Bache or Henry, he was so in the eyes of few others with the competence to judge. "His reputation," wrote a contemporary not long after the Civil War had removed Maury from the Washington scene, "was created by those writing in favor of works they did not understand."[62]

Maury's science made him unwelcome at the A.A.A.S. among Bache and his allies, but the latter could not disseminate their standards in a form that would undo his influence in the wider world. Neither in America nor in Europe was Maury's reputation diminished until long after his death. He remained powerful in America because of the emphasis on practical results rather than theoretical understanding, an emphasis that, in Tocqueville's words, put "the darting speed of a quick, superficial mind . . . at a premium, while slow deep thought is excessively undervalued."[63] This attitude may have originated, as Tocqueville suggested, in America's egalitarian ideals.[64] It may equally have arisen from the needs of a developing society, which could ill afford to invest limited resources in research whose utility could not be guaranteed in advance. The object of Bache's vision—an abstract science that was indigenously American—was in either case too esoteric to command wide support, even though it was tantalizingly close to reality.[65]

Though some among Bache's associates were recognized as equals by the leaders of European science,[66] the latter had reasons to embrace Maury as well. For in the halls of European science the contributions by Americans to the world's growing store of knowledge were still refracted through the prism of colonialism. Data, not theories, were what one expected from Americans, and data were what Maury offered in abundance. The organization of American science independently of the military proved impossible to effect in the 1850's. Only when Maury went South, on the outbreak of Civil War in 1861, could Bache and his friends triumph in Washington, and the international organization of meteorology, the one abstract science in which Americans led the world, was not revived until after Maury's death in 1873.[67]

Unable in the years of peace to force a decision between abstract, civilian science and practical, military science, Bache's generation left behind an American scientific tradition that was flawed. Their need for resources with which to build indigenous institutions had led them to rely on seafaring, which proved as supportive of Maury's military practicality as of Bache's mathematical originality. For American science is national science, the science of the nation-state, born in war and revolution, rather than the science of universal humanity.

HAROLD L. BURSTYN

CHAPTER FIVE

The Machine at Sea: Early Transatlantic Steam Travel

"Good-bye, Romance!" the Skipper said;
"He vanished with the coal we burn;
Our dial marks full steam ahead,
Our speed is timed to half a turn.
Sure as the tidal trains we ply
'Twixt port and port. Romance, good-bye!"

—RUDYARD KIPLING, "The King"

I.

HENRY ADAMS, in gloomy retrospection, anchored himself in the midstream of history and fixed the turning point between his comfortable old universe and the strange new one at May 1844. In that year, he recalled, he and his "eighteenth-century troglodytic Boston" came to a final parting. Reflecting on those significant innovations which had led to this rupture, Adams noted that several years earlier there had appeared in Boston harbor the first steamers of the Cunard Line.[1] Since the inauguration of their oceanic steam service in July 1840 these sturdy British paddlewheelers had been thrashing and puffing across the Atlantic from Liverpool to Halifax and Boston, and by that pivotal year of 1844 they had become a familiar sight on the North Atlantic sea-lanes. Yet the Cunarders had not been the first to provide a regularly scheduled transatlantic crossing by steam. Appropriately, if coincidentally, the turning point for ocean steam travel occurred in the year of Henry Adams' birth, with the almost simultaneous arrival at New York on 23 April 1838 of the British steamers *Sirius* and *Great Western.*

Steam navigation of the Atlantic Ocean had been attempted as early as 1819 with the celebrated crossing (primarily under sail alone) of the American steamer *Savannah.* But this and subsequent transoceanic efforts by steamers had been only spasmodic indications of future capability. After April 1838, however, uninterrupted oceanic travel under steam power was no longer merely a fanciful hope; the age of oceanic steam had arrived.

Following the initial success of *Sirius* and *Great Western,* transatlantic steam navigation developed swiftly. As the number of steam vessels rapidly increased, the volume of passenger traffic correspondingly expanded. And in an age of rapid technological development, the most celebrated steam packets soon fell from favor, overshadowed by larger, faster, and more luxurious steamships.

Yet the era of unexceptional, secure ocean crossings by mammoth passenger liners did not arrive at once. Until at least the 1860's, Atlantic steam navigation could be as unpredictable and at times as harrowing as the most daring voyager might demand. Before steam conquered the Atlantic there was to be a time of trial. But in 1838, in the flush of initial success, all things seemed possible; and America, celebrating her "go-ahead age," was particularly rapturous over the apparent triumph of steam.

"Hurrah for the Advance of Mind!" proudly recorded the New York diarist George Templeton Strong, in noting the arrival of the *Sirius.*[2] Within a few hours there also appeared in New York harbor the larger *Great Western* to confirm the feasibility of transatlantic steam travel. "From the arrival of these two interesting strangers," fellow-diarist Philip Hone wrote, "the city was in a ferment." Not only had the arrival of the two steamers stimulated endless discussion and speculation among "our novelty-loving population," but it also appeared that the pattern of seasonal travel was now to change. In their zest for oceanic steam voyaging, Hone predicted, Americans would forsake Virginia or Saratoga Springs and would flock to Europe.[3]

The immediate establishment of a regular schedule for the *Great Western* between New York and Liverpool confounded those who persisted in viewing such steam travel as an ephemeral novelty. Moreover, within a year after her initial spring crossing the "marine wonder" *Great Western* triumphantly refuted those who had darkly predicted disaster for any steamer which dared to face the tempestuous winter storms of the Atlantic.[4] Such undeniable success quickly effected a general preference among oceanic travelers for steamers over sailing packets. Steamer enthusiasts now maintained that transatlantic steam voyages, as the 1839 *British Almanac* expressed it, "may now be said to be as easy of accomplishment by means of ships of adequate size and power as the passage between London and Margate."[5]

By the end of 1839 anxious proponents of the sailing packets were busily spreading rumors of explosions and other steam disasters at sea in hopes of winning back the passengers and valuable cargo which had gone over so quickly to the steamers.[6] But these efforts failed to resist the competitive onrush of steam or to offset the enthusiastic and growing preference of travelers for these novel vessels. Within a few years Atlantic steam travel was securely established and proclaimed as "one of the most portentious 'signs of the times.' The Old World and the New," it was now so often observed, "are brought, as it were, side by side."[7]

Steamers offered an unprecedented predictability of time spent on the ocean voyage. From the outset they possessed an insurmountable advantage over the sailing packets, which necessarily depended on the vagaries of weather. Steam might not assure a faster passage, for under ideal wind conditions the swiftest sailing vessels would continue to outrace steamers at sea well into the late nineteenth century. Yet from the start of steam competition the average passage for a sailing ship across the Atlantic was hopelessly slower and far less predictable, especially on the westward crossing against prevailing winds; it was this inherent disadvantage of sail which guaranteed the ultimate primacy of steam.

But progress had its drawbacks. Early oceanic steamers relied on machinery which was primitive in design and construction, unreliable if not dangerous in operation, and ruinously expensive to run and maintain. The machinery, as contemporaries observed with awe, was stupendous. Indeed it was, but such size was necessary to compensate for imprecision in fabrication and serious limitations in metallurgy. The massive, two-cylinder, reciprocating steam engines of the 1840's and 1850's were constructed of wrought iron with rough tolerances between moving parts. Unlike river steamers, whose engines were supplied with steam at remarkably high pressures (often with fatal consequences, as numerous reports of disastrous explosions attest), the first ocean steamers operated on extraordinarily low steam pressures, usually less than five pounds per square inch above atmosphere. With such low pressures the threat of wrought-iron or copper-plate boilers bursting might be alleviated, but only to be replaced by another problem; on occasion the partial vacuum created by condensation and exhaustion of steam at the end of the piston stroke produced the danger of implosion. Thus for such instances engines on seagoing steamers were often fitted with a reverse safety valve to permit injection of outside air in order to equalize the pressure.[8] Low steam pressures were also necessary during these early years, because steam condensation at the end of the piston stroke was usually achieved by direct injection into the cylinder of seawater. The consequent incrustation of mineral salts, deposited by the water recirculating through the boilers, threatened to block the boiler tubes with mineral deposits. Even with low pressures, boiler explosions were thus a distinct possibility, and vessels periodically stopped at sea for several hours to "blow off" the boilers.[9]

It was common for both boilers and engines to reveal innumerable small leaks in the course of operation. Engineers disregarded most of these, on the assumption that any minor leaks in due course would be filled by the accumulation of rust. Larger leaks, however, were not to be ignored. To plug such dangerously large holes engineers employed a variety of substances; instructions for one steamer in 1839 specified that the engineers uniformly scatter two sackfuls of oatmeal down the water spaces of the boiler before filling it. For unexpected leaks at sea it was not uncommon for engineers to call upon the steward for potatoes as a filler, or even to shovel in dung obtained from the ship's cow, on board to provide fresh milk for the passengers.[10]

Maintenance of the machinery while at sea was a constant and worrisome task of the marine engineer. He lubricated moving parts usually by an extensive application of tallow, which passengers soon came to view as an unpalatable if necessary evil as it simmered away on the hot engines and exuded the pungent odor of a dirty frying pan.[11] Conscientious lubrication notwithstanding, there were frequent engine and machinery breakdowns which required stopping the vessel at sea while the engine-room crew made repairs or just simple adjustments. Aside from stopping to blow off the boilers (at that, an improvement over the earlier practice of emptying the boilers completely every third or fourth day in order that engineers could climb into them and chip away the accumulated mineral scale), steamers frequently hove to for such minor repairs as fastening the paddlewheel floats, packing the stuffing boxes, tightening innumerable bolts and screws, and adjusting a variety of machinery parts which seemed to be perpetually misaligned and overheated.[12] To be sure, with primitive machinery some problems might be relatively easy to solve. An entry in the *Britannia*'s logbook suggests the advantage of operating with steam at only a few pounds above atmosphere: "Broke the larboard steam-pipe, lapped it with canvas and ropeyarn and proceeded with low pressure."[13]

Beyond problems with the machinery, there were difficulties with the engine-powered vessel herself. Ocean steamers were ruggedly built in order to support the bulky and heavy machinery. But most of the early steamers were wooden-hulled, and as they grew in size so did the problems in carrying their motive power. Even when the hull was stiffened with increasingly intricate and massive bracing of wood and iron, the wooden vessel suffered. Furnaces subjected the wood to tremendous heat and weight. Sagging of the wooden frame was a common consequence of the battering which a steam vessel received while pounding through the seas with the weight of machinery concentrated amidships. Sagging also resulted from the shrinking of those timbers and beams in proximity to the furnaces and funnel. And as a result of the furnace heat, dry rot was so common that within three years of entering service most of the steamers on the South Atlantic run had to undergo extensive repairs in drydock.[14]

Steamers in this early period were customarily full-rigged sailing vessels as well. Sails served as a precaution against machinery breakdown, and the relatively modest speed obtainable under steam alone could often be measurably increased by hoisting sails and traveling under steam and sail together. But this reliance on both sources of power required a crew considerably larger than that for a sailing packet, and such additional manpower always on board meant a sizable extra cost of operation, even if a steamer on occasion might conserve fuel costs by running under sail alone.

The greatest direct cost for oceanic steam navigation, which for years confined the scope of such steam carriage to passengers and selected high-value, low-bulk cargo, was fuel. While wind for the sailing packet was free, if undependable, coal for the steamer was as costly as it was necessary. Moreover, the inefficient engines of early steamers required so much fuel that most of the vessel's limited carrying capacity was taken up by coal and thus was not available for income-producing cargo. The *British Queen* (1839) was designed to carry 750 tons of coal and only 500 tons of cargo; while the *Britannia* (1840), whose total capacity was 865 tons, required 640 tons of coal, leaving only 225 tons available for cargo.[15] Consequently, although a steamer, with its greater regularity and often greater speed, might do the work of two sailing packets, there remained large cost disadvantages in operation. The heavy expense for fuel, the loss of income-producing cargo capacity as a result of stowing coal, an initial construction cost three times that of a sailing packet, a larger crew, much higher maintenance costs, and a shorter operational life all combined to make the early ocean-going steamer an expensive luxury. Such vessels for years were effectively limited to carrying specialized cargo and to providing services where speed, regularity and predictability of passage, and prestige might offset the very large disadvantage in costs.[16]

Not surprisingly, the earliest ocean steamers had to sacrifice much of the luxury in accommodations common to the sailing packets, since a steamer's larger size was more than offset by the space required for machinery and fuel. Cabins and saloons were frequently smaller than those on sailing vessels, and even then space was at a premium. It was customary on the early Royal Mail steamers to the West Indies for the cargo to be piled up in the middle of the forward saloon to the point where passengers could barely edge their way into the adjoining cabins. As the coal was consumed and below-deck space became available, the cargo was systematically transferred to the hold; predictably, some of the passengers' baggage became mixed with the cargo and also vanished below.[17]

A steamer beginning an ocean voyage in these early years

rode alarmingly deep in the water. When the *Royal William* with thirty-two passengers steamed out of Liverpool for New York on a midsummer evening in July 1838, she carried no cargo; yet, as one spectator noted:

> She was so deeply laden with coal for fuel—coal that filled her bunkers, her holds, and even her well-deck—that her paddles were buried six feet, her sponsons were submerged, and it was possible by leaning over the bulwarks to wash one's hands in the water that surged at the vessel's sides.[18]

Such large amounts of coal on board were necessary. The price and quality of coal were so variable and fuel supply was often so unpredictable that vessels might have to carry far more coal than required for any single voyage. In 1841, the steamers on the West Indian run burned a combined total of two thousand tons of coal weekly, all of which had to be shipped to coaling depots on the various West Indian islands. Adequate supply was a constant concern, since the coal came in chartered sailing vessels which often were delayed by bad weather or contrary winds.[19] Thus it was customary for steamers to load as much coal as they could safely carry—or even more than that. Such overloading with coal clearly contributed to the wreck in the Gulf Stream of the steamer *San Francisco* on Christmas Day 1853. With the price of coal twenty-four dollars a ton less in New York than at the next coaling port, in South America, the steamer had taken eight hundred tons aboard. When she ran into the gale which wrecked her, she was riding so deep that her guards were less than eighteen inches above the water.[20]

As a consequence of such frequent scarcity and price variation in coal, deck officers as well as engineers were admonished to conserve fuel, to "fire *light*—give her the full benefit of the steam pressure." They were to close furnace doors as much as possible in order to keep in heat, and were to periodically measure coal consumption with care.[21] If speed were not a factor and the vessel could proceed under sail, so much the better, even if it resulted in an idle engine-room crew. To conserve fuel some shipping operators even made abortive attempts to introduce into the Atlantic service sailing vessels with only auxiliary steam power, but the general desire for increased speed and consequent prestige doomed such economizing efforts.[22] Heavy costs notwithstanding, speed and regularity were essential for the steamers to win away the oceanic traveler—first from the sailing packets, then from competitors in the ocean steam service.

II.

"Let me assure you, my dears," Harriet Beecher Stowe wrote her children, "that going to sea is not at all the thing we have taken it to be." Anticipating "the fulfillment of all our dreams of poetry and romance," she had embarked at Boston in early April 1853 for an Atlantic crossing on the steamer *Niagara*. Upon arriving at Liverpool she was decidedly less enthusiastic. The ocean crossing, Mrs. Stowe confessed, had revealed a disconcerting contrast between romance and reality. Disillusioned, she decided that "the one step from the sublime to the ridiculous is never taken with such alacrity as in a sea voyage."[23]

But if such dreams were so rudely dispelled, there was still the irresistible novelty of making a voyage under steam, and for every jaded or disappointed traveler there were many others nervously thrilled at the prospect of their first ocean crossing in a steamer. Even by the 1850's ocean steam travel retained such a considerable and well-publicized risk that only the most blasé traveler could resist that flutter of mingled apprehension and anticipation which arose at the commencement of such a transatlantic voyage.

The first glimpse of an ocean steamer was memorable. Frequently, passengers had to engage small harbor craft to take them out to their ocean-going vessel where she lay at anchor. There, in the midst of rowboats, sloops, and small steamboats which scurried about the harbor, the massive ocean steamer loomed, as Charles Dickens observed, like "an elephant among the antelopes." Departing Liverpool in early January 1842, in eager anticipation of his first ocean crossing, Dickens joined a confused throng of passengers and well-wishers to take a small steamboat out to the Cunarder *Britannia* at her moorings in the Mersey River. Like many others, he was struck by the contrast between the "panting and snorting" little steam ferry and the grand ocean steam packet from whose massive red funnel the billowing smoke signaled imminent departure.[24]

If the steamer were tied up at a dock, as was the usual case in

New York, one might walk right up to "the huge black monster." To the inexperienced her gargantuan size suggested that she must be fixed in place; yet with "an occasional strong snort, and the dash of a paddle," the steamer would suddenly reveal to the awestruck observer "that there is an element of impatient life compressed within that ponderous frame."[25]

Uneasy over the mysteries of steam and uncomfortably aware of the dangers which the Atlantic offered, many travelers brooded over the forthcoming trip. As one passenger on the *Britannia* wrote upon his departure, "A successful trip is expected by all but I cannot help wondering what we would do if the Monster exploded in mid-ocean."[26] Particularly imaginative persons might surrender briefly to panic, and few could be wholly immune to the tingle of nervous pleasure, mixed with occasional gloom and apprehension, which travelers shared with friends, relatives, and casual spectators at this momentous undertaking.[27]

Upon arrival at the wharf the most elaborate planning and careful supervision of one's luggage rarely could withstand the frantic confusion of impending departure. "Coaches drive down furiously, and nervous passengers put their heads out to see if the steamer is off before her time," Richard Henry Dana noted of a February 1859 departure of the United States mail steamer *Cahawba* for Cuba; "and on the decks, and in the gangways, inexperienced passengers run against everybody, and mistake the engineers for the steward, and come up the same stairs they go down, without knowing it." In the meantime, the boiler fires, burning for hours, have built up steam pressure so that, while the vessel is still made fast to the wharf, "the great beam of the engine moves slowly up and down, and the black hull sways at its fasts."[28]

With farewells exchanged and the initial frenzied activity of boarding having subsided, the ocean traveler endured a tiresome wait for last-minute mail or tardy passengers. At that point, a careful examination of one's cabin might produce disillusion, if not despair. For some, of course, the novelty of the occasion overrode inconvenience; the Swedish writer Fredrika Bremer was so delighted with her compact accommodations on the Cunarder *Canada* that she believed her cabin to be as "large and splendid as a little castle, and besides that, convenient in the highest degree."[29] Perhaps more typical, however, was the dismay which such passengers as Charles Dickens, with their mounds of luggage, expressed upon encountering their quarters. Traveling to the United States on the *Britannia,* the British author felt particularly aggrieved with his accommodations. He had been badly misled, he realized, by the enticing sketches of his cabin which had been displayed in the office of his travel agent. As he complained to his brother, "Our cabin is something immensely smaller than you can possibly picture to yourself. Neither of the portmanteaus could by any mechanical contrivance be got into it." With the cabin door open, he added, he couldn't turn around; and when it was shut he couldn't "put on a clean shirt, or take off a dirty one." Dark in the day and cold at night, his cabin itself was dismal enough. And as for the furnishings, "anyone of the beds, with pillows, sheet, and blankets complete, might be sent from one place to another through the Post Office, with only a double stamp." Dickens related to a friend that on such a relatively small ocean-going vessel as the *Britannia* there were so many cabins and berths that everything, including the saloon, was necessarily cramped. The ladies' cabin adjoining his own was quite commodious and well appointed, he admitted, but as for *his* cabin, "a water closet of that size would be something too ridiculous to think of."[30]

Such disenchantment was at least briefly swept aside at the moment of departure. There was scarcely enough time to rush on deck, Dickens related of another voyage, before "we, the boat become violently agitated—rumble, hum, scream, roar, and establish an immense family washing-day at each paddle box." As for the *Britannia,* she "first throbbed like a strong giant that has just received the breath of life." Her wheels then began to turn fiercely, and the steamer, quickly developing momentum, surged "proudly through the lashed and foaming water" on her way to sea.[31]

For the traveler accustomed to sailing packets, steam power was marvelously boisterous; at that, many passengers expected far worse, and some even remarked with pleasant surprise on the relatively quiet and even motion of the large sidewheels and the almost unperceived throb of the engines.[32] In this regard, Richard Henry Dana was particularly appreciative in commenting on the departure of the mail steamer to Cuba:

> Captain Bullock is sure to sail at the hour; and at the hour he is on the paddle-box, the fasts are loosed, the warp run out, the crew pull in the warp on the port quarter, and the head swings off. No word is spoken, but all is done by signs; or, if a word is necessary, a low clear tone carries it to the listener. There is no tearing and rending escape of steam, deafening and distracting all, and giving a kind of terror to a peaceful scene; but our ship swings off, gathers way, and enters upon her voyage, in a quiet like that of a bank or counting-room, almost under a spell of silence.[33]

Once in motion, an ocean steamer could be as irresistible as she was impressive. Departing New York in 1838, "amid the cheers of thousands congregated on the piers," the *Great Western* had to steer carefully through the usual swarm of small boats; as it was, she almost ran down a sailing vessel when rounding the Battery. "The quick, sharp cry 'Hard a-port!' is heard," wrote one of her passengers, "and we barely escape annihilating a Charleston schooner and her terrified crew."[34]

Running the gauntlet of small craft, the ocean steamer was often accompanied by smaller vessels bearing not only crowds of spectators but also musical groups which would blare forth such appropriate songs as "Yankee Doodle" and "Home Sweet Home."[35] Then, once free from the confines of the harbor, the transatlantic liner would delight passengers and spectators alike as she surged forward under full power. Unlike sailing vessels, which so often left passively under tow until they reached open water:

> She tramples the waters in scorn—she cleaves them with her sharp bow—she dashes them aside with her broad floats, she leaves a boiling, bubbling, seething, foaming wake behind. Away down the bay she rushes, past headland and island, and ships at anchor, heading for the open sea, resistless and imperial in her career.[36]

The first moments at sea could be inspirational: "Out of our smoke-stack," Sophia Hawthorne wrote, "poured a column of steam like a procession of snowy plumes waving off into the distance; relieved against the deep-tone sky, it was wonderfully beautiful."[37] And on a particularly calm voyage, such as Dana's trip from New York to Cuba, the ocean voyage was sublime:

> The decks are dry, the sea is calm, and the steady-going engine alone, with easy exercise of power, drives the great hull, with its freight of cargo and provisions and human beings, over the placid sea, as fast as a furious gale could drive it, and leaves her long wake of foam on the sea, and her long wake of dark smoke in the sky.[38]

But in time the initial exhilaration usually subsided, to be replaced by an uncomfortable awareness that no matter how huge and stable the vessel might have appeared in port, once on the bounding wave matters were quite different. It was at this point that, for an overwhelming majority of ocean voyagers, the romance of life at sea gave way to the grim battle, in all of its infinite stages and varieties of discomfort, with seasickness. Steamer passengers fared no better than those on sailing packets. A few might cavalierly brush off the malady, and others might remain indifferent for at least a while. But the heaving, undulating motion of the ocean-going vessel forced one traveler after another away from the dinner table and onto the deck.[39] The miserable traveler might seek refuge in his cabin, but as it opened directly onto the main saloon, there was no hope for true seclusion. Once in the full grip of seasickness, to be sure, the wretched voyager might turn indifferent to such distressing lack of privacy; at this point "life seems worthless," one sufferer grimly recalled, "and the prospect of a wreck under such circumstances, is rather agreeable."[40]

Such growing queasiness at the start of an ocean voyage, and even the full agony of seasickness which gripped the more susceptible traveler, was not peculiar to steam travel; it was merely a hazard for anyone going to sea. Was there, then, anything about these early steamers at all distinctive or that even made matters worse in this regard? "In the first place," Mrs. Stowe answers, "ship life is not at all fragrant; in short, especially on a steamer, there is a most mournful combination of grease, steam, onions, and dinners in general, either past, present, or to come, which, floating invisibly in the atmosphere, strongly predisposes to that disgust of existence which, in half an hour after sailing, begins to come upon you."[41]

For Charles Dickens seasickness on a steamer possessed its own peculiar horrors. He knew all too well when his vessel had begun her trip; once under way he soon became aware of "a stout wooden wedge driven in at my right temple and out at my left, a floating deposit of lukewarm oil in my throat, and a compression of the bridge of my nose in a blunt pair of pincers."[42]

Especially unsettling for the queasy passenger were the dubious delights of the dinner table. Steamship operators, partly to compensate for their inferior accommodations in comparison to those on sailing packets, relentlessly thrust food and drink at their passengers. For the hardy, this might serve as a welcome distraction on a tedious passage: "The lunch gong rings and I'm off for a smoked herring, a wine biscuit, and a glass of Old Stout," briskly noted one seasoned traveler. "Were it not for the animal luxury of eating often and of good things," he admitted, "a sea voyage to a passenger would be extremely irksome."[43]

If only by default, eating became a central preoccupation for those steamer passengers able to eat at all. The constant vibration of the machinery produced throughout the vessel an incessant jiggling that wracked one's nerves and made a trial out of such ordinarily simple occupations as reading and writing. Anticipating leisurely hours of contemplation or creative effort, many a traveler gave up in despair as he slipped helplessly into a state of befuddled weariness from which food and drink could at least provide frequent respite.

Yet with all of these drawbacks, life on a steamer possessed decided advantages over that on a sailing vessel. Of prime importance was freedom from dependence on the wind. As one lady observed while voyaging across the South Atlantic in mid-March 1861, "Some days the thermometer was up to 90 in the saloon, but we were fortunate enough to steam through it, while the unhappy sailing-ships we passed were flapping their sails helplessly in the calm on the Line, while their inhabitants must have been nearly roasted alive."[44] And Charles Dickens, no friend of ocean steamers after his harrowing voyage to America on the *Britannia,* had to admit during his return trip, when his sailing packet lacked wind, that steam might have its merits. Thus becalmed, passengers became peevish, lost their earlier enthusiasm for sailing ships and their officers, and became openly critical of those whom they had so recently praised. At this point there was bound to appear some sardonic traveler, Dickens explained, who now would goad the perplexed enthusiast of sail "by inquiring where he supposed the

Great Western (which left New York a week after us) was *now*; and where he supposed the 'Cunard' steam-packet was *now*; and what he thought of sailing vessels, as compared with steamships *now*."[45]

Steam engines were undeniably useful if not essential when a vessel encountered a field of icebergs drifting south across the sea-lanes. The engine of the *Great Western*, the poetess Lydia Sigourney related in grateful admiration, "accommodated itself every moment, like a living and intelligent thing, to the commands of the Captain." Arrested in its headlong rush through the waters, the *Great Western* would pause " 'till two or three of the icy squadron drifted by us," she related; then, " 'let her go!' and with the velocity of lightning we darted by another detachment of our deadly foes." After this episode, she concluded, many of those passengers initially apprehensive of steam now proclaimed its advantages.[46]

A summer passage of the North Atlantic, let alone one in midwinter, was bracing—so much so that many passengers were unable to brave the elements for very long. Yet to go below, especially when one felt a bit unsettled, was to court disaster. Thus "our favorite resort," Mrs. Stowe explained, "is by the old red smoke pipe of the steamer, which rises warm and luminous as a sort of tower of defense." There was usually a sheltered place by the funnel where one might escape the wind and warm one's feet while observing the cook at work in the pantries and the livestock milling about in their pens. "In fact," she decided, "the old smoke pipe is the domestic hearth of the ship."[47] On a blustery day, another traveler observed of an 1846 crossing, one could count on seeing a few who clung to this spot and "spent most of their time in all but bodily contact with the funnel, courting its warmth, and smoking nearly as much as it did."[48]

Of course there might be too much of a good thing. The funnel was clearly a means to keep one from freezing while on deck, one passenger noted of a late spring passage, yet "we gather round it and sit upon its hot flange until we can decide whether it is better to perish with heat or cold, for any intermediate state seems denied us." Still, the warm, bulky funnel of a steamer was a welcome alternative to the fetid atmosphere in the saloon, smoking rooms, or ladies' cabin, the only sheltered places available for those who could not bear to be closeted in their own cubicles.[49]

Steam also provided certain luxuries unavailable in the sailing packets. By the 1850's cabins and saloon were heated by steam pipes running off the ship's boilers, and on some vessels there was even a measure of heat regulation.[50] For those who feared that a steamer was more likely than a sailing ship to burst into flame, there was the compensating benefit of steam-driven pumps for the fire hoses, so that in the event of fire a great quantity of sea water could be drawn into the vessel and distributed to the endangered area.[51]

Unfortunately for the steamer passenger, there was no way of avoiding some of the other consequences of burning coal. "You cannot think how dirty everything gets," wrote one despairing traveler to her sister; "hands, clothes, everything is black. The white in my dress is in a most disastrous state. I never saw such a dirty ship."[52] For those who worked aboard the steamer matters were scarcely better. It was especially galling for men accustomed to a life of sail to be subjected to the filth of a steamer. Stationed on an open bridge running athwartships between the two paddle boxes, the deck officers found life to be a depressing change from the good old days on the quarterdeck. "The agony of it," William McFee recalled, "was that they had to command from a bridge amidships, a most unsuitable location for a sailing-ship man. There they might, with a following wind, be smothered in soot from the funnel. Sparks burned holes in the sails. The black gang, dumping ashes every watch, made life hideous with their banging and clashing of buckets and the fine ash blew across the decks and into the cabins."[53]

Cleaner-burning anthracite coal was preferable to the notoriously dirty soft bituminous variety, but still there was a sooty residue which poured from the funnel and blanketed any steamer with grime. Chuffing slowly and ponderously flailing the waters of New York Harbor at the completion of an ocean voyage in 1841, one such vessel startled an observer who recoiled at the sight of a "hull as black as night; a column of thick smoke boiling up from its low pipe—dark, frowning, begrimed with soot—unearthly, wild, murky, threatening, as if it had just wrestled with a storm upon the Stygian Gulf." For this filthy and storm-battered vessel there was "little to relieve the Cimmerian blackness but the white foam of its paddle-wheel and the red flag of England which floats above its stern." What, he wondered, could this apparition be? "It is the *President,* fifteen days from Liverpool, bringing fresh merchandise and news to this republic."[54]

Most ocean-going travelers appreciated only that much of their vessel which was visible. In particular, their understanding of steam propulsion was limited to what they might observe from the deck of their ship. Richard Henry Dana, Jr., admitted to the thrill of standing "on the high quarter-deck, the lofty sails spread before you, the great hull throbbing with the invisible power that is driving you along." Yet, he pointed out, there was a crucial part of the steamer of which the conventional passenger knew little, if anything. In their ignorance, most voyagers considered only the activity on deck and in the rigging as worthy of comment. Yet "all the time, down in the abyss of the hull, worked with ceaseless energy, day and night, the enormous, complex machinery." Here, Dana realized, was the essential source of power to which masts, rigging, and sails were merely convenient auxiliaries.

The ignorance of passengers was understandable, Dana believed, since ordinarily they were not permitted to visit the engine room while the vessel was moving under steam power. Dana, however, determined to go below "to see the great works of fire and steam." With the officers' permission he descended level after level of winding steps to "these deep and unknown regions, down by the keelson of the ship." There, in the fitful light of the furnace room, he discovered the engineers and their large crew of firemen and coal passers, "a body of grim, blackened, and oily men . . . who know as little of the upper ship, as the upper ship knows of them." Here was truly another world. "On the brick and iron floors between the walls of brick and iron," Dana wrote, "I lost all sense of being at sea, or even on shipboard." Little wonder that sailors complained of giving up going to sea to go into steamers! "For aught that I could hear or see," Dana mused, "I might have been in the subterranean recesses of a steam factory in Staffordshire."[55]

The world below decks was not necessarily an inferno, some dismal and suffocating cavern in which brutish men had been condemned to a life of endless drudgery. When the weather was bad and the nights "wet and Dreary," Dana wrote of a later voyage, "how cheerful it looks to go into the engine room, & see the engine working away briskly, the fires gleaming & the oil lamps burning bright." In fact, Dana concluded, the engine room could be quite cosy on such a stormy night.[56]

But the usual life below decks, even though few passengers might know or care, was hard. As early as 1828 firemen were issued a double allowance "of beer or other beverage" while on duty.[57] On the first trip of the *Great Western* across the Atlantic her stokers and trimmers received extra pay for hauling coal to the furnaces from those bunkers farthest away. Even with this incentive, there was scarcely enough coal for the engineers to maintain sufficient steam pressure for the engines.[58]

Drunk and abusive firemen—the notorious "black gang" which sailors and passengers alike would shun—were grim products of this toil. The incessant demands of deck officers for more speed meant unremitting, back-breaking work for the men who labored in the dingy, stifling bowels of a steamer. An occasional extra ration of food or grog was little enough recognition of their task. As William McFee observed, from his own later experiences as engineer, "Only the most muscular and hardened men could stand the life when, as we used to say, it was 'blood for steam.' "[59]

While oblivious or at least indifferent to the crew and to the machinery below decks, ocean-going passengers could scarcely ignore the most tangible evidence of steam power, the wheel. Indeed, throughout this early period of oceanic steam travel a debate raged between advocates of the side paddlewheel and those of the screw propeller. The first ocean steamers were sidewheelers, and to men of sail they were grotesque. Those who gloried in the clean and increasingly sharp lines of the swift sailing packets and the later clipper ships recoiled in disgust at the huge, protruding paddle boxes and the wheels which transformed the graceful sailing ship into a wallowing, thrashing, puffing monstrosity.

With the mammoth, iron-hulled *Great Britain*, the screw-propelled ocean steamer appeared on the Atlantic in the mid-1840's. Yet while the advantages, both aesthetic and practical, of the screw were apparent from the start, many years would elapse before the sidewheelers vanished from the sea lanes. A case could be made for the superiority of the sidewheeler over the screw in these formative years of marine steam technology, and for a time those who advocated the screw were even on the defensive.

Much of the comparison between sidewheel and screw involved a choice of the lesser evil. For those who professed satisfaction with the easier movement of the sailing ship, the motion of *any* steamer was objectionable. To be sure, after reading a number of doleful recollections of sea travel, one might reasonably conclude that instead of the peculiar faults of any steamer it was a general detestation of the ocean crossing or of a particularly violent passage which stimulated much of the criticism. Yet many travelers persisted in asserting that a steamer possessed a motion both distinctive and deplorable.

A steamer in a rolling sea, one naval officer observed, behaved like "a cat in walnut shells on ice."[60] When the weather was particularly severe an ocean steamer passage could be truly terrifying. Charles Dickens, having survived his tempestuous midwinter Atlantic crossing on the sidewheeler *Britannia,* vividly portrayed the distinctive manner in which his steamer, unlike a sailing vessel, stubbornly fought her way through the heavy seas:

> Flung down on her side in the waves, with her masts dipping into them, and that, springing up again, she rolls over on the other side, until a heavy sea strikes her with the noise of a hundred great guns, and hurls her back—that she stops, and staggers, and shivers, as though stunned, and then, with a violent throbbing at her heart, darts onward like a monster goaded into madness, to be beaten down, and battered, and crushed, and leaped on by the angry sea—.[61]

Not surprisingly, Dickens determined to return to his homeland in a sailing packet. In June, he calculated, with pleasanter weather and prevailing winds, such a passage probably would take no more than three weeks. But regardless of the time it might take, he insisted, the sailing ship was his only possible mode of travel: "I never will trust myself upon the wide ocean, if it please Heaven, in a steamer again." Reflecting upon his experiences on the *Britannia,* Dickens was appalled at the risks he had taken: "First, that if the funnel were blown overboard, the vessel must instantly be on fire, from stem to stern." The *Britannia*'s funnel, he recalled, was more than forty feet high, yet at night "you see the solid fire two or three feet above its top." What, then, might happen in a strong gale or even a sudden gust of wind?

Steamers at sea exhibited other peculiarities in their motion, Dickens noted. A twelve-hundred-ton steamer which required seven hundred tons of coal for fuel necessarily left port too deep in the water for the paddlewheels to work properly; yet if she carried less coal she would complete her trip so light that the wheels would be too far out of the water. In any event, as the coals were burned in the course of the passage, the vessel perceptibly lightened; thus "the daily difference in her rolling," Dickens explained, "is something absolutely fearful." Any steamer passenger, he concluded, might well be terrified. Trapped for days in a vessel "full of fire and people" with no boats to carry off the passengers and with the huge machinery pounding away and threatening to tear the steamer to pieces as she struggled through heavy Atlantic seas, a passenger, he decided, might very well "quake considerable" and "damn the engine."[62]

While enduring the ceaseless lurching and heaving of his vessel, the steamer passenger encountered the most dismal moments of the voyage, as Dickens phrased it, "in the dead water-gurgling waste of the night."[63] Mrs. Stowe vividly recalled that at such times "you hear every kind of odd noise in the ship—creaking, straining, crunching, scraping, pounding, whistling, blowing off steam, each of which to your unpractised ear is significant of some impending catastrophe." Grimly determined to keep the vessel afloat by her own will, she lay awake, hour after hour, listening with all her might even while admitting that her efforts were useless. At last she succumbed to fitful slumber and awoke in the morning mildly surprised to find herself alive and the vessel still in one piece. Nothing really had been the matter, she then concluded; the appalling sounds of the previous night were merely the "necessary attendants of what is called a good run."[64]

The problem with a steamer's motion, insisted one British naval officer, was not the engines or wheels but rather the hull design. Here, he confessed, the Americans were clearly superior to the British. The latter might build better machinery, but on the American Collins liners of the 1850's "there was none of that violent plunging—that sudden check usually attending a large ship in a heavy head sea." For instance, when a huge wave moved toward the Collins steamer *Baltic* her elongated bow and trim lines permitted her "to sink gently down until almost level with the water, and as gradually to rise again after passing," without taking any seas on board in the process. Yet the British Cunarders were notorious for taking in a huge volume of water over the bow even in an ordinary head sea, thanks to their heavy bowsprit, "an absolute excresence—a bow-plunging, speed-stopping, money spending, and absurd acquiescence in old-fashioned prejudice about appearance."[65]

Most passengers preferred to attribute the particular discomfort of a steamer to that which so evidently distinguished her from a sailing ship—the propelling wheel. A sidewheeler, most agreed, was bound to be a clumsy sailer because of the paddle boxes. Buffeted by winds and waves, these large and vulnerable protuberances slowed the steamer and produced a jarring motion which left passengers wretched. When under both steam and sail, a sidewheeler often heeled over so far that one wheel was revolving uselessly in the air while the other was buried in the water.[66] The consequent waste of power and difficulty in steering were obvious. To work the sails on a sidewheeler was particularly frustrating, because the bulky machinery, the cumbersome paddle boxes, and the bridge extending between the two boxes thwarted the most adept sailor.

A sidewheeler, however, had her compensations. Passengers berthed in the vessel's stern, a preferred location both by sailing-ship tradition and by being farthest away from the noise and vibration of the machinery. Sidewheelers in this early period were just as fast as screw-propelled steamers and less prone to costly and dangerous mechanical breakdowns at sea. Highly debatable was the contention that the paddlewheels afforded greater stability for the vessel than did the screw, but few would deny the psychological stability provided by the highly visible and thus reassuring presence of the paddlewheel. The wholly submerged screw, on the other hand, did its work in a far too mysterious fashion.[67]

Proponents of the screw propeller nonetheless affirmed its superiority over the sidewheel. From its inception the screw appeared to be somewhat more economical to operate than the paddlewheel. In addition, its machinery occupied far less space, and this meant correspondingly more room for fuel and cargo in an era when so little cargo space was available in a steamer. Because of its location at the stern of the vessel, the screw propeller produced far less drag under sail than did the much larger sidewheels. Moreover, drag was further reduced by using screw propellers so designed that they could be disconnected from the shaft and hoisted out of the water.[68] When possessing telescopic or collapsible funnels as well, a screw steamer could become a proper sailing ship, much to the satisfaction of old salts and penny-pinching ship operators.

Advocates of the screw believed that the motion of a screw steamer was preferable to that of a sidewheeler. Of course, they might admit, a screw vessel rolled more in a sea, but her pitch was far less—"the pitch being *the* misery at sea."[69] A number of travelers would disagree; for them the rolling of a screw steamer was her most notorious attribute. The Cunard screw steamer *Delta,* Anthony Trollope complained, exemplified this deplorable trait. So far as he was concerned, "Screws have been invented with the view of making sea-passages more disagreeable than they were." True to his convictions, he returned from New York to Liverpool on the sidewheeler *Africa.* "I have sailed in many vessels," Trollope triumphantly concluded, "but never in one that was more comfortable."[70] Others shared his dislike: "Our steamer is a screw," reported a weary Atlantic traveler in the mid-1860's, "and she has wriggled us into screws too. She rolls like a revolving auger, boring an endless gimlet-hole in the eastern horizon." But for many a suffering, sea-tossed voyager such distinctions were superfluous: "As to the question whether 'pitching' or 'rolling' is the less miserable," the weary traveler grimly concluded, "it must probably be settled by saying that the form not immediately present is the more tolerable of the two."[71]

The most serious drawback to traveling on a screw steamer, some maintained, was not her motion; instead, it was the noise and vibration of the screw propeller itself. Especially irksome were the earliest screw-propelled ocean steamers. The iron-hulled *Great Britain* initially carried a screw and engine both acclaimed as "wondrous in their vibration." Extensive bracing of her hull and modification of her machinery, which included replacing her endless-chain drive with wheel and pinion gearing, produced a refreshing improvement. One traveler enthusiastically reported that even in the stern of the vessel, where one would expect the most severe shaking, the vibration could hardly be felt; and at the forward end of the steamship the vibration was imperceptible.[72] Such an achievement, if wholly realized, was indeed extraordinary. The huge iron propeller shaft produced enormous friction as it revolved through the lignum vitae stuffing at the steamer's sternpost. At the other end of the shaft, where it met the thrust plate, engineers had to play streams of water constantly on the grinding metal in order to help reduce the heat caused by friction between those two surfaces.[73] In comparison with such iron vessels as the *Great Britain,* wooden-hulled screw steamers, heavily braced though they might be, suffered even greater problems through straining the hull and misaligning the shaft.

Screw steamers in the early period suffered from an additional disadvantage resulting from the design of their engines. Usually just modified versions of the earlier direct-acting paddlewheel engines, the engines of early screw steamers customarily ran at a slow 14 to 18 revolutions per minute. This sharply contrasted with the speed of the screw propeller, which had to make up to 150 revolutions in order to provide sufficient propulsive force for the vessel. To reconcile this discrepancy, engine builders designed ingenious gearing arrangements by which iron teeth meshed with those fabricated of such hard wood as lignum vitae. This, however, resulted in the heavy expense of a frequent engine overhaul and a bilge carpeted with wood shavings at the end of a high-speed ocean voyage.[74]

Those passengers who had been accustomed to the relative comfort of a stern cabin in a sidewheeler were appalled by the noise and shudder of the screw as it revolved directly beneath them. One young lady unconcernedly violated ship's regulations by hammering up some nails to serve as clothing hooks: "Our cabin," she explained, "is directly over the screw, so that I dare say they did not hear."[75] Yet to relocate the passengers' quarters amidships was to defy tradition and to compound the existing complexities of naval architecture. It was not until the 1860's that Atlantic travelers in screw steamers began to enjoy more comfortable accommodations amidships; until then, they remained unwilling victims of the screw.

No transatlantic traveler in this period was more trenchant in his complaints than was Charles Dickens. Evenhanded in his condemnation of steamer types, he found as much to criticize in the Cunard screw steamer *Russia* as he had earlier in the sidewheeler *Britannia.* Yet for Dickens the screw propeller became an obsession. The Screw (*sic*), Dickens explained, served the passengers on the *Russia* as a "voice of conscience . . . because it seemed to me that we were all of us, all day long, endeavouring to stifle the voice." Yet this was impossible; the Screw was "under everybody's pillow, everybody's plate, everybody's campstool, everybody's book, everybody's occupation." Attempting to ignore it, passengers busied themselves in a frenzied round of shipboard activity, but to no avail. "It was always among us in an under monotone," Dickens related, "not to be drowned in pea-soup, not to be shuffled with cards, not to be diverted by books, not to be knitted into any pattern, not to be walked away from." Neither pungent cigars nor strong drinks could dispel the voice; yet to recognize its presence openly was inadmissable, for, as Dickens explained, "It was considered (as on shore) ill-bred to acknowledge the voice of conscience." Such a breach of decorum in fact had occurred one stormy day: "An amiable gentleman in love gave much offence to a surrounding circle, including the object of his attachment, by saying of it, after it had goaded him over two easy-chairs and a skylight, 'Screw!' "

Every now and then one might almost forget this voice, during those diverting moments "when bubbles of champagne pervaded the nose" or when activity on deck became sufficiently boisterous. Yet when the clattering of pots and pans had subsided, when the gulls had wheeled away after the last of the garbage, "the instant any break or pause took place in any such diversion, the voice would be at it again, importuning us to the last extent."

At night, as with other memorable aspects of a steamer's behavior, matters grew worse. "For then," Dickens recalled, "as we fell off one by one, and, entering our several hutches, came into a peculiar atmosphere of bilge-water and Windsor soap, the voice would shake us to the centre." Once the lights were out and the passenger squeezed himself into his narrow berth, he became fully aware of his plight. "The voice grows angrier and deeper," Dickens wrote. "Under the mattress and under the pillow, under the sofa and under the washing-stand, under the ship and under the sea, seeming to rise from the foundations under the earth with every scoop of the great Atlantic (and oh! why scoop so?), always the voice." It was futile to ignore it, nor could the obsessed traveler feign deafness; "screw, screw, screw!"

During the night the voice might change—but only for the worse. "It lifts out of the water, and revolves with a whirr, like a ferocious firework," Dickens remembered, "except that it never expends itself, but is always ready to go off again." At other times the screw "seems to be in anguish and shivers"; or "it seems to be terrified by its last plunge, and has a fit which causes it to struggle, quiver, and for an instant stop."

But the voice always resumed, and day after day it droned on until the ship finally entered port and the engines stopped. "A very curious sensation, not unlike having my own ears stopped, ensued upon that silence," Dickens observed. Struck by the absence of the screw's voice, he felt compelled to go over the side of the steamer so that he could examine "the outer hull of the gracious monster that the voice had inhabited," much, he admitted, as he might observe the corpse of a fellow-human by whose death the voice of conscience had finally been put to rest.[76]

The incessant noise and vibration of a steamer, the smells and the motion, the soot and the cramped quarters—these might be bearable for a while, but there came a time when all but the most energetic or insensitive traveler yearned for an end to the Atlantic voyage. On the ocean crossing a steamer might cut by more than half the usual time for a sailing packet, a period which, granting considerable unpredictability, still was at least three weeks on the eastward passage. Nevertheless, after a week on board a steamer complaints of boredom became frequent.[77]

If an uneventful passage was tedious, the alternatives were even less palatable. Storms, fires, machinery breakdowns, collisions with icebergs or other vessels—such frequent and serious hazards made the Atlantic voyage a formidable undertaking. In a period when steamer losses and accidents were widely publicized, no passenger could easily remain unaware of the considerable risk involved in an ocean steam trip. A particularly severe storm, such as Charles Dickens experienced on the *Britannia* or as the huge *Great Eastern* barely survived in September 1861, was a possibility never to be entirely discounted. Whether it was better to ride through storms in a steamer rather than in a sailing vessel was debatable. Sidewheelers, in particular, might take such a beating that major injury to the machinery would occur. A heavy sea could snap a paddlewheel shaft; if the wheel fell out of the vessel she might then capsize.[78] Yet such a steamer could also be safer than a sailing vessel. Making a passage in an autumn gale on the *Britannia* in 1845, several sailing-ship captains on board preferred the steamer to any of their own sailing packets. She was light in the rigging, they explained, and her small sails would not be so easily carried away in a sudden gust of wind. Moreover, her steam power permitted her to maintain headway in the worst of seas. By keeping her head to the wind she could avoid the fate of so many sailing ships—being pooped or becoming swamped by a wave coming broadside.[79]

A sailing ship not only had less chance than a steamer to be set afire in the normal course of operations; sailers also avoided the chronic problem of early steamers—machinery breakdown. On her first return passage from New York to Bristol, the *Great Western* had been at sea only two hours when a connecting rod bearing pad broke; the repairs required completely disconnecting a piston while the steamer limped along on one engine. Such difficulties recurred several times on the same passage, and even when making minor repairs the steamer had to heave to in the midst of the ocean while engineers worked frantically on her machinery.[80] At that, her passage home was no more perplexing than her initial crossing when, according to the Engineer's log, "a knocking noise existing in the larboard wheel, stopped engines. Found one semi outer paddle adrift at one end. In both wheels found several nuts loosed and two bolts gone." Although he made these repairs uneventfully, the Engineer's good fortune ceased abruptly when the *Great Western* arrived at New York. While the vessel tied up at the wharf, he busied himself with shutting down the engines. Perhaps distracted by the cheering crowd or by the magnitude of this epoch-making ocean voyage, he attempted to blow steam out of the boilers and was scalded to death.[81]

On a return voyage from New York to Liverpool, the captain of the celebrated iron screw steamer *Great Britain* noted "something wrong with the propeller and striking the stern post very hard." He thereupon reversed the engines, but, he observed, "after two or three good thumps, the arm broke off." Resuming the voyage, the captain used as little steam and as much sail as he could afford. His vessel still moved along at a quite respectable speed, between seven and nine knots, but the captain grew increasingly concerned when, on the following day, "another propeller arm broke, leaving only one and a half." Now resorting entirely to his sails, he maintained his course for five more days, at the end of which time the last complete propeller arm snapped off. This left the steamer to complete her transatlantic voyage with only a single stump at the end of her propeller shaft, but with a number of passengers and crew properly grateful for her capabilities under sail.[82]

At times steamers suffered accidents which bordered on the ludicrous, as one inexperienced junior deck officer discovered to his chagrin. During an October 1844 passage from Madeira to Barbados, the Royal Mail steamer *Tweed* was under steam and sail power when the wind died. Perhaps flustered at the novelty of steaming along faster than the wind, the deck officer failed to take in his sails in proper order. As a result, one of those on board recalled:

> The lee topmast studding-sail tack hooked on to one of the floats of the paddle wheel, and in much less time than it has taken to write it, wound down the topmast and topgallant studding-sail booms and the sails. The inside end of the topmast studding-sail boom got in between two floats and forced itself up through the bottom of the starboard paddle-box boat—sail, gear and all being wound round the wheel.

At this point, the engineer on watch, hearing "a commotion in the wheel," prudently stopped the engines before going to see what was the matter. It was difficult to make out just what *was* wrong, except that a mast improbably appeared to be projecting from the bottom of a lifeboat. Fitted upside down over the paddlewheel, and thus serving as the top of the paddle box, the starboard boat had been neatly speared and was in no condition to be put to sea. For that matter, the steamer was also out of commission until the following morning; it took that long to remove the gear which had been so tightly wound around the outer end of the paddlewheel shaft.[83]

Fears of collision, especially with an iceberg, had long hounded passengers of sailing packets on the fog-shrouded Atlantic run. Steamers, many insisted, were safer because they could maneuver around the icy peril, regardless of wind conditions. But this advantage, it soon appeared, was too often illusory. The precious reputation of a shipping line, of an individual steamer, and of a skipper, was increasingly dependent on speed. Commanding officers were consequently loath to slow down, let alone stop, for anything. They frequently took unconscionable risks, especially when fog compounded the dangers of collision as steamers raced through the ice fields. Too often the only concession to prudence, even in the reputedly safety-conscious Cunarders, was to increase the watch when going through a field of icebergs. Thus the *Britannia,* Sir Charles Lyell somberly recalled, maintained her speed of nine miles an hour although at one point during the night she came dangerously close to a large iceberg. A naval officer on board assured Lyell that they had been in imminent peril: "He had weathered a typhoon in the Chinese Seas, and would rather brave another than sail so fast in the night through a pack of icebergs."[84]

The American Collins liners of the 1850's were notorious for their heedless pursuit of transatlantic speed records. The result, while deplorable, was predictable. The tragic collision and sinking of the Collins steamer *Arctic* was bad enough. The subsequent disappearance of her sister ship *Pacific,* presumably through collision with an iceberg, not only discouraged further Federal Government support of the Collins Line, but also confirmed the dangers of the Atlantic crossing in even the most celebrated steamers.[85] Little wonder that the fear of collision preoccupied many a querulous traveler—especially at night when, as Dickens lugubriously recalled, one might "put aside the rolling and the rush of water, and think of darting through such darkness with such velocity. Think," he added, "of any other similar object coming in the opposite direction."[86]

Often this "similar object" was a hapless sailing vessel which could scarcely survive a ramming by a heavy ocean steamer. Typical was an incident involving the *Persia,* the Cunard Line's most popular steamer in the late 1850's. On the first night out from Liverpool she collided with a small brig. "Although the shock was hardly perceptible to us on board the *Persia,*" a passenger recorded, it was not so for the brig. She had been struck so hard by the steamer that she promptly sank under the interested gaze of the steamer's passengers. As was usual in such cases, the *Persia* stopped barely long enough to rescue the brig's survivors and then resumed her swift Atlantic passage. "It created quite a gloom on board," admitted the passenger, "but like railway accidents on land, such things are never talked about on board ship, as no doubt there was great neglect on the part of the watch."[87]

Speed was essential. Despite collisions and fog, ocean steamers rarely slackened their pace. After a collision with a sailing vessel in a dense fog, the Cunarder *Canada* resumed steaming at top speed, eliciting one passenger's pensive comment: "It is strange how soon one gets hardened to this state of things, and we began to feel as much confidence in the blind rush of the ship over the sea as in the world itself rolling through space."[88]

Of course there were exceptions. Some captains grew suitably cautious when their vessels encountered hazardous conditions, and at times such caution even exceeded that of their impatient passengers. Voyaging to England in July 1856 on the Cunarder *America,* Richard Henry Dana observed that upon steaming into foggy weather and ice-strewn seas his vessel reduced her speed and blew whistles and horns constantly in order to locate icebergs by the echo. Even then the steamer almost collided with an iceberg, after which the passengers, Dana remarked, were "now better satisfied with the slackened speed of the boat, and praise the captain for his careful watch."[89]

The safe arrival of an ocean steamer was not to be taken for granted in the early years of steam. For those many Americans who took an avid if vicarious interest in ocean steam travel and who considered the superiority of the Collins steamers over the Cunarders to be a matter of national honor, a steamer's scheduled appearance was cause for widespread satisfaction.[90] An overdue steamer, correspondingly, was a matter of intense public concern, as a troublesome winter crossing of the steamer *Atlantic* reveals.

Departing Liverpool on 12 December 1850, the *Atlantic* encountered such a gale that she was unable to let off the pilot. Persisting through winds of hurricane force, she was nearly lost on 6 January when a huge wave pounded into her larboard paddlewheel, broke its main shaft, and disabled both her engines. In imminent danger of capsizing, helpless without steam power, and far out to sea, the *Atlantic* struggled to remain afloat while her captain stubbornly worked to maintain her westward course. But her two auxiliary sails, which according to one passenger "looked like handkerchiefs in comparison with our immense craft," were insufficient to give her headway. She turned back to the British Isles, where she finally arrived on 22 January—almost six weeks after her departure—with an exhausted crew and a group of thoroughly disgruntled passengers who had been reduced to two meals daily in place of the usual four.[91]

Meanwhile, no news of the overdue *Atlantic* had arrived at New York, her intended destination. Public concern mounted as the weeks passed into mid-February, still with no word of the steamer.[92] Back in England some of the *Atlantic's* passengers had resumed their efforts to get to America; scarcely more than a week after the *Atlantic's* ignominious return, they embarked on the Cunarder *Africa* for what turned out to be an unexceptional two-week passage from Liverpool to New York. With them and the *Africa* came the belated news that the *Atlantic* was safe. It was evening when the *Africa* arrived at New York, recalled the editor of *Harper's:*

> And the Extras, in a moment sowed the exciting news broadcast over the town. Men stopped each other in the streets, and told the glad tidings as of some great victory which had secured peace and prosperity to the land. Crowds gathered under the lanterns, while some loud voice read out the happy news. People looked in at shops and up at windows, saying, "The *Atlantic* is safe!" In the theatres the managers rushed upon the stage in the midst of the performance, and announced to the audience what everyone was rejoiced to hear.

"For that evening," he concluded reverently, "men stood upon the ground of a common manhood, sure of individual sympathy, in the universal joy."[93]

Passengers disembarking from the *Africa* were struck by the tumultuous response to the news. "A newspaper, which costs only 2 cents was sold for and eagerly paid with fifty cents," one of them marveled. And New Yorkers, he added, were not alone in their relief; the "joyful intelligence" had been telegraphed directly "to Louisiana and Mississippi, to Cincinnati and Michigan."[94]

New Yorkers understandably developed avid interest in the fortunes of each transatlantic steamer. Any deviation from the normal schedule was quickly noted and endlessly discussed. Writing in his diary on 14 February, weeks beyond the *Atlantic's* scheduled arrival, George Templeton Strong remarked how Wall

Street that day had been convulsed with excitement when a horde of newsboys rushed in with what at first appeared to be fresh intelligence of the long-overdue *Atlantic*. And all it was, he remarked in exasperation, was a late bit of news that the steamer had been spoken when four days out of Liverpool. One may then imagine the public frenzy which greeted the final word of her safety. "Communicated to Gramercy Square at about 11:30 by a herd of highly excited newsboys," the good news brought New Yorkers tumbling out of bed, downstairs, and onto the streets. Strong himself appeared in "an ethereal costume," he admitted, in his haste to obtain a copy of the extra.[95]

Such general and profound relief over the safety of a steamer was matched in intensity by the public agony when one was lost. Contemporary accounts of the *Arctic* tragedy in 1854 attest to the successive shock, horror, and doleful reflection which followed the news of such a disaster. And this consuming public interest in the early ocean steamers was far from superficial or sporadic. Ocean steamers were more than passing fads; they were even more than objects of awe and pride. In America's "go-ahead age" they stood both as evocative symbols and as tangible expressions of power, progress, national purpose, and mankind's newly attained mastery of nature.

III.

The ultimate triumph of oceanic steam navigation had been forecast with confidence even before the successful Atlantic crossings of *Sirius* and *Great Western*. Yet in these early years of steam there were doubts as well about the consequences of such achievement. Throughout the formative period of ocean steam travel, contemporary opinions ran through the full spectrum from ebullient acceptance to indignant rejection, from giddy optimism to doleful apprehension. And within this variety of response to ocean steam, many an individual commentator revealed an uneasy ambivalence toward this marvel of the age.

Some, of course, relished the prospect of steam voyaging and hesitated little, if at all, in asserting its undoubted benefits. Traveling to England on the *Great Western* in 1838, Frederick Delano quickly made up his mind: "Sailing packets for passengers are not the thing," he declared. "Steamers will supersede them altogether." He would never make such a trip in a sailing vessel again, he added, unless a steamer comparable to the *Great Western* was unavailable. The customary forty-five-day winter passage of a sailing packet against prevailing winds would be a bore, especially after one had experienced the exhilarating power of a steamer. As it turned out, Delano failed to obtain return passage to America on a steamer; "in despair," he struggled home in a sailing packet.[96]

But Charles Dickens, speaking for the disenchanted steam traveler, emphatically disagreed. After his terrifying January passage on the *Britannia* he made sure that he would return safely to England on a sailer. His euphoric description of that homeward passage (occasional lack of wind notwithstanding) emphasized the contrast of such a relaxed trip with his harrowing ordeal on a transatlantic steamer. When the wind rose, he fondly remembered, then the sailing packet truly came into her own: "Away we went before it, with every stick of canvas set, slashing through the water boldly." Indeed, Dickens insisted, there was "a grandeur in the motion of the splendid ship, as overshadowed by her mass of sails, she rode at a furious pace upon the waves, which filled one with an indescribable sense of pride and exultation."[97]

Billowing clouds of canvas might enrapture the sea-dreamer; yet the compelling reality of ocean travel was the need for regularity and speed, and here the steamer was supreme. The very idea of crossing the Atlantic in just a week, one steam advocate pointed out in 1857, "robs the trip of half the dread. " Statistics on steam passenger traffic confirmed such confidence. Only 5330 Americans crossed the Atlantic in 1850, but for 1854 the number of such travelers had increased to 32,631, to a great extent because of the speedy and luxurious Collins steamers.[98] "The Atlantic is now so completely bridged by the magnificent steamers of Cunard and Collins," a British naval observer insisted in 1853, "that a voyage across the ocean has become a mere pleasure trip."[99] Indeed, wrote one traveler, steam assured security without detracting from "the vague mystery" of ocean travel. "No drifting at the pleasure of the elements, with our vessel," he boasted, "but a straight path and a steady one."[100] And with a particularly characteristic observation for 1851, a popular magazine proclaimed: "What a revolution has been brought about in commerce, through the means of these immense traversers of the deep! Time and space are annihilated. . . . What a miracle!"[101]

Was there any limit to what man might achieve through steam power? None whatsoever, some asserted with lighthearted conviction:

> "Oh dear, think of a scheme, *odd though* it may seem—
> 'Tis sure to succeed if you work it by steam."[102]

And in this era of such remarkable ingenuity, they asked, why heed the skeptics? In the mid-1830's such doubters had firmly rejected the possibility of crossing the Atlantic entirely under steam power—and then came the *Great Western* to prove both that it could be done and that it could continue on a regular basis. Even by the late 1850's critics stubbornly persisted in maintaining that no steamer over ten thousand tons could ever be operated profitably by hauling mail, freight, and passengers across the Atlantic; but wasn't it just a matter of time before technology once again would triumph? And what of those opponents of steam who insisted that the clipper ships of the early 1850's had achieved such speeds as "no freighting steamer" could ever hope to match at sea? How many knowledgeable observers of oceanic steam navigation could agree with one maritime authority who proclaimed in 1858 that "it is utterly idle to suppose that steam in any form can take the place of sail upon the ocean."?[103] Today's impossibility became tomorrow's actuality too often for a mid-nineteenth-century advocate of steam to accept such dismal estimations.

But skeptics persisted. Steam, they argued, was not always the tractable servant of mankind. Too often men failed to understand the forces they attempted to bring under control, or even the mechanisms they had developed to exploit these forces. Any new mechanical experiment might succeed in such "days of successful enterprise," Philip Hone admitted in 1837. But he had reservations about steam power for ocean-going vessels. In moderate winds and seas, no doubt the steamer excelled, "wheezing and puffing alongside of the proudest ship in the British or American navy, and passing, laugh her to scorn." Yet what would happen in a great storm at sea when the waves reared up to the topmast of "this long stiff vessel, over-burthened with the weight of machinery, with a burning volcano in her bowels?"[104]

Such uneasiness as Philip Hone expressed would not dissipate by midcentury, regardless of how many passengers might successfully cross the Atlantic in steamers. After all, those impressive speeds achieved in the devil-may-care competition among ocean steam liners meant hazardous as well as costly voyages. No one could reasonably deny that ocean steam still had its limitations.

Such limitations notwithstanding, the steamship was still revolutionary. Like all revolutionary innovations, it exacted from human society a formidable price, regardless of the benefits it might produce. And upon this point, so often, rational discourse ceased and the lamentations began. For steam was a destroyer, not just of ships and humans on occasion, but of an entire way of life. Steam irreparably tore the fabric of human values, institutions, and relationships which had flourished in the age of sail. Steam was both unnatural and dehumanizing; it ruined sea life and corrupted those "genuine sailors of story and song."

One might correctly argue, of course, that many of the best sailing-ship men moved with alacrity to steamers, while stubborn resistance came from the diehards, "these elder merchant-masters . . . whose briny saturation has been invariably acquired under sail . . . some so deep and dyed in it that if you scratch them they ooze tar."[105] And few would wholly deny the occasional brutality and frequently mindless drudgery of sailing-packet life. But at least the sailing ship, as one naval historian recently observed, was a "paradise of spick-and-spanness" in contrast to the steamer, "from whose grotesque and clumsy engines, from whose monstrous smoke-stacks, there belched forth the smuts, the concentrated mess from the combustion of filthy Newcastle coal, and the first smell and contamination of Oil."[106]

Steamer passengers, while often admitting the conveniences of their vessel, often shared the regrets of the sailing-ship man. The ocean steamship might be vastly more reliable than the sailing packet; it might offer unprecedented regularity and speed with at least bearable if not luxurious accommodations; it might, on balance, be safer, especially in the treacherous Atlantic ice fields or in furious ocean storms. But sailing vessels, as Fredrika Bremer concluded, "are so infinitely more beautiful and more poetical than steam-vessels. On board the latter one never hears the song of the wind or the billows, because of the noise caused by the machinery, and one can enjoy no sea-air which is free from the fumes of the chimney or the kitchen." On rivers, she conceded, steamboats were desirable, "but on the sea—the sailing-ship forever!"[107]

Steam might be faulty, noisy, shuddery, dangerous, expensive, inefficient, and squalid. Still, it would triumph. As the nineteenth century wore on, steam conquered the Atlantic as it had finally vanquished the sailing packets. The implacable advance of steam technology brought ocean liners to a point of size, power, and luxurious complexity where the Atlantic passage seemed to be reduced to a humdrum, hothouse affair, far removed from the novel and frequently perilous crossings of the first ocean steamers.

For many who traveled or worked on the sea, this onset of steam brought an end to romance. To those who gloried in that special communion between man and nature which the sailing ship inspired, the machine at sea from the start had appeared as a noxious, unnatural intruder. But for many others romance did not vanish so suddenly with the introduction of steam on the Atlantic; rather, if romance ever did depart it was in those later years when steam came to dominate the oceans.

Then, once the risk appeared to be over and the Atlantic won, with the real adventure at an end, where was the romance? Turned into a seagoing pleasure palace whose very sumptuousness betrayed an arrogant if overly confident assertion of man's mastery of wind and wave, the modern ocean steamer sought to insulate its human cargo from all but the most tempestuous moods of the sea. And in that achievement lay the final irony. For with a nostalgia born of frustration and bewilderment with the onrush of progress, men turned away from the triumphant machine and reached with romantic yearning for their vanishing world of sail.

EDWARD W. SLOAN, III

CHAPTER SIX

The American Merchant Marine as an Expression of Foreign Policy

Woodrow Wilson and the Genesis of Modern Maritime Diplomacy

RECENT YEARS have seen the historical analysis of the American merchant marine assume broadened dimensions. There continues to be an important emphasis on the merchant marine as a storied institution with its own unique aspects, colorfully symbolized in ships and ships' people, and as a major business enterprise and vitally essential arm of the nation's domestic and foreign economy. But today, in an age of extraordinary internationalism and deep interest in comprehending the nature of American global influence, the analysis takes on new meaning by recognizing shipping's significance as a notable expression and instrument of United States foreign policy.

Nothing makes this so clear as the recent proposals in favor of a maritime growth necessary not only to meet the vast requirements of America's foreign trade, but to what is viewed as an obligatory strengthening of the national security in a world dominated by power politics. As Helen Delich Bentley, chairman of the Federal Maritime Commission, put it in 1970, nations do not build ships merely for the sake of building them, for history demonstrates that "no nation achieves greatness or maintains it without also being a major maritime power." Inasmuch as the Soviet Union employed its ships "as an inherent instrument of national policy," so too had the United States a vital and overriding responsibility to utilize its own in the interests of the Free World.[1]

Such concepts are not new, of course: America's colonial and early national shipping industry has received due recognition as a force of international importance. However, in the drastic decline that shook the American merchant marine in the late nineteenth and early twentieth centuries, the United States fell to all-time lows in global maritime involvement and prestige. How and when American ships became once again a source of worldwide economic influence has been discussed often. How they became a resource of international political significance has not. It is the purpose of this essay to demonstrate how the first twentieth-century President to emphasize shipping in diplomacy, Woodrow Wilson, rationalized and employed maritime growth and policy as an agent in foreign affairs as he reacted to the crises and opportunities brought about by World War I and its aftermath.

Imperial in character, Woodrow Wilson's world view had supported a vigorous American expansion into the world marketplace as early as the turn of the century.[2] Grounded upon the conviction that there was an immutable bond between the nation's social, economic, and political welfare and the extent of its foreign trade,[3] Wilson's initial efforts as the nation's new chief executive were to achieve commercial growth through reform in three major areas. First, he emphasized the necessity of lower tariffs as central to the release of American surpluses. Second, he determined to democratize the domestic economy, to break down the inelastic and parochial power of the New York-centered money and banking trust in order to redistribute and utilize its credit facilities to greater advantage in foreign trade. Lastly, Wilson scored America's failure to develop adequate shipping services and facilities for the overseas carriage of American products—less than 10 per cent of the nation's foreign trade was then shipped in American bottoms. It was foolhardy, he argued, to expect efficiency and profits in foreign trade if one depended upon his competitors to deliver his produce. "Without a great merchant marine," he asserted, "we cannot take our rightful place in the commerce of the world."[4]

Wilson's insistence upon change in these three areas was hardly novel: a variety of interests, group and individual, had argued similarly for over half a century.[5] But Wilson differed from those before him by putting theory into practice. In each case he broke fifty-year deadlocks to obtain ground-breaking reforms: the Underwood Tariff and Federal Reserve Act were passed in 1913, and the Shipping Act in 1916. While the first two were conceived and actuated as peacetime measures, the Shipping Act was a product of the war itself, took on shape derived from war activity, and produced an important means by which Wilson endeavored to strengthen his war and postwar international position.

The advent of world war in the summer of 1914 brought the United States both serious economic dislocation and unforeseen economic opportunity. A direct product of both was the two-year political campaign by the Wilson administration during 1914-1916 to create a national merchant marine. In action this program was two-pronged. On the one hand, America endeavored to maintain and expand its economic lifeline with Europe. On the other, the United States labored feverishly to obtain influence in new markets and in those previously dominated by the belligerents but now perforce abandoned. This form of trade opportunism received strong governmental support and constituted the heart of the Wilsonian effort to create a governmental commercial fleet during the period of neutrality. Although the administration and the private sector agreed on the ends, for almost two years the means were in constant debate. American shipping and finance, reaping enormous profits through neutral trade, lobbied hard and successfully against public intervention in the economy, despite the administration's efforts to convince big business that even greater and permanent commercial rewards could be attained with a government-operated overseas transportation network.

However, during 1915-1916 the European deadlock fostered the need for new perspectives. In contemplation of a prolonged military confrontation, the nature of which continued to intensify in unforeseen ways, the belligerents began to prepare for a resumption of the commercial rivalries most Americans believed had prompted the war initially. Responding, Wilson moved from a position of strict neutrality to one of preparedness in order to cover the increasing probability of American military and commercial participation. Within this context the barriers to shipping legislation were broken down.

While some mention of the need for preparedness had been made in 1914, the crisis created by Germany's submarine policy generated a strong movement toward American armament in the spring and summer of 1915. The sinking of the *Lusitania* on 7 May turned the tide. While the impact made clearer than ever how ill-equipped the nation was to wage war, commercial interests predicted that an effective undersea blockade of Europe would destroy America's transatlantic trades. As the Secretary of Commerce pessimistically noted, if German efforts at control succeeded, "the jaws of disaster would close upon our foreign trade like a trap."[6] Men with broad commercial vision anticipated these possibilities and directed their attention to alternative goals. One such person was William Gibbs McAdoo, Secretary of the Treasury. Sharing Wilson's rationale for an American merchant marine, McAdoo saw a vehicle by which a solution could be achieved in preparedness. First, he nailed together a platform from which he lobbied for a maritime fleet as an auxiliary force necessary to buttress the United States Navy. Second, he attached the issue to the increasing efforts of the administration to use the war experience as a means of creating pan-American, or hemispheric, ties. While Pan-Americanism was essentially an effort to pioneer business in undeveloped fields or in areas formerly controlled by the European belligerents, Wilson and McAdoo had designs beyond the simple concern for profits. Both saw in the political and economic connections forthcoming from hemispheric solidarity a powerful means by which to influence Old World affairs. As McAdoo expressed it, Pan-Americanism had the potential of becoming a "powerful agency for world peace." By the simple denial of its collective resources, by sheer market weight, it could "exercise a persuasive power of irresistible force upon other nations of the world in the settling of international disputes." All of this depended, however, upon a "wholesome materialism" concerning the basic essentials of trade and communication. No such policy, therefore, could hope to function without the development of commercial self-sufficiency in the way of ships.[7]

Wilson confirmed the new direction before the Sixty-fourth Congress in late 1915. What the United States desired was a commonality of interests with Latin America. Hence the prosecution of a program of preparedness so as to protect and encourage the unfettered development of the hemisphere's economic and political interests. It was a program that went beyond the conventional stockpiling of arms by defining the appropriate function of national defense as involving not only military matters, but domestic and foreign commerce and transportation, the conservation and mobilization of the nation's industrial and natural resources, and the cooperative defense of all Latin America. The keystone, however, was represented by ships, the "only shuttles that can weave the delicate fabric of sympathy, comprehension, confidence, and mutual dependence in which we wish to clothe our policy of America for Americans," and the only way the hemisphere could hope to remain removed from the corrosive elements of European influence. Wilson had skillfully blended preparedness, Pan-Americanism, and the question of ships into one convenient package.[8]

The chief executive and his treasury head had also demonstrated how ships had come to represent the full circle of Wilson's foreign policy as it had evolved during the months of neutrality. In short, by 1915 United States reaction to the conflict had promoted a consensus among Wilsonians demanding the creation of a peacefully liberal, lawful, and procapitalistic world, secure from the disorders of imperialism (and later, revolutionary socialism), within which, as one historian has aptly put it, "America could serve mankind from a position of political and economic pre-eminence."[9] For most Wilsonians had concluded by this time that a truly stable, moral, and constitutional world order was beyond the means of European concoction and was achievable only if the United States assumed the role of leadership as based upon the principles and power of an expanding American political economy. Hence the emphasis on shipping, for maritime growth increased the national power by giving the economy greater flexibility, freeing it from former commercial dependencies, and increasing the national wealth through the expansion of foreign trade. Wilson had concluded that the United States could not achieve world influence, nor maintain it, "without also being a major maritime power."

Hence also the deep concern in Washington over indications in 1915-1916 that the belligerents would not accede with equanimity to the growth of United States overseas commerce, despite its moral overtones. The Allies in particular had been demonstrably piqued over having lost trade during the war to the United States. And while the war involvement promised to hamstring their efforts to regain that trade immediately, there was no question but that with the cessation of hostilities they would give the United States a virulent run for its money, not only south of the border but on a worldwide basis. Goaded by the fact that the Allies had not lessened but had intensified the severity of their restrictions governing America's neutral trades during the war, had nationalized their commercial fleets, and were formulating plans to coordinate their economic and commercial programs, Americans were spurred into broadening preparedness to include a strong commercial arm in early 1916.

McAdoo had expressed the administration's concerns at shipping bill hearings held in late winter by the House Committee on the Merchant Marine and Fisheries. A member of the Committee discussed with him the growing concern with European preparation for the so-called commercial "war-after-the-war":

> Is not this primarily the thought back of this whole legislation, that inasmuch as the European Governments now at war have taken over practically all of the railway and steamship transportation lines, and the same being nationalized—usurping, so to speak, the functions and rights of private and corporate interests that formerly owned them—that when the war is over there will be the greatest commercial rivalry the world has ever seen, and the nations that have lost their trade will seek to regain it and to extend it, and every country will attempt to be in the vanguard of this commercial activity, and inasmuch as European countries have nationalized those activities, thus overcoming and outstripping private and even corporate interests, that therefore they are outstripping us in this commercial conquest so long as we permit our commerce to remain exclusively in the hands of private and corporate interests, and therefore we should ourselves nationalize in a measure, or seek to do so, so as to give an impetus to that increased activity which we ourselves expect to take part in?

To which McAdoo replied: "I think that is undoubtedly true and that it is essentially a part of preparedness," adding that "to the extent the foreign governments have extended their powers over the shipping of their respective countries, it is absolutely necessary that we organize and concentrate the powers of this Nation to enable us to protect our own commerce."[10]

With commercial preparedness building up steam, Congressional opposition to the bill steadily eroded. With a decided emphasis on the need for a shipping board with broad regulatory and developmentary powers to serve as a counterpart to policies proposed by the British Board of Trade, the bill passed the House on 20 May. In the meantime, Senator William Stone of Missouri, as Wilson's floor leader for the bill in the upper branch, pounded home the now familiar theme: "I want to see the ship bill—the merchant marine measures—brought to the front and kept there until some great policy of commercial preparedness is definitely entered upon."[11]

Two additional events of import added impetus to the Senate's deliberations. The first concerned Wilson's effort to arbitrate the European war through the representations of Colonel Edward M. House. House had made an unsuccessful trip to Europe in 1915 in an attempt to bring about a peace conference, and had journeyed back across the Atlantic a year later in pursuit of the same. But prospects for fruitful negotiation appeared as bleak in May 1916 as they had the previous year. House expressed dire concern: it appeared to him that the Allies had no intention of seeking an armistice, but had determined to fight it out in anticipation of winning and reaping the rewards, a policy which would have ramifications beyond the redefinition of European affairs. An Allied victory could mean considerable trouble for American interests, he warned his President.[12] Arthur J. Balfour, First Lord of the Admiralty, confirmed House's fears: the best chance for Wilson's plan would be American entry on the Allied side in favor of Allied interests; whereas the worst chance would be represented by a status quo (or pro-German) peace "accompanied, perhaps even promoted," by continued United States efforts to champion neutral shipping privileges.[13] Wilson recalled House in disgust, his determination all the more steeled to accept the alternative of preparedness as a means of emphasizing America's views.

On the heels of that blow came another. The advent of the Paris Economic Conference of 14-17 June served to certify American convictions that the Allies planned to subject the United States to postwar trade discriminations. The stipulations of the Conference indicated clearly that the Allies were intent upon establishing an exclusive economic union which, while ostensibly a declaration of economic war on the Central Powers and their similar *Mitteleuropa* plan, was to be utilized additionally for special worldwide trade privileges in the reconstruction period following the war. Discriminations were the key to its workings, and the neutrals were by no means to be exempted from liability to their application. Moreover, the provisions outlined at Paris openly declared the Allies' intent to recapture by any means at hand the trade privileges and holdings possessed by them before the war.[14] The Paris resolves, as a member of the U.S. Federal Trade Commission described them, were sheer "militarism translated into commercial warfare."[15]

Secretary of State Robert Lansing summarized the administration's apprehension a week later. It appeared to him, he informed Wilson, that the harsh postwar commercial strategy outlined at Paris would prolong, rather than terminate, the war. For neutral nations, such as the United States, the commercial combinations provided for in the agreements had onerous implications. The result would be the creation of a powerful combination of Allied states, "which on account of their colonies and great merchant marine" would be able, he feared, to execute their preferential programs. The end product would cause a "serious, if not critical, situation for the nations outside the union by creating unusual and artificial economic conditions." No doubt bearing in mind already severe restraints imposed upon the neutrals by the Allies through ever increased blacklisting, nonexportation agreements, repressive influence upon steamship companies, monopoly control over maritime insurance rates and ratings, and the censorship of mail, Lansing maintained the Paris Conference had created a situation requiring a strong antidote.[16]

All factors combined, support for the shipping bill crescendoed in midsummer. A large cross section of the country had now become vitally aware of the issue. Farming interests jumped on the bandwagon after years of resistance to maritime subsidies when they realized that the regulatory provisions of the bill would aid them significantly in restricting, even reducing, prohibitive freight rates, largely exacted by foreign carriers; and business elements which had previously opposed the measure as socialistic turned face under the promise of a rigorous postwar commercial competition which they could not possibly entertain without public assistance.[17] With practically all of Theodore Roosevelt's Progressives joining a unified Democracy in support of the bill as part of a comprehensive economic and military preparedness package, the measure passed the Senate of 18 August 1916 and received the President's signature on 7 September.

While it is true that the bill compromised some of McAdoo's and Wilson's efforts to maximize government operation (e.g., by stipulating that lines operated by the new United States Shipping Board would have to cease business five years after the end of the war, by forbidding Cabinet participation on the Board, and by making illegal the purchase of belligerent vessels), its strengths were considerable. Foremost, the groundwork had been laid for the development of an efficient, scientifically managed foreign trade shipping program. To the administration's profound appreciation, the act represented the first time an organizational, regulatory overseer along the lines of the Interstate Commerce Commission was instituted in maritime transportation. The act's concern for the larger needs of America's transoceanic commerce was explicit in its authority over the main violators of the "public trust," the service lines, and its specific exemption of the much-needed tramp shipping which was so crucial to the maintenance of a flexible trade system. Discriminations by foreign shipping companies against American exporters were forbidden, and the Board was given the power to "disapprove, cancel, or modify" any shipping agreements between service lines which could be construed as inimical to the commercial interests of the nation. Finally, the new shipping act authorized the creation of an Emergency Fleet Corporation for the purpose of purchasing, constructing, and operating vessels for the government in time of national need. It was this particular function that would provide the merchant marine with the size it needed to become a practical diplomatic resource.[18]

Following American entry into the war in April 1917, at once a rationale and framework for growth, the administration fleshed out its new maritime power in unprecedented fashion. For example, over three million tons of ships, or as much as the total world output of any prewar year, were launched by the USSB's Emergency Fleet Corporation in 1918, almost all in the last four months alone. In addition to these prodigious figures, the administration confiscated over 700,000 deadweight tons of German ships, leased an additional 58,000 tons of Austrian ships from various sources, and acquired over 250,000 tons of Japanese vessels on charters. It also commandeered over 1.5 million tons of ships building for foreign contract in American yards, and through economic leverage obtained charters to almost 2 million tons of neutral vessels. Finally, the Shipping Board requisitioned every steel ocean-going cargo and passenger ship of American registry in excess of 2500 tons, or 657 bottoms. By the summer of 1918 the United States had not only put together a massive fleet from foreign and domestic sources in unparalleled time, but was producing in its own shipyards, some 158 of them manned by a work force of over 300,000 men, the greatest profusion of ships the modern world had ever seen.[19]

While the tremendous growth of the fleet was significant in the first instance as a war expedient, Wilsonians, as previously described, simultaneously considered it a means by which to bring about an American solution to the peace that would follow. No one was more convinced of this than the third primary figure in the Wilson maritime picture, Edward N. Hurley, chairman of the new Shipping Board and member of Wilson's War Cabinet. Hurley had had extensive experience in foreign trade and foreign trade associations, and he believed absolutely in the need for governmental aid to business and in the utter ineffaceability of increased overseas commerce. External market expansion was axiomatic, he pointed out, if the nation hoped to dispose of its huge surpluses and avoid economic and social stagnation. But like Wilson, Hurley held the altruistic view that the nation had additional responsibilities beyond the fundamental goal of economic and social equilibrium. What was at stake was the liberal mission, he argued, selling America to the rest of the world, selling her ideals and her hopes as well as her goods. Ships were a vital adjunct. Built originally by the United States as instruments of war, they were "designed to serve equally well as the instruments of an enduring peace." "We are building ships not alone for the war, but for the future of world trade," Hurley argued. America's pride in the undertaking would be measured by the degree to which its ships brought prosperity to its neighbors as well as to itself. In short, Hurley believed that just as the railroad had restructured America in the late nineteenth century, United States maritime development during and after the war would highlight an oceanic transportational "touchstone for a new world" in the early twentieth.[20]

At the same time Hurley had become convinced, as had most Wilsonians, of the belligerents' incapability of arranging for a democratic and nonpartisan peace. Arguing that in his judgment the European conflict represented to the contesting powers primarily an interlude in a Darwinian struggle for commercial supremacy, and that "we are the only nation that has taken a completely unselfish position in the war," Hurley endeavored to add weight to America's call for a liberal peace by increasing its maritime strength. "My whole thought is to get a fleet of large sized ships . . . so that we may be able to compete with Germany and England after the war," he confided at the height of hostilities.[21] For Hurley was certain that if the United States failed to obtain at least parity levels with its maritime competitors there could be little hope of eliminating international trade rivalries and of bringing about a universal acceptance of the principles of the "freedom of the seas." Consequently, with the coming of the armistice, and deeply distrustful of Allied postwar political and economic plans, Wilson and Hurley determined to maximize their drive for the legal embodiment of these lofty, yet self-interested, maxims by employing the new United States maritime power as a bargaining agent at the Versailles peace talks.

The policy chosen was to persuade the Allies that United States maritime growth and competition was a permanent undertaking by three means: by continuing a very large shipbuilding program, by refusing the Allies use of American shipping and shipbuilding facilities (badly needed for the purpose of replacing enormous wartime losses), and by extending the USSB's authority over American maritime services. While Wilson and Hurley had agreed on the ultimate desirability of returning most of the ships to private enterprise, they rationalized that, so long as this could be held undisclosed, the Allies' fear of a governmentally owned American shipping industry would make them more pliable at Versailles. It would serve the additional function of denying to the

Allies a procedural base upon which to restructure their own commercial fleets for a return to private enterprise and commercial rivalry, thereby allowing the United States additional time to strengthen its bargaining position through broadened postwar commercial maritime networks of its own. As Hurley summed up, there would be "no arrangements for any part of shipping until there had been at least a tentative agreement on a League of Nations."[22]

To this Hurley added a plan which demonstrated the absolute degree to which shipping had become part of the Wilsonian liberal-capitalistic-messianic world view. Noting that American maritime working standards were by far superior to the rest of the world's, Hurley argued for their application on an international basis. He also contended that the American peace delegation should demand the creation of a universal uniformity in freight rates. "With uniform freight rates and uniform wages to seamen," he noted to Wilson, "the trade would go to the efficient manufacturer, and not to the favored manufacturer." It would be identical to an application of the Interstate Commerce Commission to the world's seas. It would "solve the problem of trade wars" and "would give reality and force to the 'freedom of the seas.' " Hurley made no argument that the proposal would be gratefully received by European shipping interests, who would give up their advantages of low wages and high freight rates reluctantly, but he concluded that the humanitarian aspects of the proposal, coupled with America's new power in the realm of shipping, would carry the plan over its opposition to fulfillment as a great service to the world.[23]

With all these tactics put together, Wilson and Hurley had synthesized altruism and tough business talk into a plan to strengthen their hand at the Paris deliberations. But if the American peace mission thought its awesome economic and political power gave it an impregnable position from which to force a favorable peace in Europe, such expectations soon proved illusory. Notwithstanding the American contention that its mercantile growth was designed as much for the enrichment of the world as of the United States, the Allies maneuvered to divide Germany's merchant and liner fleet on a basis detrimental to the United States, and received with absolute hostility Hurley's scheme to create international regularization in freight rates and seamen's wages and working conditions—increasing your competitors' costs, as the Allies interpreted it. As Hurley shortly pointed out to Wilson, it was America's new shipping and financial position that frightened the Allies, not the League of Nations, an International Court, or even the "freedom of the seas."[24]

Radical changes in postarmistice requirements for American vessels further complicated matters. The pressures on the USSB were immense. Domestic private interests demanded a return of their war-commandeered vessels for the resumption of foreign trade, the American people insisted upon the early return of their military kinfolk stationed overseas, and labor and the shipbuilding industry strongly resisted the moratorium on foreign contracts and other cancellations related to war. At the same time the neutrals clamored for the immediate restoration of their ships on charter, and the political requirements for the rehabilitation of Europe called for an emphasis on the allocation of vessels for relief. Moreover, there appeared to be no early solution in the offing regarding Germany's remaining merchant fleet, which, if put to use, could have solved many of the Shipping Board's problems. Finally, there was a public and private outcry that unless the Board moved quickly Great Britain would leap into the breach and capture prime trades before the American foreign-trade mechanism could be brought into adequate function.[25]

It was an extremely difficult situation in which Hurley was left, as he saw it, with basically two alternatives. The first suggested a continued effort to sit on the shipping lid until the League question had been settled, formal proceedings for which had not even commenced. The other invited a revision of the means but not the ends, for Hurley reasoned that the concept of a universal peace backed by American economic and moral strength would be meaningless if in the adoption of a holding action the Shipping Board allowed American industry and foreign trade to wither for want of jobs and transportation. Moving quickly to the second alternative, Hurley made his initial move in mid-December when he reassigned vessels from repatriation and relief to the American export trade to relieve congestion at ocean ports.[26] Secondly, he questioned the logic of continuing an embargo on Allied contracts, despite Wilson's League position. Noting that pressure from the shipyards was increasing every day, Hurley inquired of the President if his Paris plan might not be served better by reaching an immediate accord with French and Italian shipbuilding needs. To agree to contracts for both would not only decrease social pressure and benefit the shipbuilding trades in the United States, but would constitute an act of international good will at a most propitious moment. Otherwise, Hurley warned, "if we keep our fist closed until they open theirs, the result may be a delay in the settlement of the larger issues."[27]

But Wilson turned down Hurley's request, remarking that he understood the Board's problems, but still held that the League policy was paramountly important and that no concessions should be made until peace terms were actually formalized. Wilson then ordered the USSB to meet Allied maritime competition by lowering its shipping rates, a policy put into effect at the first of the year. Shortly thereafter, Hurley also began to return commandeered vessels to private control. While resulting in a final jettisoning of the feigned policy of full public ownership, this move responded directly to Great Britain's decision to call Wilson's bluff by releasing its own requisitioned tonnage for competitive trade.[28]

All of this confirmed the growing animosity between British and United States representatives over shipping. While Hurley's delegation was considerably put out by what it interpreted as British efforts to cripple American foreign trade interests, the American naval contingent at Paris bordered on complete distraction. Its head, Navy Chief of Staff Admiral William S. Benson, painted a picture of Versailles in which British commercial intrigue dominated the landscape. So vehement was Benson over what he defined as British attempts "to block our Naval building program, and also to put every possible obstacle in the way of the development of our merchant marine," that on one fiery occasion in early January 1919 he very nearly exchanged blows with the First Lord of the British Admiralty. Later that month Naval Operations summed up for both American groups: Great Britain was "out to capture the lion's share" of the world's carrying trades, and unless the United States moved to get its shipping organized and into competition quickly and efficiently it would be so severely handicapped "that it will be impossible for us to get in the running at all."[29]

Even though Hurley's personal assessment of this need emphasized a non-European shipping solution (only 18 per cent of the USSB's vessels were assigned to the continent in February), serious political deterioration in Germany and Eastern Europe brought his command back onto the North Atlantic on a vitally important basis. By the turn of the year, Wilsonians had agreed on the necessity of getting immediate food relief into Germany and East Europe to contain revolutionary socialism through support to more moderate political groups. Herbert Hoover, director of relief, was the leading advocate of this effort to combat Bolshevism with food. At first, however, French opposition to any program designed to alleviate pressure on Germany prior to a peace settlement was sufficiently effective to prevent the actuation of a relief program. Then in late winter 1919 the European situation deteriorated suddenly and to such an extent that Hoover's needs were increased geometrically overnight. The Allied blockade was lifted, but not before the most anarchistic forms of disorder came to Germany and the countries of the former Austro-Hungarian Empire. March in particular was a month of blackness. Hoover emphatically argued that with food and supplies transported from America in American ships he could halt the red tide. Wilson agreed and ordered Hurley to divert shipping from other foreign trades back to the European theatre.[30] Hurley balked at these demands, but not because he had lost sight of the long-range diplomatic objectives.

In fact, Hurley and Hoover strongly endorsed Wilsonian ends: it was the means over which they differed. To Hurley, stabilizing and strengthening America's postwar position meant the immediate establishment of shipping services for the complete panoply of American exports. Securing outlets for these surpluses in new markets removed from prostrated Europe was his primary objective. Social disorder was countered by attacking it at home through continued ship construction (meaning full employment) and increased exportation. On the other hand, Hoover's goals were tied primarily to a single segment of the exporting economy, American agriculture, and to the disposition of its enormous war-induced surpluses. Ravaged Europe, not the Western Hemisphere, offered the Food Administration its best market and, in terms of relief, one justified by humanitarian and political requirements. Likewise, Hoover's experiences convinced him that arresting Bolshevism in its native context with food relief was overwhelmingly important.

These differences, however, were not sufficient to prevent the USSB from accomplishing both ends—by continuing to construct ships and expand trade, and by reallocating vast numbers of ships to fill relief requirements, all at the same time. While Hurley remarked with irritation to Wilson that the relief program "greatly interfered" with the Shipping Board's plan to put the country back on a commercial basis,[31] his reassignment of ships to relief broke the back of the crisis. By late April it was apparent that European economic and political stabilization had been satisfactorily achieved and Bolshevism adequately contained as the result of the relief program and Hurley's shipping support, however reluctantly given. In fact, while Hurley redirected over 2 million tons of ships into Hoover's program between February and May, in the identical period he actually augmented the nonrelief national foreign-trade fleet by 900,000 tons.[32] In full perspective, Hurley's and Hoover's emphases did not clash, but expressed jointly the major theme in Wilsonian thought: that the requirements of America's expanding capitalism necessitated coincidentally a universal obligation to the creation of a humane and, above all, orderly world system.

In the end, Wilson's maritime diplomacy did not have the positive and salutary effect at Versailles that was intended. A principal concern of the American peace delegation's shipping group had been to obtain the immediate use of Germany's impounded merchant fleet. American shipping power and influence had not been sufficient, however, to force the distribution of those vessels before March, or before a point at which their value to America had been sizably diminished. Nor had Wilson been able to persuade the Allies to allow Germany active use of its merchant fleet so as to reintegrate that country more readily into the commercial commonwealth of nations he sought. Additionally significant, the "freedom of the seas," a principle originally considered to be one of Wilson's primary aims, was utterly abandoned in the final reckoning, suffering the same fate as most other neutrality issues in the overriding quest for a League. And while Wilson did retain the 700,000 tons of German ships confiscated by the

United States in 1917, he severely antagonized the Allies who had sought to obtain their distribution on a pro rata basis according to actual war losses. Perhaps the only thing Wilson had to show for his maritime work at Paris was the Shipping Board's success in obtaining 200,000 tons of Germany's largest liners for the purpose of repatriating the still more than a million American servicemen remaining in Europe. But this was accomplished only upon the understanding that the vessels would be returned to the Allied shipping pool as soon as their services had been completed.

So it was a vastly disappointed shipping delegation that finally returned to the United States in the late spring of 1919. To American maritime proponents, the peace settlement did not reflect a basic interest in the creation of a moral, cooperative, and stable internationalism, but expressed in the main the avaricious economic aims of the Allies. As Benson put it in late April to Wilson, "It is evident that commercial interest is underlying every factor under consideration by the various nations, except ourselves," adding that this was particularly true of Great Britain. A nation that had systematically crushed maritime competition for centuries and was now threatened by another, England stood poised to add America to the list of victims. It was a situation, he advised the President, requiring extraordinary vigilance and the utmost in safeguards. When nothing in the following week occurred to assuage Benson's concern, he actually warned the Secretary of the Navy of the possibility of war with Great Britain and urged him to keep the American fleet fully manned, "and in every respect ready for action."[33] While few others desired to go to such extremes, by late spring no one with real authority in governmental shipping circles cared to express American nautical policy in the old utopian terms. The concept of an American maritime growth conceived as a benefit for the world was tarnished considerably at Versailles, and much of the remaining two years of Wilson's shipping program reflected the ensuing bitterness.

With Edward Hurley's resignation on 31 July 1919, Wilson appointed a chairman relatively inexperienced in maritime affairs, Judge John Barton Payne, formerly of the United States Railroad Administration. But what Payne lacked in shipping experience and knowledge he compensated for by applying a rancorous policy aimed firmly at preventing the Allies from gaining undue commercial advantage at America's expense. While Payne's tenure in office was quite short, just seven months, it featured important shipping issues illustrative of the intensified Anglo-American hostility. The primary one involved the disposition of the major portion of Germany's oil-tanker and passenger-liner fleets, including in the latter category the world's largest ship, the *Imperator*. In every case Payne's policy carried out what Benson and others had resolved at Paris: America, he would prove, could be just as economically nationalistic as the Allies.

The *Imperator* case was a complicated one. Enmeshed in it were not only now fundamental Allied-American maritime rivalries, but the fast-rising subject of control of the world's oil supplies, unresolved shipping controversies inherited from Versailles, all topped off by the prostration of Presidential action caused by Wilson's illness in the fall of 1919. Central was the concern over oil. Much as the Allies and the United States had clashed over maritime growth and policy, the two groups envisioned a postwar period rife with struggles to corner the sources of world petroleum. Hurley and the Shipping Board had worried over this for months when Payne came into office. When an issue arose concerning the Standard Oil Company's claim that it held title to nine German tankers impounded in European ports, the new shipping head moved quickly to lend his support.

The hassle involved the legality of the company's sale of the ships, formerly registered under the German flag, but disposed of to German shipping interests during the war to avoid confiscation by the German war government. The Allies argued that Standard Oil no longer owned these vessels, but upon the basis of a technicality the corporation contended the sale was invalid. The stakes were high, for the nation that triumphed would add to its national oil-tanker fleet on a large scale. Resentment on the Allied side stemmed from the knowledge that with the USSB already in possession of seventeen German tankers commandeered in American ports in 1917, the addition of nine more would give the United States twenty-six of the thirty-two German tankers still operative after the war. On the other hand, rumors that the French, on the basis of a clandestine deal with the British, would take the tankers to support a state oil monopoly caused apoplexy in American shipping and diplomatic circles. That the tankers in contention were under actual Allied naval control and on the verge of being moved to British waters for safekeeping did nothing to strengthen the American position. Then two factors enabled Payne to move. The first came when Wilson suffered a nervous-physical breakdown on 25 September 1919 while campaigning for the League. Profiting by the shock and confusion caused by the President's subsequent stroke and by the absolute breakdown in authority, Payne put into effect a plan geared to counter the possibilities of Allied discrimination.

Basic to it was the disposition of the eight German passenger liners obtained on temporary assignment by the United States through peace conference negotiation the previous March. Including the *Imperator,* at 52,117 deadweight tons the largest vessel afloat, these ships had just terminated their assigned tasks of repatriating American servicemen for the War Department and were in process of being transferred to the USSB for turnover to Great Britain, in whose custody the Allied Reparations Council had determined they would permanently reside. Receiving the ships in mid-September, Payne sensed he had a powerful means by which to pressure the Allies into releasing the tankers to Standard Oil, or at least in obtaining a favorable settlement—so long as the liners remained in United States possession. Though scheduled for turnover in New York Harbor beginning at the end of the month, on 27 September, two days after Wilson's collapse in Pueblo, Colorado, Payne simply and arbitrarily refused to release the vessels to British shipping authorities.[34]

Payne's decision caused anguish on both sides of the Atlantic. From his vantage point as the last important American representative in Europe, Undersecretary of State Frank Polk cabled that in the major case the Shipping Board's position was illegal and in every case sure to widen the chasm in Anglo-American relations. Irritation in England was immense, he reported. Not only were Britishers aware of the blatant unlawfulness of Payne's act and that the United States already retained the majority of Germany's tankers, they were still seething over having been unable to obtain all of America's confiscated German tonnage for equitable distribution on the basis of shipping lost during the war.[35] To these grievances Polk might well have added British displeasure at having sent over more than a thousand crewmen to New York to work the liners back across the Atlantic. Without employment, the men not only caused social woe in the metropolitan area, but the British government was faced with paying royally for their upkeep while Payne dallied. In addition, by retaining the *Imperator,* it was painfully clear that the United States now possessed not only the largest vessel in the world but the *two* largest, for it had confiscated the *Vaterland* (renamed the *Leviathan*), sister ship to the *Imperator,* at the time of American entry into the war.

Though initially Lansing's inclination had been to support Payne in his consternation over Allied shipping discrimination, Polk's protestations had to be reckoned with. Payne's handling of the affair was a clear case of blackmail, would never stand up in court, and would possibly provoke the British into an impossible position on the tankers issue. By mid-October Lansing argued that the coupling of the *Imperator* and the tankers by the Shipping Board was causing great difficulty: a clear case of expediency without reference to legality. But the Secretary of State was unable to obtain an audience with the prostrated President, who not only had sole authority to veto Payne's decision but had come to despise Lansing to boot. Compromised as well by increasing Anglophobia on the domestic political scene, Lansing could do little more than express his disapproval to those who would listen.[36] Payne took full advantage of the situation. When asked by Lansing to explain his position before the Cabinet, the shipping chairman justified his action upon the grounds that Great Britain was obstructing American maritime growth and then took refuge behind the statement he could not act otherwise except by direction of the President.[37] With Payne determined to maintain an uncompromising attitude, Lansing intensified his effort to make his point to Wilson. But Wilson's long-awaited reply resolved nothing. On 17 November Lansing was informed indirectly that Wilson was not prepared to consider the *Imperator* affair until he was stronger physically. At the same time the Allies had resolved to move the tankers to the Firth of Forth and to refuse a commitment on Standard Oil's claim until further discussion.[38]

At this point Payne moved slightly toward an accommodation, releasing the *Imperator* without a *quid pro quo,* but not because he desired to, as he carefully pointed out to the Board: the Navy's threat to remove its crews and the growing burden of maintenance forced him to do so. The remaining vessels, however, were to be held up on the original bargaining terms.[39] A month later neither side had budged. The British Embassy had made absolutely evident its refusal to act on the tankers so long as the Shipping Board connected the two issues, and Payne was still adamant in his unwillingness to negotiate.[40]

Ultimately, in realization of the futility of prolonging the deadlock, Wilson broke it himself four days before Christmas. Agreeing reluctantly with Lansing that the Shipping Board's seizure of the *Imperator* group had "embarrassed action of our diplomatic representatives in the settlement of certain matters of interest to the United States and Great Britain," and had "become the most effective obstacle to a solution of the tanker controversy itself," the President, through his wife Edith Bolling Wilson, informed Payne that "much to his regret" he found "no ground for differing from the Sec[retary] of State's judgment in this important matter."[41] Payne forthwith delivered the formerly German passenger liners, but the tankers question was not settled for half a year, and then only to allocate the vessels to the Standard Oil Company on a temporary two-voyage basis.

Wilson's disinclined acquiescence in the *Imperator* case did not signal in any way a diminution in the nation's resolve to strengthen its maritime position. One of the first Congressional items of business in the winter of 1919-1920 was a new merchant marine bill to replace the Shipping Act of 1916. Since the former act had stipulated that the government was to relinquish its shipping business within five years after the war, the need to create a permanent national fleet took on major importance. Hearings to assist Congress in the formulation of a bill were opened in January by the chairman of the Senate Committee on Commerce, Wesley Jones, from the maritime state of Washington. Archetypical of the men who had become involved in the maritime program, Jones was obsessed with trade rivalries and foreign discriminations. Maintaining that the effort to create a lasting and effective American merchant marine would have to be accomplished "in the face of the most determined opposition and the fiercest competition," Jones insisted upon reading into the hearings an abstract from a recent issue of the British magazine *Fairplay*. It was his way of substantiating the hostile environment in which the maritime program would have to function:

> Thanks to vigorous instruction from President Wilson and Mr. Hurley. . . [we know] that our friends on the other side have this common with ourselves that they never put their hand to the plow without the fullest intention of driving the furrow to the bitter end, regardless of what may happen to interfering competitors. . . . When it has been a question of the survival of the fittest, we have invariably done our level best to crush or mold opposition, and, as regards America's new merchant marine, we shall go on doing it, and expect her to do the same to us.[42]

While Payne had demonstrated a respectable appreciation for Jones' concerns, his transfer to the Interior Department in March 1920 gave Wilson the opportunity to appoint a man superbly capable of living up to the *Fairplay* game plan. More than ever convinced that the world was "on the eve of a commercial war of the severest sort," Wilson elevated the xenophobic Admiral William S. Benson, now retired and a member of the Shipping Board, to its chairmanship.[43] Benson's antipathy for Great Britain and the Allies had been made apparent at the Paris talks. But it went beyond that: reflecting an age highly sympathetic toward the concept of America for Americans, Benson intensely disliked and distrusted anything not of national origin. No sooner had he taken office than he assumed an aggressive leadership in pushing through a shipping bill aimed at guaranteeing American mercantile interests the most calculated forms of antiforeign discrimination.

Upon the argument that every second wasted would only benefit America's competitors, Benson and Jones cleared a bill through Congress that reached Wilson's desk only thirty minutes before the close of the session. Commonly known as the Jones Bill, it was a measure clearly intended, as Benson described it, "to meet and offset the countless discriminations by other nations against American shipping with which Shipping Board ships and privately owned vessels of the United States have had to contend."[44] Amongst its provisions were clauses extending the coastal monopoly to the Philippines and other American insular possessions; giving the USSB authority to supervise the rules and regulations of all governmental departments, boards, bureaus, or agencies directly or indirectly involved with shipping matters in foreign trade; and creating a circumvention of Lloyd's of London's maritime insurance monopoly by improving American insurance conditions and allowing American maritime insurance companies waivers from the Sherman Anti-Trust Act. Most important was Section 28, personally inserted by Benson, which granted preferential railway rates to American cargoes carried in American vessels, provided there was a plethora of American tonnage to handle a port's foreign trade.

A final clause, Section 34, instructed the President to abrogate all treaties in conflict with the right of the United States to impose discriminations. As Jones put it, "They say it will drive foreign shipping from our ports. Granted; I want it to do it."[45] Congressional sentiment warmly endorsed this position. And characteristically, as tough as the bill was, Benson complained that it was not tough enough; it did not stipulate that in all ways concerning ownership and personnel United States ships would be 100 per cent American. He hoped the next Congress would correct the deficiency.[46] As it turned out, such an inclusion probably would have only intensified difficulties, for Wilson's signature affixed to the bill on 5 June 1920 signaled the opening of a veritable hornet's nest.

Controversy focused on one major point, which Section 34 was intended to remedy. The discriminatory provisions of Section 28 violated no less than thirty-two of America's foreign treaties. The protest that resulted came not only from predicted foreign and commercial sources, but from a quarter Benson had not anticipated—the White House. Section 28 had strength only if Wilson translated it into policy by abrogating treaties in ninety days as directed by Section 34. But no sooner had the President signed the bill than it became obvious that he was hesitant to use its authority to destroy what had taken much time and labor to build up through international negotiation, despite Congressional arguments that he had no choice. Benson and Jones toiled throughout July and August to persuade the President to use the prerogative, but they were unanswered. In early September Benson had no alternative but to extend the ninety-day period to the first of the coming year.

The President's verdict was released finally on 24 September. Denying that Congress had the power to issue such directives as were embodied in Section 34, Wilson authorized the State Department to announce that his endorsement of that section would have been "wholly irreconcilable with the historical respect which the United States has shown for its international engagements and would falsify every profession of our belief in the binding force and the reciprocal obligations of treaties in general." Wilson had signed the bill in June in the rush of time, the new Secretary of State Bainbridge Colby pointed out, and in the belief that his subsequent refusal to carry out the discriminatory mandate of Congress would not effect the over-all validity and operation of the measure which contained a great many "sound and enlightened provisions."[47] A week later Colby insisted that the chief executive's resolve to build up the merchant marine had not diminished in the least. The action had been intended primarily to relieve tension in international commercial and shipping circles, for there were indications that Section 34 had been interpreted globally as a challenge to one of the greatest economic conflicts the world had ever known. Wilson, Colby asserted, had taken a position "that will stand out as one of the most valuable acts of his administration for the people of this nation."[48] The President put it in its larger perspective shortly thereafter. There were two ways in which the nation could assist in fostering a spiritual and pure world democracy: by applying equality of treatment in domestic legislation, and by "standing for right and justice as toward individual nations."[49]

While Wilson did pull some of its teeth, the Jones Act remained a substantive conclusion to his eight-year campaign to strengthen the nation's domestic economy, and therefore its international standing, through maritime development and expansion. Aside from its discriminations, the measure marked the creation of an "essential trade routes" plan, directed the Shipping Board to devise means by which to maintain these selected sea-lanes, and if private enterprise was unable to provide the services, to operate ships in them until it was. Over all, the purpose of the act was to encourage American shippers and shipowners to undertake permanent trades with foreign markets deemed necessary by the government for various economic and political reasons, to prove the economic feasibility of doing it, and by employing private businessmen in the management of these public lines, to help pave the way for an efficient transition to eventual private ownership. That the measure had lasting significance is evidenced in the fact that its provisions and aims provide the fundamental principles upon which maritime policy is based today.[50]

Despite the disastrous slump that struck the world's economy, in particular shipping, in the last months of his administration, Woodrow Wilson had devoted a large and rewarding portion of his Presidential work to raising the merchant marine to a level from which it would finally view the world's commercial horizons with some satisfaction. While by no means solving all of shipping's problems, "no man [had] done more in recent years," as Colby, a former Shipping Board Commissioner himself, put it, "for the development and upbuilding of the American merchant marine."[51] That this accomplishment proceeded from the requirements of Wilson's world view and from the callings of its diplomacy distinguished it beyond all other considerations. This was best expressed by Benson, who spent his last days in office, as he recorded it, anxiously attempting to assist the incoming Harding administration "in its efforts to build up an American merchant marine and in carrying out a strong foreign policy."[52] To Wilsonians these two were inseparable—as they remain today.

JEFFREY J. SAFFORD

CHAPTER SEVEN

The British Strategic Inheritance in American Naval Policy, 1775-1975

IN THE REALM of strategy, the navies of the United States and Great Britain have shared common interests and therefore mutual missions over the two hundred years since the American declaration of political independence from the British Empire. The initial differences between the two peoples were primarily economic—commercial independence being proclaimed in April 1776, three months before the political act—from which all other separations stemmed, including the tendency of American historians to overstate the differences between them.[1] Nevertheless, the Anglo-Americans shared a desire for profits through maritime trade, with the mother country's closed mercantilistic policies leading to the War of Independence and the War of 1812,[2] after which it adopted a policy of free trade which fostered a shared economic endeavor with the young offspring nation that has persisted down to the present.

A fortuitous similar geographic insularity is part of the explanation, a natural isolation which separated both from continental Europe and from each other and which, says Nef, "encouraged the very confidence which facilitated the expansion of both industry and commerce, a confidence largely denied from 1792 to 1815 to the other leading Western nations."[3] As Mahan observed, the original colonies' intimate economic dependence on the sea was typically English, giving the Americans "an inborn love of the sea, the pulse of that English blood which still beat[s] in their veins . . .[and an] inherited aptitude for self-government and independent growth."[4] As American shippers began to share with Britain the worldwide markets forbidden them before 1776, they required the same naval protection theretofore provided by the Royal Navy. Gradually, over the ensuing two centuries, the new United States Navy (created in 1798) joined in this role, first depending on Royal Navy leadership and finally assuming the leadership itself. Common strategic aims therefore complemented the strong cultural, political, and economic ties between the two peoples.[5] In this way, the Americans inherited Britain's naval strategy both in general objectives and in many of the particulars.

British naval influences on the United States Navy are difficult to discern for several reasons. First, the general state of Western naval developments has always been followed closely by the United States Navy, and the British contribution to this is not easy to separate from other navies' impact. Second, proud American naval officers have been generally loath to give real credit to their doctrinal dependence on the British naval example, a characteristic of general American Anglophobia throughout much of American history.[6] Finally, France has loomed overlarge in the American military experience, particularly in its first century.

The French-American political and military alliances of 1778-1783 and 1812-1814 and the Napoleonic-Jominian example inspired generations of officers of the senior service in the United States Army, through the Civil War and beyond.[7] French philosophical notions of the Enlightenment influenced the Jeffersonians to disparage standing armies and navies, and Americans' continental preoccupations throughout the nineteenth century made their defensive policies susceptible to the continental French example. Indeed, the fledgling American naval doctrine followed French strategic practices of emphasizing *guerre de course* (commerce raiding) for the first century of United States history, and then fell under the spell of French naval and historical scholarship in the late nineteenth century: the inshore, torpedo-centered ideas of the French *jeune école* and the history of France's seventeenth-century maritime empire inspired by Colbert.[8]

Nevertheless, it was the Royal Navy more than any other that most directly influenced American naval doctrine and strategy. Throughout the eighteenth, nineteenth, and early twentieth centuries, general naval development was dominated by the awesomeness of British naval superiority in all its aspects: administration, technology, science and medicine, tactics and strategic aspirations.[9] Abroad, American naval squadrons acted in concert with British units far more than with other navies—and without regret.[10] Though the French alliances and naval practices were in fact utilized by the United States Navy whenever convenient and in such specifics as naval architecture or tactics, the present essay will show that the British example continually predominated. For instance, in just one area, that of administration, the United States Navy persisted in a long campaign to create a Board of Admiralty on the general British model that was not finally achieved until 1945 with the centralization of the Office of the Chief of Naval Operations and its several Deputy Chiefs, comparable to the British Sea Lords who made up the Admiralty Board.[11] British naval practices were always under the watchful scrutiny of the offspring navy, but most significantly in the area of strategy, missions, and doctrine.

The British strategic inheritance in American naval policy may be divided roughly into three chronological periods. The first period stemmed from the colonial era through the Revolution and early national years and encompassed the nineteenth century, all the while that Britain policed the sea lanes of the world and often accepted American naval participation due to mutual interests. The second period, about 1900 to 1947, generally featured Anglo-American naval cooperation, partnership, and equality—if often reluctant and even stormy. The final period, since 1947, has been one of American domination at sea with the Royal Navy as junior partner but still exerting powerful doctrinal influences.

1. BRITISH LEADERSHIP, 1775-1900

"New" England as a title aptly befitted the maritime section of the American republic during the first century of its history, for the merchants of primarily Massachusetts and its neighbors labored mightily to remain within the economic sphere of the British Empire, and under the protection of the Royal Navy, as revealed by their impact on the Federal Constitution in protecting private property and by their general Federalism—all very English and thus rarely shared by their agricultural brethren in the South and West.[12] Ironically, during the initial four decades when New England enjoyed its greatest political prestige, the

United States fought two wars against the mother country for political as well as economic independence. After 1815, having finally achieved both, New England declined in political influence just as its merchants found themselves virtually reincorporated into the British strategic domain. While the new nation expanded throughout the nineteenth century, New England's shippers plied the seven seas relatively secure from harassment due to a Royal Navy whose friendship was reciprocated by support from a fledgling United States Navy. New England remained more British than the rest of the country in its thalassocratic traditions and cultural cosmopolitanism, giving the region "a special flavor that has remained to this day."[13]

More than any other individual, John Adams represented the New England attitude—to maintain close ties with Britain without succumbing to English economic greed. Like the American merchant class in general, he at first sought only to reform English mercantilism, then viewed the Revolution as "the occasion of a reformation in the maritime law of nations of so much importance to a free communication among mankind by the sea."[14] Genuinely regretting that the war had been necessary, Adams struggled unsuccessfully after its end for trade reciprocity with Britain.[15] Antagonistic to an alliance with either Britain or France, and finding the French Revolution more repugnant to international order than British economic arrogance, Adams turned to diplomacy and naval power to restore economic normalcy with both of these nations. Though Britain's wars with France from 1793, the unsettled Canadian frontier, the impressment issue, and Britain's mercantilistic persistence frustrated any real commercial rapport until after the War of 1812, Adams initially preferred to pay the relatively inexpensive tribute to the Barbary states. But he then led in the creation of the small United States Navy in 1798, in order to thwart French depredations and to impress the British with American naval capabilities. Between American diplomacy and limited naval prestige, Adams along with Alexander Hamilton hoped that the United States could act as the fulcrum in a balance of power between Britain and France.[16]

Adams' efforts to create a real naval presence were frustrated as much by his own countrymen as by events abroad. On the one extreme, the more conservative Hamilton supported a strong merchant marine and wanted a navy to protect it but not in the role senior to the Army that Adams envisioned, and Hamilton preferred outright alliance with Britain. On the other extreme, the more liberal Thomas Jefferson ideally wanted no navy at all, but supported it whenever the Barbary pirates plundered American shipping, a navy of expediency built around coast-defense gunboats and an occasional frigate.[17] Adams, like New Englanders in general, viewed both the pro-British army-oriented Hamiltonians and pro-French agrarian-minded Jeffersonians as if both belonged to the same nonmaritime "landed" camp. With a full appreciation of why the seventeenth-century maritime aspirations of both France and the Netherlands had failed, he observed in 1812, "The landed interest in Holland depressed their Navy. The landed interest in France always starved theirs. And we see the consequences. The landed interest in America has done the same and we feel the Effects."[18] Fearing the ultimate effect of any war with Britain on American commerce, Adams counseled President Washington in 1790 to avoid such a conflict at all costs, welcomed the rapprochement of 1794 following the otherwise unsatisfactory Jay Treaty, recalled his part in the creation of the Navy Department as his greatest achievement, and chafed at American helplessness before British and French economic sanctions during the Napoleonic wars; but he still supported war with Britain rather than with France in 1812.[19] War seemed to favor the notion that a French victory would right the balance of power so important to American neutrality, a view probably held by President James Madison.[20]

"If the War of 1812 . . . accomplished nothing else," in Albion's words, it showed "the folly of two trading nations fighting each other."[21] Shipping interests in Old and New England alike sought profits under a common capitalist system which lacked success only in the face of the old anomalies which eventually precipitated that war. In both countries, Adam Smith's new gospel of free trade increasingly found ardent champions. John Adams believed that the adoption of free trade by the British would eliminate Britain's need for a navy, a naïve view made particularly irrelevant by the long Napoleonic wars.[22] But free trade between Britain and the United States was urgently desired by the shipping interests on both sides of the Atlantic, to the point where American merchants tried to quiet public passions over British impressments dramatized by the *Chesapeake* affair in 1807, and the British actually encouraged continuing Anglo-American trade even during the height of hostilities in 1812-1814.[23] American markets for British goods profited both sides, so much so that the Royal Navy exempted the New England coast from the general blockade, and the New Englanders, frustrated by the economic dislocations caused by Jefferson's embargo and other matters, flirted with separatism at the Hartford Convention of 1814 which sought Anglo-American accommodation at any price.[24] All that the latter endeavor demonstrated was the growing minority position of New England within the expanding nation and its government.

Actual American naval doctrine of the colonial period, the Revolution, and the early national years reflected British training and experience. Historians have disagreed on just how well versed the Founding Fathers were in understanding the virtues of naval power. Millis believed, "The authors of the Constitution were as familiar with the concepts and significance of sea power as if they had all sat for Captain Mahan's lectures at the Naval War College a century later," whereas the Sprouts saw Congressional leaders both in 1798 and 1812 generally ignorant of naval warfare and strategy, save for a vague appreciation of the naval dimension of British imperial greatness.[25] The truth lies somewhere between, with the executive branch under the Federalist leadership being intimately involved with naval matters, whereas the non-Federalist majorities in Congress from the late 1790's reflected the demise of New England's leadership and the usual more narrow interests of elected regional representatives. Before the Revolution, the American colonists had merely augmented the mighty Royal Navy in fighting the French and pirates alike, developing doctrinal habits of relying on privateers and armed merchantmen that persisted through the Revolution and the War of 1812.[26]

In naval practice, Adams in 1775 authored the first regulations book of what became the Continental Navy and in 1778-1779 articulated the strategy that would insure independence, namely French assertion of command over North American waters in cooperation with the Continental Army from the landward side.[27] Washington realized the same thing and accomplished it in the Yorktown campaign of 1781.[28] Adams as President was quite willing to allow the Royal Navy to convoy American merchantmen during the Quasi-War with France and to follow British naval leadership in the West Indies during and after that struggle.[29] In the construction of vessels for war, the Americans did nothing (save for developing the fast schooner) to initiate original designs during or after the Revolution and depended to a large extent on the work of an English-trained shipwright, Josiah Fox, between 1793 and 1809 to lead in the building of the fine forty-four-gun frigates which characterized the early United States Navy. Also, Chapelle has shown that British rather than French designs most influenced American naval architecture during this period.[30]

Small wonder, then, that the War of 1812 was a tragic interlude for two nations whose economic and strategic policies—like so much else—were so inextricably intertwined. The British abandonment of the impressment of American sailors after 1815 and the gradual extension of commercial reciprocity to the United States by 1830 preceded Britain's endorsement of free trade by 1850, to the delight of the New England merchant class. Indeed, New England immediately in 1815 entered upon its "golden age," which lasted half a century and during which it absorbed the key port of New York into its commercial block, dominating not only American trade but coming—by the early 1850's—very close to surpassing British maritime trade. Such prosperity also created revenues for badly needed economic surpluses that went into internal improvements such as canals and turnpikes.[31] In addition, New England blossomed in thalassocratic cultural grandeur through the transcendental philosopher writers of this "renaissance" age and came ever closer to British cultural life.[32] New England and New York prospered, and with them the nation.

But such American prosperity did not occur in a strategic vacuum, although most Americans at the time "passed into the new peace . . . more or less convinced that [their] military institutions were fundamentally sound. In relation to the actual problems of the day, the temper of the times and the situations confronting [them], perhaps they were."[33] The American Congress authorized nine ships of the line and twelve forty-four-gun frigates in 1816 to make up for the wartime weaknesses, a program not lost on the British, who from 1826, when the United States had seven of the line in commission, "began constructing ships to equal or surpass the best that the Americans could build."[34] Such British action can be viewed more as respect for the former colony's naval prowess than as anti-American feeling. For, indeed, from 1815 the merchants of Old and New England restored their trade associations with a will as a prelude to open reciprocity, which made the Liverpool-to-New York run the busiest economic route between the two countries, passively protected by British naval control of the North Atlantic. Between 1815 and 1825, in fact, the British disarmed their forces on the Great Lakes, trusting to American friendship as expressed in the Rush-Bagot agreement; and in Latin America the diplomatic policies of George Canning, James Monroe, and John Quincy Adams coincided under the rubric of the Monroe Doctrine to exclude all the powers but Britain and the United States from political or economic intervention in the region. All of which is to say that the United States from 1815 enjoyed a privileged economic and strategic place within the *Pax Britannica* as it began to work again in common naval concert with and within the British Empire.[35]

To be sure, diplomatic incidents constantly jarred Anglo-American relations but never to the extent that they interfered with the growing naval coalition policing the sea lanes against pirates, slavers, and smugglers in the protection of aggressive Anglo-American trade and political interests. In the Mediterranean, American and Anglo-Dutch squadrons bombarded Algiers in 1815 and 1816 respectively, leading to a small but permanent American squadron in the middle sea and the stationing of a solitary British ship of the line there to match it. As the Mediterranean became a region of international unrest during the 1820's and 1830's, with the Americans providing naval advice and friendliness to Ottoman Turkey, Britain increased its naval forces to major proportions, especially to offset potential French and Russian expansion at the expense of Turkey (a problem which led to the Crimean War of the 1850's).[36] In the Baltic, Britain further resisted Russian expansion from 1835 by policing that sea, also to the profit of the Americans who secured naval stores there; it was the United States, in fact, which in 1855 refused to pay the ancient Sound tolls to Denmark, leading to a general international conference which eliminated them altogether—a measure in the true spirit of Anglo-American free trade.[37] In the Caribbean, British and American naval vessels and personnel covertly assisted the

Latin American republics to achieve their independence from Spain and Portugal and thereby gained privileged trade status. Britain opened British West Indies trade to the United States in 1820, while in the last Spanish colonies, Cuba and Puerto Rico, American trade outdistanced that of Britain. Augmenting the antislaving efforts of the British South American and African squadrons, the United States created its Brazil (or South Atlantic) squadron in 1826 and African squadron in 1843.[38] In the Far East, American traders and warships followed closely their British brethren, battling Chinese pirates and coastal warlords, the British East Indies squadron being joined by an American one of the same title in 1835, both acting in virtual concert during the Arrow War of the late 1850's.[39] Indeed, the Americans, more legitimately a Pacific power than Britain after the Oregon compromise and the acquisition of California in 1846-1848, took the lead in opening Japan to the West in a display of naval force in 1853. So the English-speaking navies shared their global enterprises, with the United States imitating Royal Navy practices.

The irony in such early nineteenth-century American strategic practices lay in the fact that between 1820 and 1860 New England (and New York) gradually lost prestige in the national government, epitomized by the failure of the unpopular New England President John Quincy Adams to make the United States into "a great naval power."[40] The increasing predominance of the Western and Southern non- and antimaritime elements, from Jefferson to Andrew Jackson, culminated in the period 1842-1861 when, paradoxically, "the naval affairs of the United States were largely under the influence of Southern men."[41] It may be said that New England and New York got cruisers for the essential protection of their trade while the Western and Southern men utilized the Navy chiefly for purposes of continental protection—coastal defense and support of overland expansion, an entirely realistic strategy for the young republic. The Navy asserted American primacy in the Gulf of Mexico by assisting the Army in pacifying the Seminole Indians, encouraging Texas independence, and demonstrating against the British with the creation of the Home Squadron in 1841. Victory over Mexico in the war of 1846-1848 was made possible largely because of the Navy's blockade, sealift, and amphibious efforts in close concert with the Army.[42] Importantly, however, the United States was saved the expense of a big navy and allowed to concentrate on overland expansion by virtue of its protection under Britain's strategic umbrella.[43]

Just as the interior states rose to dominate the Federal government, so too did they place the Army in the position of the senior service, from Washington, Winfield Scott, and the Lees of Virginia through the frontier-militia types of the Andy Jackson-Zack Taylor mold. Such individuals generally appreciated the utilities of the Navy in wartime, but their training was Napoleonic and their experience continental rather than maritime.[44] Such a political-military education was manifested by both sides in the Civil War, where any British strategic influence was indirect. The North knew from the two wars with Britain and the Mexican War the importance of a blockade against the South, and General Scott joined a naval strategy board in recommending it early in the war; but while the Abraham Lincoln administration adopted it, the Army, Secretary of the Navy Gideon Welles, and indeed the nation at large preferred the direct and seemingly quicker approach of an assault on Richmond.[45] The North enjoyed command of the sea by virtual default as in 1846, although two engineering bureau chiefs recommended, but in vain, a seagoing fleet of modern ironclads for "keeping command of the open sea" rather than mere coastal waters, clearly following British practice.[46] The blockade proved more successful than the repeated efforts against Richmond, but it was accomplished largely by an inshore navy in the continental tradition and not an ocean-going one like Britain's. The wartime Navy's eventual sheer size, however, helped—with the Union army—to impress Britain sufficiently to remain neutral and officially friendly.

The South's major maritime effort lay in convincing Britain to switch her political-naval favoritism from the United States to the Confederate States, principally in legal arguments (the declared blockade being recognition of full belligerence). The Southern naval effort resembled those of 1775 and 1812—*guerre de course* and coast defense. But even in the latter endeavor, Southern Army-bred strategists erred. When Union expeditionary forces took isolated beaches early in the war, coast defender Robert E. Lee mistook these thrusts for bridgeheads for direct invasion rather than as blockading base enclaves and kept his forces in the interior awaiting the seaborne invasion that never came.[47] Convinced from the outset of Union naval prowess, Great Britain let neither diplomatic incidents like the *Trent* affair nor Napoleon III's foray into Mexico disturb the Anglo-American *pax status quo ante bellum*.[48]

In addition to being reluctant maritime strategists, the leaders of the Federal government before, during, and after the Civil War also failed to learn from Britain the importance of sufficiently protecting the merchant marine, thus making the United States ever more dependent on the British economic and maritime system. A number of dramatic changes during the 1850's all combined to arrest, then reverse, the upward growth of American shipping: the financial panic of 1857, the diverting of investments and services from coastal vessels to the new railroads, the overproduction of the initially profitable clipper ships, and the failure of the Federal government to subsidize American shipbuilders for the new and expensive iron and steam ships to keep up with their British government-subsidized competitors. In addition, the few Confederate commerce-raiding cruisers of the early 1860's drove Yankee traders temporarily to halt their activities or permanently to change their registry to Britain for the cheaper marine insurance rates befitting a neutral carrier and for the protection of the Royal Navy. And an irritated but shortsighted Congress refused to allow their postwar return to American registry. Such actions, plus actual captures and sinkings, cost New England and New York about half their prewar tonnage, while many of the older industries like whaling simply suffered a natural demise (in this case, competition from petroleum), and the dogged preference for sail over steam led to an emphasis on coastal schooners over oceanic vessels. And yet the American wartime and postwar economy did not suffer. It boomed (in spite of the Panic of 1873), but relied on English rather than Yankee bottoms. The old sailing warships returned to their distant stations after the war, but were little more than token auxiliaries to an ever-modernizing British navy.[49]

The post-Civil War United States Navy accompanied the merchant marine back into the shade of the British strategic umbrella, where it remained until the 1890's. As long as the *Pax Britannica* guaranteed free American global trade profits, and only incidentally the shores of American continents (and thus the Monroe Doctrine), no ocean-going United States fleet was really necessary. Consequently, the Navy and Congress realistically demobilized the wartime squadrons during the late 1860's and kept the Navy in an almost antiquated presteam condition throughout the 1870's.[50] And as long as neither American soil nor territorial regions vital to American capitalism were threatened by invasion, the American people were content with what Huntington has called their "business pacifism."[51] The Royal Navy remained the measure of naval excellence to Americans simply because of its prominence and because diplomatic incidents with Britain inevitably raised the question of a possible naval confrontation between the two countries.[52] Given the utter American dependence on the "peace of Britain" and the consequently feeble American Navy of the late nineteenth century, the United States—realistically—based its military policies on the traditional adherence to coast defense with fortifications and monitors and commerce-raiding cruisers. In such straits, American strategy closely resembled that of Britain's arch enemy, continental France, whose naval architects and theorists provided additional rationales for a nonmaritime continental-style defensive policy, especially in the 1880's, when France's *jeune école* reformers argued that the underwater torpedo had neutralized British sea power.[53]

The relatively tranquil *Pax Britannica* and the passive American strategic position within it, like free trade in general, might have continued indefinitely but for the rise of challengers and a new round of imperialism. Economic progress, especially in Germany but also in Italy, France, and Japan, "forced the two leading commercial and industrial nations—Great Britain and the United States—out of their geographical isolation and put them into the orbit of deadly struggle."[54] That struggle until the 1880's largely escaped both the British and American governments, but not their naval officers. "Blue water" admirals and pundits in Britain battled their Army-oriented "bolt from the blue" antagonists who favored a defensive strategy at the coasts and colonies in this age of steam bridging the English Channel,[55] just as American naval officers argued forcibly for an open-ocean capability with offensive battleships, overseas bases in the Caribbean and the Pacific—from the *Virginius* affair in Cuba in 1873 to the Samoan incident of 1889—and for a modern staff and command system in order to compete effectively with Britain and the other powers. The 1880's became a transition period, as imperialism erupted from Europe outward, and these arguments were institutionalized in the Naval War College just as American industry was developing to the point where it could indeed create a modern steel-steam fleet. An additional factor was the growth of the discipline of naval history, particularly in Britain, whose eighteenth-century imperial achievements were virtually sanctified by Captain Mahan of the United States Navy in 1890, creating a powerful if "indirect influence of British naval history on American naval policy and development in the 1890's and 1900's."[56]

To be sure, the American transition from strategic dependence to strategic unilateralism was very gradual but no slower than Germany's or Japan's, both of which unabashedly imitated the Royal Navy. The American Naval Appropriations acts of 1883 and 1890 authorized the first modern United States cruisers and battleships, just as the British Naval Act of 1889 called for a two-power standard of battleships.[57] And yet the only naval enemy the United States could envisage until the early 1890's was Britain, and naval planners went through the motions of preparing exceedingly unlikely war plans against Britain.[58] But, following the Venezuelan crisis of 1896, "the Anglo-American rapprochement made war appear less likely year by year."[59] Such an attitude fitted comfortably into British strategy, for the Franco-Russian entente and the growth of the Italian and German navies caused Britain to stress home defense over any serious activities in the Western Hemisphere. With the Royal Navy providing a strategic shield in the North Atlantic as always, the United States in the 1890's began to face the realization that it could no longer passively depend upon that same shield in the Caribbean and the Pacific, particularly as the jingoistic imperialists at home were calling for expanded overseas trade, colonies and bases, and a transisthmian Panama canal to connect the lot. Spain's repressive actions in her Cuban colony led to war in 1898 and a strengthened American position in the Caribbean, but German, French, Russian, and Japanese expansion in the Far East led to real apprehensions about the security of American trade and defenses there.[60]

From the American victory over Spain and the first German Naval Act in 1898 until the Boxer Rebellion in China and the second and more important German Naval Act in 1900, new strategic realities became apparent that made Anglo-American naval partnership exceedingly desirable. The United States could no longer rely on an *ad hoc* system of strategic decision-making that took for granted the naval protection of an evaporating *Pax Britannica,* no more than Britain could afford the luxury of maintaining international police forces far away from the North Atlantic. The reduction of strong British base garrisons and naval squadrons in the Mediterranean, Canada, the Caribbean, and the Far East meant that political vacuums would be created. The American naval response to this new reality in 1898-1900 was the creation of naval bases in Cuba and Puerto Rico in the Caribbean, the acquisition of the Hawaiian Islands and the development of Pearl Harbor, the occupation of Wake Island, and the first steps toward defending Guam and the Philippine Islands obtained as spoils of war from Spain. In addition, Germany and Russia were threatening China, the American position in the Philippines, and Anglo-American Far Eastern trade in general. The United States Navy began to respond to the challenges of this new world system with the creation of the strategy-oriented General Board in 1900 and a growing overt feeling of common purpose with the Royal Navy.[61]

2. ANGLO-AMERICAN PARTNERSHIP, 1900-1947

"British interests are not American interests, no," Alfred Thayer Mahan told Theodore Roosevelt in 1906. "But taking the constitution of the British Empire and the trade interests of the British islands, the United States has certainty of a very high order that the British Empire will stand substantially on the same line of world policy as ourselves."[62] Such an expression typified opinion in the United States Navy toward the British, not only in the first decade of the twentieth century[63] but ever since. Between 1900 and 1947, however, though the United States and Great Britain officially maintained unilateral and separate foreign and defensive stances in their over-all strategies, in practice they shared a common aim: superiority at sea to thwart aggression by avowed usurpers of free Anglo-American trade who threatened the stability of balanced international order. The major source of irritation between the two nations lay in the goals of each to have its own navy "second to none."[64] Nevertheless, the British and American navies worked in more or less close concert immediately before and during World Wars I and II as allies against Germany and Japan, shared naval parity between the wars, and cooperated in both immediate postwar periods against Communist Russia. In so doing, the Royal and United States navies comprised a strategic partnership of unparalleled might that continued to command the seas as during the nineteenth century, but now on a quantitatively and qualitatively equal basis and usually under wartime conditions.[65]

The United States was not a colonial empire like Britain and—with the demise of New England[66] and the American merchant marine—no longer a leading maritime carrier, but in the strategic sphere the defensive policies of both nations became virtually identical. And since neither one had sufficient naval power to command the seas against the rival navies of Germany, Japan, and Italy, both used diplomacy and warship distribution schemes to complement each other by recognizing mutual spheres of influence. Consequently, Britain between 1900 and 1906 reconcentrated its fleet in the North Atlantic against Germany and secondarily in the Mediterranean against Italy, assisted by the French.[67] To keep this shield against Germany intact, the United States intervened in both world wars on the side of Britain.[68] For its part, the United States filled the strategic vacuum left by the British withdrawal from the Caribbean and gradually shifted major fleet units into the Pacific to counter Japanese expansion. Because of the primacy of the Atlantic-Caribbean hub of Anglo-American trade, however, the major naval area of peacetime deterrence and wartime operational theatre remained there, with the Pacific being treated on a secondary basis by diplomatic moves and occasional shows of force by Britain and the United States until World War II.

American strategic reciprocity in allowing Britain to look after American interests on the other side of the Atlantic was more reluctant and less obvious. Theodore Roosevelt's avowed unilateralism led him to dispatch new American battle-fleet units on several cruises to European ports as displays of American naval strength between 1904 and 1912. Nevertheless, several of these were decidedly anti-German, being designed to pressure Germany directly in the Caribbean and indirectly in Europe and the Mediterranean—and thus, coincidentally, to strengthen the British naval position vis-à-vis Germany. "The European powers," observes Livermore, correctly, ". . .equated every movement [of the United States fleet] with the precarious international situation in which the weight of the United States constantly tipped the balance against the pretensions of Germany."[69] Still, in all, it was the British (and some French) naval power that countered the Germans in the North Atlantic and Mediterranean before and during World War I.[70] During the early years of that conflict, the United States and its admirals doggedly professed naval neutrality but in fact practiced a generally anti-German strategy and doctrine against a possible German invasion somewhere in the Western Hemisphere.[71] American naval unilateralism persisted, however, with battleship construction, looking to the day when the United States fleet would have to fight the German High Seas Fleet should Britain be defeated.[72]

Britain's naval withdrawal from the Western Hemisphere coincided with the "big navy" expansionism of the Roosevelt administration in the United States.[73] Conveniently, therefore, between 1901 and 1907 both nations aimed at thwarting German expansion so that their strategies overlapped to the point where they appeared to be under common direction. By treaty, Britain yielded to America the rights of building, operating, and fortifying the Panama Canal. By strategic actions, namely the permanent recall of the North American squadron to home waters, Britain also surrendered political-economic-military hegemony over the Caribbean to America. The Roosevelt administration lost no time in building a strong battleship navy, in proclaiming the "corollary" to the Monroe Doctrine of exclusive rights of intervention in the affairs of the Latin American states, and in turning the Caribbean into an American lake.[74] When Germany threatened to intervene in Santo Domingo and Venezuela, the British were quite content to let the Americans take the lead in pressuring the Germans into withdrawing.[75] Britain quietly turned over her northernmost naval bases to Canadian administration and let the United States police the rest of the Hemisphere, by which British economic interests and the last few colonies were protected—a policy which has continued through both world wars to the present.[76]

By April 1917, when the United States entered World War I against Germany, not only had the admirals made absolutely no preparations for coalition warfare alongside Britain, but that month the General Board advocated a two-power standard against Germany and Japan.[77] Nevertheless, according to Trask, "Basic disagreements between Great Britain and the United States did not materialize precisely because both countries saw the requirements of sea warfare in broadly the same light."[78] Despite a Chief of Naval Operations, Admiral William S. Benson, who was "deeply suspicious of the British," the American theatre commander in England, Admiral William S. Sims, "a notorious Anglophile,"[79] and Captain William V. Pratt,[80] Benson's own key assistant, prevailed upon the administration of Woodrow Wilson and the Navy Department at large to postpone capital-ship construction in favor of supporting the all-out British antisubmarine effort. To help the British Grand Fleet contain the German High Seas Fleet, however, the United States Navy subordinated one battleship squadron to British tactical command. The American navy became so enamoured with the antisub campaign that it even outdid the Royal Navy by inaugurating its own undersea effort, the Northern Mine Barrage, however dubious its effectiveness. During Anglo-American naval operations in 1917-1918 both navies worked in the closest possible concert, with the Americans generally following British leadership on the basis of the common goal: command of the sea over Germany.[81]

Because of the Anglo-American preoccupation with Germany between 1900 and 1918, the rise of Japan in the Pacific could not be confronted directly by either English-speaking nation—neither separately nor, had they wished, together. Britain's recall of her Far Eastern fleet units in 1904 resembled her withdrawal from the Caribbean in intent and effect, only here a formal alliance with Japan in 1902 guaranteed the protection of Britain's interests and possessions by Japan against particularly Russia but also Germany. Japan virtually eliminated the Russian menace in the war of 1904-1905 and forced the German East Asian squadron to flee Oriental waters in 1914. The United States—geographically a

Pacific power—had more immediate concerns and an unusually strong commitment to the future of China. The American seizure of the Philippine Islands, Guam, and Wake in 1898, the annexation of Hawaii in 1899, and the declaration of the Open Door policy for China in 1899-1900 had all established the American position in the Far East. But the tiny Asiatic Fleet at Manila and the Yangtze gunboat patrol were no match for Japan should that nation choose to attack China or the new American possessions.[82]

Presidents Theodore Roosevelt, William Howard Taft, and Woodrow Wilson, lacking a two-ocean navy in the face of the dual German-Japanese threat, tried to contain Japan by relying on mutual interests with Britain in the Pacific, unilateral displays of force such as the voyage of the Great White Fleet in 1907-1909, and unofficial diplomatic concessions which steadily eroded the Open Door by recognizing Japan's hegemony over Korea and "special interests" in China. Roosevelt's search for British "moral support and even material assistance" was frustrated by his false assumption "that Anglo-American actions were based upon identical interests in the Pacific as well as in the Atlantic." Still, in Braisted's words, "American naval and civilian leaders [between 1901 and 1909, Roosevelt's terms] regarded Britain and the British navy as potent factors for peace and for the welfare of the United States."[83] This easygoing relationship began to deteriorate under Roosevelt's successors as the Japanese menace grew, and the United States Navy drew up its Orange Plan for a possible war in the Pacific against Britain's ally. Such a possibility exacerbated Anglo-American naval relations before and during World War I, the British outright rejecting American overtures for guarantees against potential Japanese aggression in the Pacific aimed at China and/or the United States. In fact, both Britain and the United States were buying time in the Pacific through flimsy diplomatic deals and inaction while they countered Germany.[84]

In the turbulent postwar period of 1918-1922 the United States and Britain in varying degrees tried to re-establish some semblance of international order upon the seas not unlike the prewar era, though differing—as usual—over economic policies and neutral shipping rights in time of war. But Britain with France reasserted its leadership in the Atlantic and European waters, while the United States finally faced westward against

Japan. The wartime alliance dissolved, the United States retired to unilateralism by withdrawing both from the abortive interventions in the Russian Civil War and from the peace conference at Versailles, and war-weary Britain faced the unhappy economic prospects of a battleship-building race with the United States and Japan. Britain's marriage of convenience with Japan now forced her to recognize her first loyalty to her English-speaking partners—not only the United States but the now vociferous Empire governments of Canada, Australia, and New Zealand, which also feared Japanese expansionism. So Britain—ever so begrudgingly—accepted the American invitation to attend the Washington naval arms limitation conference of 1921-1922. From that emerged naval parity between Britain and the United States with Japan third, also two vague multilateral treaties whose chief consequences were the supersession of the Anglo-Japanese alliance and the recognition of separate spheres of influence in the Pacific. A fragile balance of power thus restored the Anglo-American naval partnership, however tenuous, in the world.[85]

The naval rapprochement encouraged by the parity allowed Britain and the United States by the Washington agreements did not come to pass until the late 1930's; neither did any global *Pax Anglo-Americana* eliminate the seeds of renewed world war. The chief reason lay in major antagonisms between both powers throughout the 1920's, "the fundamental causes of which," says Roskill, "lay in the challenge of the United States to the long-standing maritime and mercantile predominance enjoyed by Britain."[86] And, the Sprouts saw, "the possibility of such a Pax Anglo-Americana [depended] not only on the cordiality of British-American relations but also on the security of the British Isles and of the sea routes radiating therefrom."[87] The competitiveness which divided both differed from the pre-World War I years only in magnitude—that is, the *potential* size and thus prestige—of the United States Navy. The American merchant marine had declined to near impotence, but there had been no decline of Anglo-American trade nor of the community of strategic interests which provided for the security not only of the British Isles but of the continental United States "and of the sea routes radiating therefrom" as well. Britain reasserted its maritime supremacy in the Atlantic, and the United States in the Caribbean, both generally passive assertions for lack of real enemies. Exceptions came during the Ethiopian war when Britain refused to check Italy partially because France failed to support her,[88] and when Britain surrendered to Germany the right to rearm at sea by treaty in 1935.

Where the absence of real Anglo-American naval cooperation hurt most was in the Pacific, in which the United States concentrated its major fleet units to balance off Japanese naval power. But the United States failed to build up to treaty strength, even after the London accords of 1930, and had neither the power nor the will to deter alone Japanese aggression in the 1930's. The world depression further hampered the English-speaking nations, while President Franklin D. Roosevelt in 1933-1935 supported Congressional measures to improve the fleet and build to treaty strength, but not to go beyond it. He further remained, like the earlier Roosevelt, committed to a unilateral strategy and gave no serious consideration to bilateral naval action alongside Britain.[89] Only "the rise of the dictatorships" and their aggression—especially Japan's in China from 1937 and Germany's in Europe from the Munich crisis of 1938—"gradually produced the realization [again, one might add] that Britain and America had common interests, traditions and outlook which transcended the issue of which country should possess the more powerful navy."[90]

World War II dramatically brought the Anglo-American naval strategies under unified, coequal direction, with the British continuing to lead in the Atlantic and Mediterranean and the Americans virtually monopolizing the Caribbean and Pacific.[91] The Alliance now pooled its resources and doctrine in the closest possible coalition of its history, which also included the Commonwealth navies of Canada, Australia, and New Zealand. Winston Churchill, British Prime Minister but also First Lord of the Admiralty in 1911-1915 and 1939-1940, not surprisingly dominated Allied naval strategic planning in the Atlantic and Mediterranean and was a strong advocate of both the British and United States navies.[92] However, American Admiral Ernest J. King, Commander-in-Chief of the United States Fleet and Chief of Naval Operations, exerted strong influence over Atlantic antisubmarine operations and over Allied naval strategy in the Pacific. Needless to say, the usual antagonisms arose from particular national interests and biases, but most overtly in the person of Admiral King, an outspoken advocate of American naval unilateralism and just as suspicious of the British as his predecessor Admiral Benson had been. In the Pacific, theatre commander Admiral Chester W. Nimitz followed the example of Admiral Sims by quietly promoting completely successful joint operations, only this time with the British in the subordinate role.[93] The Baltic and Black seas fell within the strategic jurisdiction of the third ally of the Great Coalition, Soviet Russia, whose major contribution was on the land rather than at sea.

The maritime aspects of the Atlantic wartime strategic goals included restoring peaceful trade upon the seas in the postwar world, but as in the past no formal plans were ever made for a long-range sharing of such strategic responsibilities. Instead, the British merely assumed that they would dominate the North Atlantic and Mediterranean, which the American admirals were quite willing to let them do.[94] The Americans would undoubtedly police the Pacific following the demise of imperial Japan, and the Baltic and Black seas would have to be negotiated as part of the postwar settlement with Russia. When, after V-E Day, the Russians began to make political demands for hegemony over those two seas adjacent to Eastern Europe and even beyond—the Dardanelles, Iran, and the former Italian colonies in the Mediterranean—Britain and the United States hastened naval units into the eastern Mediterranean (though they could do little in the Baltic as long as the Russians occupied East Germany and Poland). Such Anglo-American naval demonstrations thwarted Russian designs in late 1945 and throughout 1946, but such temporary arrangements were not to last.[95] When, early in 1947, Britain declared its economic inability to shoulder such enormous postwar responsibilities, the burden fell squarely on the United States—and Britain became the junior partner.

3. AMERICAN LEADERSHIP, SINCE 1947

Contemplating a possible *Pax Americana,* the Sprouts in 1940 had envisioned that "the American people, with their immeasurably greater resources, might conceivably succeed in establishing a virtually global dominance" but not without a "desperate armed conflict leading to the military defeat of Great Britain and

Japan."[96] World War II resulted in the military defeat of Japan and with the Cold War led to Britain's demise as a major naval power, reducing it to a secondary position alongside the American military colossus. As during the *Pax Britannica* of the preceding century, the maritime powers have had to reassert their traditional command of the sea for global economic and political stability but with new ideological and technological overtones. Ideologically, Communism has contributed importantly to the political challenge of Russia and China in the global balance of power and has influenced the wars of national liberation that have destroyed the European overseas empires, including Britain's. Technologically, the advent of nuclear weapons has altered diplomatic relationships but also the nature of naval forces that act as launching vehicles for many such weapons. Such challenges have been met by the Anglo-American coalition, but now as a formal peacetime alliance.

Formal alliance under American leadership became necessary when Britain revealed in 1947 her inability to maintain strategic control over her traditional sphere, the waters around Europe, and thus to deter any Russian advance on the Continent. The United States took up the challenge with the Truman Doctrine and policy of containment, and Anglo-American naval forces therefore continued to operate informally together in the Atlantic and Mediterranean until the formal creation of the North Atlantic Treaty Organization (NATO) in 1949.[97] Despite extreme British displeasure, not unlike that over parity with the United States granted by the Washington treaties in 1922, the nine chiefs of staff of the NATO countries two years later selected an American admiral—the Commander-in-Chief of the United States Atlantic Fleet—permanently to be Supreme Allied Commander, Atlantic.[98] Of the European members, Britain has remained the strongest naval and maritime nation, while the American merchant marine declined further when the United States gave over its surplus wartime merchantmen to its NATO allies until less than 10 per cent of American trade traveled in American hulls.[99] But the cheaper merchant registries of Panama, Liberia, Honduras, and Greece lie within the general American-NATO strategic camp. And all NATO navies, including the Royal Navy, have remained quite small under the American strategic umbrella. Even with small flotillas, says Martin, "The present posture [1967] of Western European navies makes sense only so long as they are auxiliaries to the United States in European and Atlantic waters."[100]

Of course European and Mediterranean waters have constituted only part—the NATO element—of the maritime requirements of the Anglo-American naval coalition under the *Pax Americana*. The nuclear dimension has been both European and global, with the United States not only eventually leading in quantity and quality but by the Nassau agreement of 1962 making Britain utterly dependent on the American Polaris underwater-launched strategic-missile system. British aircraft carriers briefly deployed with atomic weapons from 1959—a full decade after American carriers had them—and during the 1960's Britain constructed five Polaris submarines alongside the United States Navy's forty-one, but, as British Admiral B. B. Schofield observed in 1963, "Without the backing of the United States it is impossible for Britain to enter the nuclear arena in a contest with Russia, whatever the issue."[101] Policing of sea lanes beyond Europe has been another dimension of Anglo-American maritime strategy. The United States has continued to dominate the Western Hemisphere as before and in 1945 filled the vacuum left by the demise of Japan throughout the Pacific, while Britain and her Commonwealth colleagues generally policed the Indian Ocean until the beginning of the 1970's.

Where both American and British naval policies have been most erratic and uneven has been in the waging of limited wars in the peripheral Eurasian waters between the Suez Canal and Korea, actions which have borne significantly on their policies. In the late 1940's both nations tried to demobilize their conventional naval forces (save for antisubmarine elements to counter the considerable Russian sub fleet), even in the face of the Communist victory in China and the revolutionary wars throughout Southeast Asia and the Middle East. The Korean War (1950-1953) challenged such a retrenchment and provided the political lever for naval rearmament with not only conventional but nuclear-war forces. Indeed, Anglo-American-Commonwealth naval forces under strategic United States Navy direction operated successfully in Korea, only to revert to a general preoccupation with nuclear weapons when that war ended. The United States created a nuclear-armed carrier force and initiated the Polaris program, and the Royal Navy deployed a limited carrier force that would seek to utilize nuclear weapons. In practice, however, both navies—especially Britain's—found themselves employed more in conventional roles. Britain's respectable naval posture even encouraged her into unilateral naval adventurism that came to grief in 1956. Without consulting its senior ally, Britain joined France and Israel in attacking Egypt, exposing its own strategic as well as tactical inabilities for such latter-day gunboat diplomacy. By contrast, the American amphibious intervention in Lebanon two years later was successful though not a consistent part of any American limited-war doctrine.[102]

This Suez debacle shook the British nation and military into replacing its traditional naval diplomacy with the necessity "to work even more closely with the United States to produce alliance harmony in these regions of the world where British and American interests partly diverged," but with Britain now decidedly in the subordinate role.[103] In particular, in addition to the heavier reliance on American nuclear systems, Suez prompted the British to focus their major naval energies on improving their conventional war forces and capabilities. From 1957 the British increased their amphibious-commando forces, building their limited carrier units into them, including in 1964 the purchase of American Phantom II carrier fighters.[104] As a result, the Royal Navy was able to demonstrate successfully in the Persian Gulf (Kuwait), off Tanzania and Rhodesia, and in the Indonesian confrontation during the 1960's—all independently of the United States but within the general strategic context of the *Pax Americana,* containing Communism and/or maintaining political stability upon the seas and coastal waters. Unfortunately for the coalition, the British between 1967 and 1971 withdrew their last major naval units from all waters east of Suez, leaving the United States to assume the burden of stabilizing the Indian Ocean and Persian Gulf.[105]

Despite considerable American naval demonstrations in the Middle East and off Quemoy-Matsu along the Chinese coast during the late 1950's, the United States Navy did not discover the weakness of its preoccupation with nuclear war strategy until the 1960's. The "quarantine" blockade of Cuba during the missile crisis of 1962—incidentally quietly opposed by the junior British partner[106]—restored the efficacy of naval blockade, while the growing American involvement in the Vietnam War (1965-1973) renewed the need for conventional inshore naval forces. Both events, though unilateral, did not undermine the alliance, while the Russian naval buildup and the announced British withdrawal from the Indian Ocean served to strengthen it, for the Russian penetration into that ocean after the Arab-Israeli war of 1967 led the Anglo-American-Commonwealth navies to seek common bases for action in the region. In addition, the United States and Britain began to shore up Iran as a buffer to Russian efforts in Iraq and the Persian Gulf. The American inability to fill the British vacuum in the Indian Ocean immediately, in fact, helped to induce the British to keep at least a token military force at Commonwealth Singapore during the 1970's. The Arab reaction (economic oil boycott) to American—and thus British—support of Israel during the October war of 1973, as well as increasing strains in the NATO arrangement, require renewed examination of the over-all strategy of the Anglo-American oceanic policy.[107]

The future of the Anglo-American partnership, whether under a continuing *Pax Americana* or within some new multilateral balance-of-power arrangement, will depend at least partly on the two-century-old traditions of a common maritime and strategic heritage. Much depends on the ability of American leaders to appreciate and apply the international rights of a maritime power. During the Cuban blockade of 1962 the United States did so, but would not blockade China during the Korean War and applied a full naval blockade to North Vietnam only very late in that war (1972).[108] Also, the actual British contribution continues to diminish, which has raised very legitimate fears over the future viability of British naval authority even in the Channel. Says Cable, "Unless the British Government can appear capable at least of disputing the rule of the Narrow Seas, the conduct of British foreign policy could become uncomfortably dependent on detailed American approval—and the availability of American warships."[109] Historically, it almost seems as if a cycle has been completed, with the Britain of 1975 virtually reliant upon the strength of American naval power just as the reverse was true in 1775. And yet, even should the official bonds of NATO be broken just as the political ties of Empire were shattered in the War of the American Revolution, one may assume that like maritime interests will forever link the Anglo-American peoples in common cause—in the Atlantic and throughout the world.

Between 1775 and 1975 the general strategic goals of the Anglo-American peoples have never changed, although over these two centuries the preponderance of the actual responsibility has shifted completely from the Royal Navy to the United States Navy. Cultural and ideological affinity may be explained as an essential part of this phenomenon, but more important has been the common desire to keep the seas free of forces dangerous to the survival of Anglo-American political freedom of action and economic prosperity made possible by seaborne trade. The essential goal of such a maritime strategy—command of the seas—has not changed appreciably over these years. In a very real sense, these two centuries have comprised an uneven record of both the British relearning the strengths of such a maritime strategy and the Americans learning them from the British.

By controlling the seas, Great Britain and the United States have contained, frustrated, and/or dictated international maritime law to France, Germany, Italy, Japan, and Russia (both tsarist and Soviet). In this strategic sense, then, the nineteenth and twentieth centuries have been aptly regarded respectively as the *Pax Britannica* and the *Pax Americana,* bringing international law and order to the high seas while chaos and upheaval have been more than norm ashore. If lessons may be gleaned from history, the English-speaking peoples have learned that they neglect their navies and a sagacious strategic use of them only at their peril.

Clark G. Reynolds

CHAPTER EIGHT

The Atlantic Paradox

THE ATLANTIC OCEAN has played a paradoxical role throughout the history of North America. From the beginning it has been a barrier, a moat isolating the continent from Europe and Africa and giving specific meaning to the term "New World." Yet at the same time the Atlantic has been a bridge between the Old World and the New. Moat and bridge—two contradictory themes which together have woven into the American fabric a special theme—the maritime way of life.

Man has always felt insecure upon the seas. For Aristotle, Homer, Vergil, and the writers of the Old Testament man's proper domain was clearly the land. In the Judaic-Christian story of the creation God first brought into being the seas, which He then "gathered together in one place and let the dry land appear." Man's world was thus encircled by a body of water which kept him within proper bounds. Significantly, the greatest disaster in the Old Testament was the flood of waters which the Jews believed God had called forth to destroy man's sinful world. Indeed, so terrifying was the idea of a flood in the minds of the Jews that they took pains to record God's promise never again to unleash such a calamity upon mankind.[1]

Through the early years of the Christian era western man explored the farthest corners of his land mass; by the fifteenth century most Europeans who thought about the matter agreed that the world had three parts—Europe, Asia, and Africa—connected to each other and bounded all around by a hostile sea. We know now that during this period some Europeans probed beyond these limits—Norsemen certainly and perhaps others as well. But any record of these voyages failed to find its way into the general body of knowledge and therefore had no effect on the world view of most Europeans. Columbus merely reflected the prevailing belief of his time when he assumed that the land he had reached by sailing west was the "backside," as it were, of the known world. Indeed, what else could he have considered it to be, given the cosmology of his time? As Edmundo O'Gorman has so brilliantly explained, nearly a generation passed before Europeans "invented America," convincing themselves that what Columbus encountered was not simply another part of the known world but literally a "new" world, unconnected to other land masses at any point. Thus from the beginning America was distinctly different *because* of the Atlantic Ocean.[2]

The Americans first affected by the fact of the Atlantic were of course the Indians. Lands into which they moved were vacant primarily because the Atlantic moat had prevented migrating Europeans from reaching America before them. More than that, the vastness of the ocean had isolated the Americas from the Old World in botanical and zoological terms as well. As Alfred W. Crosby has noted in his provocative work *The Columbian Exchange*, even Columbus, who after all believed himself simply to be in another part of the known world, still remarked that "all of the trees were as different from ours as day from night, and so the fruits, the herbage, the rocks, and all things." These variations proved very difficult to explain. It is not surprising that so many Europeans toyed with the heretical idea of multiple creation, a belief that both accepted and reinforced the concept that America had been from the beginning an island in the midst of an impassable sea. Buffon's contention that New World species were inferior to those of the Old gave new life to the concept of separate creation as late as the 1780's.[3]

Behind their protective moat for thousands of years the native Americans developed their distinctive cultures free from the influence of Old World institutions—without feudalism, without manorial estates, without religious wars pitting one sect against another. The first Americans were in the view of Alfred Crosby "more different from the rest of mankind in 1492 than any other major group of humanity" except for Australian aborigines. Scientists have concluded from the preponderance of O-type blood among American natives that they also possessed a genetic uniformity unmatched by any other group of humans spread over such a large area.[4]

But this cultural and biological isolation left the Indians totally defenseless against the European invaders who followed Columbus. No horse, no effective armor, no gunpowder. Far more significant, however, was the fact that the Atlantic moat had prevented the Indian from developing the defense he needed most—immunity against major European diseases like influenza, measles, and especially smallpox. The New World was conquered not so much by the gun as by the microbe. To cite but a single example, within fifty years after the first Spaniards reached the island of Hispaniola its native population fell from about one million to around five hundred, almost entirely the result of devastating epidemics.

For most Europeans the primary significance of the New World lay in the opportunity to exploit its largely untouched natural resources—gold, silver, fish, timber, and furs—and to bring Christianity to its heathen inhabitants. But England's Sir Thomas More thought otherwise. Writing in 1516, he placed his *Utopia* ("Nowhere") among the newly discovered lands across the western Atlantic. Its distance would isolate Utopia from the ills of European society—greed, warfare, misery, injustice. Its spaciousness would break the cycle of land hunger, war, and crime which led in More's view to Europe's repressive social order. Instead, Utopians would renounce gold and silver in favor of tilling the soil. Security and space were the conditions necessary for More's ideal society—conditions that could be found only in the newly discovered lands across the sea. But sixteenth-century England was not ready for Sir Thomas More's ideas. Not for another one hundred years would a group of his countrymen share his vision of what lay beyond the tempestuous Atlantic.

For the English Puritans the remoteness of America created still another meaning, the idea of the New World as a sanctuary for God's chosen people. The fact that in English eyes North America was vacant strengthened the conviction that God had intended it to be their promised land, as Canaan had been for the Hebrews. While John Winthrop and other Puritan leaders watched what they considered the decay of English society during the 1620's, they concluded that the old country was marked for eternal punishment by a wrathful God. By the end of the decade a considerable number of Englishmen agreed with Winthrop that withdrawal to New England was their best hope for perpetuating God's purified church.

Immigration to America, however, meant a permanent commitment to the New World, for few people would cross the ocean merely to seek temporary refuge during hard times. Especially in the seventeenth century, when vessels were small and ocean passages a novelty, the idea of such a crossing terrified otherwise brave men and women. Those among the Puritans who may have minimized the sea's dangers before their crossing had good reason to alter their opinions afterward. Winthrop admitted to his wife in England that his fleet had "a longe and troublesome passage," although in his journal he wrote in more positive terms of his experience. Other accounts spoke of bad weather, illness among the passengers, and death to more than one-third of the cattle being transported. Some saw in the necessity of crossing the Atlantic a divine test of their faith, the successful fulfillment of which confirmed in their minds that God had indeed protected them en route. Winthrop, for instance, likened the undertaking to the crossing of the Red Sea by the Jews. Others referred to the North Atlantic as a Sinai desert. One observer concluded that God had made the passage stormy so that New England "might not be deserted by them at first entrance, which sure it would have been by many."[5]

Another measure of the persistent impression made by the Atlantic crossing on New England Puritans was the continuing use of nautical references in the sermons of their ministers, most of whom had no contact with the sea before or after their own crossing. From his new pulpit deep in the Connecticut valley the Reverend Thomas Hooker warned his congregation of the "shipwrack" of heretical thought endangering its adherents "as a ship that is foundered in the midst of the main Ocean without the sight of any succor, or hope of Relief." Such errors were "as violent and boistrous winds and raging waves, [which] force the Vessel out of the channel" and lift "it upon the shore and shelves where it is set on ground, if not split." John Cotton cautioned those among his congregation who went to sea that their safety "lieth not on ropes or cables . . . , but in the name and hand of the Lord." The minister of inland Concord likened the man who depended on good works for salvation to "a wave of the Sea, tossed and tumbled up and down and [who] finds no rest." "People will accept of a quiet harbor," suggested another minister, "rather than be afflicted with continual tossings in stormy seas." The Reverend Thomas Shepard suffered such a difficult crossing himself that the experience of having "stood many a week within six inches of death" marked his sermons for twenty years thereafter. The now familiar metaphor "ship of state" appeared in numerous Puritan political writings of the seventeenth century, to suggest that the political establishment was like a vessel that bore its people safely through the seas of anarchy.[6]

The idea of crossing the Atlantic as a test was perpetuated by the American-born descendants of the Puritans as an indication of their forefathers' determination to be free of Old World restrictions. Thus the Reverend Thomas Allen of Pittsfield could write in 1775 that "our forefathers left the delightful abodes of their native country, passed a raging sea that in these then solitary climes they might enjoy civil and religious liberty, and never more feel the hand of tyranny and persecution." By the era of the Revolution, a willingness to brave the "raging sea" had become a part of the shared historical past that made Americans perceive themselves as a unique people—different from their English and European cousins.[7]

The crossing remained throughout the long era of immigration one of the most significant influences of the Atlantic on American life. Especially during the age of sail the course across the North Atlantic was fraught with danger. Prevailing winds and currents headed the westward voyagers much of the way; autumn hurricanes, winter gales, and springtime fogs limited the favorable season to a few short months. Even after steam replaced sail as the primary means of Atlantic navigation, the passage was sometimes dangerous and usually uncomfortable. But for the forty million immigrants to America an ocean crossing was the only way to reach the promised land. Few of them forgot the traumatic experience. Immigrant literature abounds with references to storms, shipwrecks, inedible food or none at all, arrogant captains and cruel sailors. The more impoverished the immigrant, the more helpless he was to protect himself and his family against these conditions. One vessel arrived at Philadelphia in 1805 with tales of the captain turning some of his passengers over to impressment gangs in England, then whipping and deliberately starving those who refused to go. In January 1868 the immigrant ship *Leibnitz* entered New York after a passage of about ten weeks, during which nearly 20 per cent of the original 554 German passengers on board had died. Upon inspection by the New York authorities the lower steerage was found to be so foul that their lanterns would hardly stay lighted. And for Africans forced to make the crossing on board the slave vessels of the eighteenth and early nineteenth centuries, conditions reached the very depths of inhumanity.

Year in and year out, disease, starvation, and shipwreck took a toll of from 10 to 20 per cent of all passengers, slave and free alike. Still more perished later from effects of the ocean passage. In 1847, for instance, ten thousand immigrants died in Quebec shortly after their arrival in the New World. Death at sea was a frightening prospect. Wrote one Irishman:

> Ah, we thought we couldn't be worse off than we war [in Ireland] but now to our sorrow we know the differ; for supposin we *war* dyin of starvation [at home], it would still not be dyin like rotten sheep thrown into a pit; and the minit the breath is out of our bodies, flung into the sea to be eaten up by them horrid sharks.[8]

Toward the end of the nineteenth century some of the worst conditions had been ameliorated by the strict enforcement of sanitary regulations, but crossing the Atlantic still retained its grim moments. In 1879 Robert Louis Stevenson described what life was like in the steerage of a steamer during a storm on the North Atlantic:

> A more forlorn party, a more dismal circumstance, it would be hard to imagine. The motion here in the ship's nose was very violent; the uproar of the sea often overpoweringly loud. . . .The air was hot, but it struck a chill from its foetor. From all around in the dark bunks the scarcely human noises of the sick joined in a kind of farmyard chorus. . . . I heard a man run wild with terror, beseeching his friend for encouragement. "The ship is going down!" he cried with a thrill of agony. "The ship is going down."[9]

The Atlantic Ocean proved to be a brutal filter for future Americans. Only those Europeans most desperate to reach the New World were willing to uproot themselves, scrape up the necessary funds, and take the chance of an ocean crossing. Yet so great was the commitment of some that they sold themselves into temporary servitude to pay off the cost of the passage. The harshness of the crossing itself eliminated those weak in body or spirit and left a residue of men and women toughened by the experience of what might almost be viewed as a national initiation rite. And perhaps the lingering memory of this rite gave those who went through it a special sense of belonging to America—which they might not have gained had the process of reaching this country been as simple as, say, crossing the border between Belgium and France. At the least, recollection of the crossing discouraged thoughts of returning home even among the many immigrants disappointed in their New World life.

The impact of this experience on American life becomes even more apparent when one realizes that as recently as 1930 one out of every three American families included at least one parent who had made the passage. Even now the third generation of the nation's last immigrant families vividly remembers grandparents telling of their trepidation at boarding the vessel that would take them across the ocean—an anxiety born not only from a fear of the sea itself but from the sense that they would probably never see their homeland again.

The same ocean that had preserved North America as a virgin land before the Europeans' arrival thereafter, with the interior wilderness, formed a great hedge which the Puritans believed God had thrown up around them in New England. The hedge simultaneously preserved the promised land from evil influences of the outside world and prevented dissidents within the community from escaping their responsibilities by fleeing. The Atlantic moat shielded the Puritans against whatever punishment God might ultimately visit upon the inhabitants of the decadent Old World. More specifically, with the ocean protecting their rear they could concentrate their defenses against the Indians along the land frontier. The folklore historian Richard M. Dorson has observed that later immigrant groups seemed to remember the demons and other supernatural beings of their culture only in relation to Old Country habitats. When asked why these beings were never seen in America, one immigrant explained with an embarrassed laugh that "they're scared to pass the ocean; it's too far."[10]

In short, the ocean barrier strengthened the migrants' original commitment to America and reinforced their conviction that as residents of a distinctive New World they were themselves a distinctive, chosen people. The Atlantic moat also compelled these new Americans to look to their future in the New World, not to their past in the Old. As for the Puritans, so also for the millions of immigrants who followed them across the Atlantic. Few of them would return to their homeland; many would come to believe themselves a special people (and certainly their descendants have done so); and almost all have been conditioned to be future-oriented in their outlook.

Of these several themes, perhaps the isolation of America from the Old World has remained one of the Atlantic's most persistent functions. As long as they remained colonists of Great Britain, the Americans did become embroiled in numerous European wars, but rarely in more than a peripheral role. The devastating Indian wars resulted more from American expansion than from the instigation of Frenchman and Spaniard. The Atlantic itself, and the supremacy of the British fleet upon it, minimized the number of direct attacks from French, Spanish, or Dutch forces against American settlements. At the same time, the vast expanse of the Atlantic worked its inexorable force against effective English governance in the American colonies. Edmund Burke put it clearly enough in his speech to Parliament "On Conciliation with America" in 1775:

> Three thousand miles of ocean lie between you and them. No contrivance can prevent the effect of this distance in weakening government. Seas roll, and months pass, between the order and the execution; and the want of a speedy explanation of a single point is enough to defeat the whole system. . . . In large bodies, the circulation of power must be less vigorous at the extremities. Nature has said it.[11]

Thomas Paine was only the most articulate of many pamphleteers who carried the theme still further to justify American independence. "Even the distance at which the Almighty hath placed England and America," he wrote in *Common Sense,* "is a strong and natural proof that the authority of the one over the other was never the design of Heaven."[12] When the War of Independence erupted in 1775, the vast expanse of the Atlantic proved a most difficult obstacle to British forces. Although they maintained command of the seas for most of the war, the one time they lost it off the Chesapeake at the end of August 1781, the loss proved fatal to their cause.

The presence of the Atlantic was felt not by political figures alone. One of the phrases most frequently used by English and American correspondents during the eighteenth century was "your side the water." That is, men of both countries routinely recognized that the ocean was a line of demarcation between them, and both came to expect that Americans would have different interests from the mother country, even different customs and institutions. For despite the conscious effort of most first-generation immigrants to model their new society on English forms, through the passage of time many of them forgot just how things were done in the Old World. For their children and grandchildren, knowledge of European experience depended on hearsay, though some tried to keep up through books, magazines, and other indirect contact with the Old World.

Furthermore, unique American conditions led to different institutions and practices, even different meanings for the same words and different words for the same objects or concepts. One example will do. In eighteenth-century England the idea of political representation meant that all the major interests of the realm—royalty, aristocracy, church, military, and in time the mercantile and manufacturing interests—should have a voice in shaping national policy. In America, however, the concept has meant from the beginning a delegation of authority from towns, counties, and other grass-roots communities to a central law-making body. In America, it was people who were represented; in England, interests. Such a difference in meaning had little significance until the question of "no taxation without representation" arose in the 1760's. The British argued that the American interest was "virtually" represented in Parliament through the various members who were merchants trading with the colonies. Americans, however, knew that they were not actually represented, nor, because of the Atlantic Ocean, could they be, in the sense of sending delegates to that body.

The presence of the Atlantic encouraged other differences between mother country and colonies as well. England in fact expected the colonies to be different and considered them inferior political and economic communities to the mother country. Fair enough: that was what an empire was all about. But the idea of inferiority did not stop at political or economic considerations. Many eighteenth-century Englishmen regarded the colonists themselves as inferior people, whose demands for equality were "insolent" and "arrogant," to note but two descriptive adjectives commonly used. Britons especially resented the fact that the New Englanders rebelling against the mother country were descended from those Puritans who had "run out" on their fellow countrymen in the 1630's when obstensibly stauncher patriots remained in England to fight the good fight against the Stuart tyranny. Of course many Americans have in turn felt inferior to Englishmen, and some still do. Thomas Paine, on the other hand, saw the Atlantic moat in quite a different light soon after his arrival in America in 1774:

> Degeneracy here is almost a useless word. Those who are conversant with Europe would be tempted to believe that even the air of the Atlantic disagrees with the constitution of foreign vices; if they survive the voyage they either expire on their arrival or linger away in an incurable consumption.[13]

For both Englishmen and Americans, the Atlantic moat seriously impaired the mutual understanding on which good relations depended.

To Americans of the early Republic the Atlantic Ocean seemed an adequate bulwark against whatever they considered the most serious manifestation of European depravity—monarchy, Jacobinism, Catholicism, poverty. Clearly the nation turned inland during the course of the nineteenth century for reasons having little directly to do with the ocean. But the freedom to move west resulted in part from the sense of security that the Atlantic moat created. The idea of America as a special land emerged as a cardinal principle in American foreign policy in the Monroe Doctrine during this period. "The political system of the allied powers [France, Austria, and Russia] is essentially different . . . from that of America," the President declared, and henceforth the Western Hemisphere was to be considered closed to further colonization by European nations. Monroe pledged in return a continuation of his government's policy toward Europe "not to interfere in the internal concerns of any of its powers." In declaring that the Americas were different from Europe, Monroe was also saying that the two New World continents had much in common, a proposition that most North Americans refused to honor at the time or, indeed, for many generations thereafter.[14]

The Atlantic barrier had profound cultural influence on the young nation in the nineteenth century. In making America geographically distinctive, the Atlantic compelled Americans to become culturally distinctive as well. For most this was a welcome opportunity; for some, like poets Philip Freneau, Joel Barlow, and philosopher Ralph Waldo Emerson, it was a necessary companion to political independence. Henry David Thoreau considered the Atlantic as America's "opportunity to forget the Old World." Whatever the conscious efforts of writers and other cultural pacesetters, however, the isolated situation of Americans continued under its own momentum to add original and unique customs and institutions to the national pattern, free from the ill effects of the wars, revolutions, and class turmoil that periodically erupted on the continent of Europe. No matter what his origin—Irish, German, Italian, or Polish—the nineteenth-century immigrant seemed to take on the ways of America with alacrity. The very fact that newcomers streamed across the Atlantic throughout the century in ever increasing numbers stood as incontrovertible proof that America's unique role as a sanctuary remained valid to millions of Europeans.

Long after the Atlantic moat had begun to lose its effectiveness in cultural respects, it seemed to retain validity in matters pertaining to foreign affairs. As the United States emerged at the end of the nineteenth century as a world power, its first efforts at imperial diplomacy pointed south into the Caribbean and west across the Pacific. With only a few exceptions, Americans remained aloof from the diplomatic affairs of the Old World, even while making war (and peace) with the ancient European power, Spain. This century's first new President, Theodore Roosevelt, did not hesitate to take a major role in the diplomacy of Asia when the opportunity to mediate the Russo-Japanese War presented itself. Among the numerous reasons for these patterns of diplomatic behavior, I think, is the fact that most Americans continued to view the world on the other side of the Atlantic as a threat, while Asian matters seemed far less dangerous. This attitude of course continued well into the era of World War I, through the interbellum period to the end of 1941. When one reads through the debates surrounding the ratification of the Versailles treaty and the League of Nations, he realizes how great a departure was the entry of the United States into World War I after all. Surely it is no coincidence that active American participation in World War II came not as a result of any European confrontation but rather from an act of aggression on the opposite side of the globe. The Atlantic still separated the United States from the European war; when we finally intervened, it was in response to a declaration of war by Germany, not by our own initiative.

The significance of the Atlantic Ocean in the foreign affairs of the United States well illustrates the paradoxical role that it has played in the nation's past. The irony lies in the extent to which our involvement in European wars has actually resulted from our dependence upon the Atlantic. It was the series of affronts to American national pride beginning with the *Chesapeake-Leopard* affair that led to the War of 1812, not lust for Canadian lands or for Florida. In supporting an increase in the naval establishment in January 1812, Kentucky's senator Henry Clay told his fellows: "If you wish to avoid foreign collision, you had better abandon the ocean—surrender all your commerce; give up all your prosperity. . . . Commerce engenders collision."[15] American entry into World War I would be difficult to explain without reference to Germany's policy of unrestricted submarine warfare announced in February 1917. The case is not quite so clear for World War II, since by then ideological ties with England, and revulsion against Nazi Germany, had become major forces within the American political arena. Yet some historians have recently suggested that a congressional majority favoring war with Germany might have been hard to muster even after Pearl Harbor had Hitler not made the decision for us. And it is worth noting that at least some of the pro-war sentiment that did develop in Congress during the fall of 1941 came not from a desire to help Great Britain or to stem the expansion of Nazism in Europe, but out of resentment against such confrontations on the Atlantic as resulted in the *Kearney* and *Reuben James* affairs.

At the same time that for most Americans the Atlantic remained a moat separating them from the Old World, for others the sea became a bridge to new opportunities. Americans' first significant experience with the Atlantic after the initial crossing involved fishing voyages and coastwise trading ventures. While some of the southern colonists engaged in a little fishing in the bays and rivers of their region, the best grounds lay off the coast of New England and Canada. Although fish was not the colonists' favorite food, it was no less welcome in their households as a dependable source of nutrition. With the rapid expansion of plantations in southern and Caribbean colonies during the eighteenth century came a greatly increased demand for fish as a cheap item in the diet of slaves. As a commodity in overseas trade, fish ranked close behind tobacco and rice by the eve of the Revolution. More directly, of course, this widening demand brought increased opportunity for the fishermen of New England, and for the men who built their vessels and marketed their catch. A more specialized activity, whaling, gave work to the crews of over three hundred vessels and provided valuable cargoes for sale on the London market.

From the first settlements in the seventeenth century, the colonists depended heavily upon water transportation along the Atlantic seaboard. Uneven terrain, broad rivers, mud, and snow all inhibited the cartage of goods by land. Water routes between many ports were actually shorter, and transportation by water, especially of bulk commodities, cost far less (and still does). Coastwise traffic was at first largely limited to local areas, but by the late seventeenth century northern merchants began to exchange the products of their region for the produce of the southern plantations to obtain the returns they needed for their growing trade with the mother country. The coastwise commerce continued to expand throughout the eighteenth century. Besides fish, New England shipped quantities of rum and various timber products south, while the middle colonies sent out bread, flour, and provisions. In addition to tobacco, indigo, and rice for export to Europe, the northerners also acquired for themseves wheat and corn from the Chesapeake and naval stores from the Carolinas. Meanwhile, coastal routes expanded to include English and foreign West Indian islands and the Maritime Provinces after they had been won from France. Now sugar and molasses were added to the list of goods suitable for returns in the English trade, as American merchants found their fish, timber, provisions, and breadstuffs in great demand among the Caribbean plantations.

It is not so much the commerce itself which is interesting here, for that is an old story, but only recently have historians recognized the full significance of coastal and West Indian trade as a stimulus to the colonial economy and as a force for change during the first half of the eighteenth century. Wheat farmers of the middle colonies, timber merchants and rum manufacturers of New England, and even planters of the Chesapeake all profited from the fact that the western margin of the Atlantic provided cheap access to markets for their produce in other American colonies. The consequences of this expansion profoundly altered the way of life in many a New England village, hastening the change from a closed Puritan corporation to an open Yankee community. Wheat and corn gave the planters of Virginia and Maryland a much needed alternative to the tobacco which was fast exhausting the soil of the tidewater. By the 1760's for instance, George Washington had almost completely switched over his Mount Vernon farms to the production of grains, and he continued to experiment with new crops for the remainder of the century. In Pennsylvania the expanding market for flour led to what one historian has regarded as the first real factories in the colonies, the large merchant mills in and around Philadelphia. On a less tangible level, coastwise commerce brought an exchange of cultural influences among the continental colonies, ranging from the furniture trade to the exchange of newspapers and pamphlets. Without the line of communications developed through decades of coastwise commerce, the degree of political cooperation necessary for revolution would have been far more difficult to establish in the 1770's.

Meanwhile, an Atlantic community that transcended national boundaries had begun to take shape in the mid-seventeenth century. Its foundation rested on the mutual dependence of Europe upon America for staples like tobacco, sugar, indigo, fish, and rice, and the New World's need for the manufactured goods of the Old. The mutual interest of commerce gradually drew together merchants in England's major ports, in Ireland, the Maritime Provinces, the mainland American colonies, as well as in the West Indies, the Atlantic islands, the Iberian peninsula, and the ports of northern Europe. As Bernard Bailyn has shown, many of these commercial contacts were established among mercantile brothers, sons, and other kinship relations. The Winthrop family, for instance, from beginnings in England and Massachusetts, soon had representatives in Rhode Island, Connecticut, Antigua, and the Canary Islands. Whenever any member of a commercial family moved to a new location, he and his descendants became potential factors in the expansion of commercial interests. And both Englishmen and Frenchmen were especially mobile during the seventeenth and eighteenth centuries.[16]

The men who carried on these activities soon shed their provincial origins and became sophisticated men of the world. Unlike other colonists, the merchants and planters who regularly traded across the Atlantic could order their clothes, books, and household furnishings directly from the mother country and even send their sons across for a proper education under the watchful eye of a business associate. Their economic success was easily translated into political and social power within their local regions. Preferential treatment from governors, legislatures, and other political authorities in turn reinforced their economic strength. All over the Atlantic world the merchants became a new force within societies that had previously been dominated almost entirely by the landed interest.[17]

Although severely strained during the half-century of the American Revolution and Napoleonic Wars, the commercial threads that knit together this Atlantic world survived the crisis. American merchants continued their intercourse with English correspondents whenever conditions allowed vessels to sail. Mercantile houses on the Iberian peninsula similarly maintained contact with English and American associates through the turmoil of war and revolution. Retiring merchants handed down these special connections to successors from generation to generation—relationships that were jealously maintained, for they gave older mercantile houses a distinct advantage over would-be competitors. Newcomers were often forced into other more risky (but potentially more profitable) ventures beyond the Atlantic world into the Mediterranean, the Indian Ocean, and particularly the Pacific. Despite the more glamorous aspects of these distant routes, however, the main line across the North Atlantic remained the predominant maritime interest of both Great Britain and the United States. Only the commodities involved changed somewhat, tobacco giving way to cotton, and coffee becoming more important.

The Asian trade was one exception to the general rule that the commerce of the Atlantic world centered on the exchange of goods grown or manufactured within that area. As early as the seventeenth century English, Dutch, and French East India companies had brought in numerous Asian commodities, including tea, silks and other cloth goods, and spices. And as we have seen, after the Revolution American merchants also began to introduce various Asian goods into the Atlantic trading world, but this business was never so important as was commerce within the community itself. A far more significant exception, however, was the forcible transportation of some ten million Africans from their homelands beyond the North Atlantic world into the European colonies of America. The cultivation of staple crops in the Caribbean and southern continental plantations would have been impossible without such workers, but the cost in human terms is beyond calculation. For blacks the Atlantic was first a bridge to the hell of New World enslavement, then a moat that cut them off from their African homes thereafter. The Atlantic was in fact a far more formidable barrier for Afro-Americans than for transplanted Europeans, who had at least some opportunity to keep alive their Old World roots through occasional communications. The survival of an Afro-American heritage within the culture of the New World becomes thereby a truly remarkable feat.

By the beginning of the nineteenth century the fruits of Atlantic commerce began to acquire new dimensions. The only significant path to wealth in preindustrial America was through the merchant's counting house. Southern planters lived high enough, but they were almost always in debt. Artisans rarely achieved more than a modest middle-class prosperity, even during the best of times. Land speculators were at the mercy of a boom-and-bust economy. But for a merchant to make it big in America was no longer unusual even by the eighteenth century. Thomas Hancock had amassed an estate of £100,000 at his death in 1764. During the years of neutral trade from 1793 to 1812 truly large fortunes were made. Even in a small outport such as Newburyport, the son of a cordwainer, William Bartlet, could parlay already impressive stakes of about $100,000 to a total of $500,000 by the eve of the War of 1812. Much of Bartlet's property was relatively liquid. In addition to his warehouses, vessels, and stock in trade, he owned shares in a bank, an insurance company, a turnpike, and a woolen manufactory.[18]

Like so many other New England merchants, Bartlet began to invest much of his capital in the manufacture of cotton goods in the years after the War of 1812, an example of the well-known shift from wharf to waterfall. Perhaps the reason was simply to maximize profits, as most historians have assumed, but Robert F. Dalzell has suggested other possible motives. For one thing, the manufacture of cheap cotton goods was a far less risky investment in the first half of the nineteenth century than was overseas commerce. Those who have already acquired a fortune, as Bartlet had, tend to think of ways to preserve it rather than to increase it. Furthermore, agents could be hired to run factories, while mercantile houses required the constant attention of the firm's senior partners. Many of New England's merchants were anxious to buy more leisure with their investment in cotton mills so that they could devote more time to their charitable and cultural interests. Bartlet, for instance, had commitments to a local academy, a library, and a Bible society, and he was also a major supporter of the Andover Theological Seminary, an institution that took much of his time and money. The number of Boston merchants who turned simultaneously to factories and charitable activities—Lawrence, Perkins, Howe, and others—is too great to be discounted. Capital earned in the Atlantic trade not only transformed New England's economy but gave significant support to a wide range of social reforms and other activities. Considering the fact that so much of this wealth originated in the plantation trade, it is ironic that profits should underwrite the work of various antislavery societies among other reforms.[19]

As the nineteenth century progressed, the effect of the Atlantic trade began to reach far into the interior of the American continent. Foodstuffs such as coffee, tea, and sugar; textiles like cotton and woolen goods; chinaware, cutlery, and other tools remained high on the list of imports into the nation's economy. In addition to the cotton which vessels carried to England and France in vast quantities, tobacco, wheat and flour, beef and pork products, and the first fruits of America's infant factories found markets in the West Indies, South America, and Europe. Vessels plying the coastal routes from Maine to Texas carried goods from one part of the expanding nation to the other. With the discovery of gold in California at mid-century "coastal" commerce took on a new dimension. And within a decade gold and silver bullion had risen to second place in value among the nation's exports, much of it used to purchase imports from England and France. As of 1860, the position of the Atlantic in America's over-all trade remained unchallenged—its routes represented more than 80 per cent of the nation's commerce by value. This economic exchange gave further impetus to the gradual transformation of both England and America. The former was already on its way to becoming a nation of shopkeepers. As Lewis Namier pointed out: "Trade was acknowledged to be the great concern of the [British] nation; and money was honored, the mystic, common denominator of all values." America would remain predominantly rural for the first century after independence, but its farmers, unlike those of Europe, already aspired to the possession of commodities obtainable at that time only by trade across the Atlantic.[20]

During the first half of the nineteenth century American farmers were becoming even more dependent upon other nations of the Atlantic community as markets for their surplus production. The rich lands of Indiana, Illinois, Iowa, and Wisconsin produced far more wheat and corn than the Americans themselves could consume. Even more significant were the remarkably fertile cotton lands opening up in the Mississippi delta and eastern Texas in the 1840's and 1850's. By 1860 America was exporting about $250 million worth of agricultural produce (out of exports totaling $316 million), mostly across the Atlantic to Great Britain and France, of which cotton amounted to about four-fifths. Without cheap water transportation to the voracious markets of Europe, clearly the expansion of market farming into the northwest and southwest would have been severely limited. The famed "westward movement" owes a debt to the Atlantic ocean not often acknowledged by landbound historians.

In addition to the manufactured goods brought back to the United States (to the annual value of over $200 million in 1860), American ships carried over five million immigrants into the new nation in the four decades between 1820 and 1860. In an era when the indenture was no longer deemed appropriate, few of these German, Irish, and English immigrants could have reached their New World destination without the availability of cheap westbound transportation on board the ships that had carried the produce of American farms and plantations to Europe. The significance of this human commerce transcends the numerical terminology of the economist and becomes a part of the national fabric, as these immigrants became new citizens of the United States.

Commerce on the Atlantic provided markets for farm produce, supplied manufactured articles for American consumers, and generated surplus capital for investment in industries. But there were less direct benefits as well. Particularly in the early decades of the nineteenth century, maritime commerce provided a nursery for businessmen, giving them the opportunity to learn the skills of management which so many would later apply to land-based industrial activities. Not only did a fair amount of capital shift from wharf to waterfall but—equally important—experienced businessmen made the change as well. Measured in yet other economic terms, the value of American commerce becomes still more extraordinary. With the exception of only a few years, until the 1890's the federal government derived over half its annual revenue from customs duties. In only two years during that century-long period did the sale of public lands bring a higher return than duties on imports. And in a banner year for commerce, like 1854, customs accounted for about seven out of every eight dollars received by the federal treasury. Almost all of the dutiable goods entered through Atlantic ports.

Yet another result of this burgeoning Atlantic trade in the two hundred years from the mid-seventeenth to the mid-nineteenth century was the development of the seaport. Most port towns of England and northern Europe had developed gradually through many centuries of relatively short-haul trade amongst themselves across the English Channel and North Sea. The rise of Atlantic commerce merely built upon these medieval foundations. Europe, in short, already had cities before the rise of maritime expansion. For America, however, the seaport and the city were synonymous until well into the nineteenth century. Of the twenty largest population centers before the American Revolution, only Lancaster, Pennsylvania, was not on Atlantic tidewater. Atlantic commerce not only accounted for the founding and growth of most of these urban centers, it prevented some of them from disappearing altogether as population moved inland. Compare Plymouth with Jamestown, for instance. The Pilgrim town might well have gone the way of its sister pioneer community on the James had not the sea continued to offer the men of Plymouth a livelihood. The proliferation of such communities along the Atlantic seaboard from Passamaquoddy to Delaware Bay, long after interior regions with their superior soil had become safely settled, suggests that their inhabitants looked to the Atlantic for their future.

In his two-volume study of five American seaports during the colonial period, Carl Bridenbaugh was bold enough to label these communities "cities." Three of them, Boston, New York, and Philadelphia, along with Baltimore, continued to grow rapidly after the Revolution, and by 1800 each of the four could boast a population of at least twenty-five thousand inhabitants, enough to meet any reasonable definition of a city in the early nineteenth century. All of the major problems which we have since identified with urban life—housing, sanitation, public safety—challenged the inhabitants of these Atlantic communities. Furthermore, with the exception of Philadelphia, their seaboard locations severely limited the direction of their growth. Greater Boston, New York, and Baltimore were all intersected with rivers and inlets which necessitated reliance on numerous ferries and bridges for internal communication. Yet the economic opportunity offered by the Atlantic world encouraged growth despite these handicaps and despite the mounting competition from inland regions for both capital and people.

But seaports developed rather differently from inland communities. For one thing, they were laid out around a harbor, and because waterfront space was severely limited, the heart of a seaport town became far more compact than the typical inland city of similar population. Warehouses, shops, and other commercial buildings crowded into every square foot of space within walking or carting distance of the waterfront, as construction went up three, four, or more stories. The harbor itself remained common public property, belonging to the community as a whole long after the common lands of inland towns had been distributed to private owners. The fact that the seaport community had a stake in the harbor produced a degree of cohesiveness in its social and political structure. Initial responsibility for such projects as the construction of jetties and lighthouses, the establishment of buoys and other navigational aids, and the maintenance of a piloting service fell to local public authorities doing what they considered best for the community. Likewise, along the waterfront itself were publicly maintained wharves and landing places and publicly built marketplaces. Inland towns by contrast were far more diffuse, with their centrifugal force-lines reaching out in all directions to the privately owned farms around the center, while the seaport held its population in close around the public domain of the harbor, which was the only gateway to the Atlantic world beyond.

These differences between seaports and inland towns point to a more fundamental contrast that I have called the Atlantic paradox. We have already noted that for most Americans the Atlantic has been a moat cutting them off from the rest of the world. Paradoxically, however, for a small number of citizens living in seaports and other coastal communities, the sea has been a bridge to opportunity and to new and different experiences. Like most paradoxes, the juxtaposition of the Atlantic's roles as both moat and bridge has never been resolved for most Americans, nor is it ever likely to be. Yet it is precisely this paradox that has made the maritime way of life a subject of such enduring interest. *Because* millions of landbound Americans view the sea as an impassable moat, the lives of those who paradoxically use it as a bridge are that much more fascinating. For only in their lives can the Atlantic paradox find resolution.

The maritime way of life has intrigued landsmen for a number of reasons. For one, going to sea has always been an uncommon experience in this nation. Mariners, fishermen, and others who work on the sea have never comprised more than a small minority within the labor force. At the height of maritime enterprise in the mid-nineteenth century, fewer than 1 per cent of the work-force of ten millions went to sea for a living. Furthermore, seafaring has been one of the most dangerous of all occupations. Specific mortality figures are difficult to compile, but the experience of Gloucester's fishing fleet suggests the risks involved. In the twenty-two-year period 1861-1882, almost two thousand Gloucester fishermen lost their lives at sea—an annual average of eighty-eight. This figure represents one fatality for every seventy fishermen of the port as of 1885. In contrast, another dangerous occupation, railroading, reached about half that rate at its worst, while still another high-risk endeavor, mining, proved even less devastating to its workers.[21]

Yet another fascinating aspect of the mariners' way of life was how utterly different it was from anything experienced by those who worked ashore. The sailor committed himself totally to his vessel—he had no other existence for the duration of the voyage, no contact with family or friends, no privacy, no personal freedom. From the moment he stepped aboard he became part of a rigidly structured work-force under that most authoritarian of all bosses, the shipmaster. In contrast, a very large number of landsmen worked for themselves as farmers, small entrepreneurs, or skilled craftsmen, and self-employment remained a realizable dream for at least some of those who worked for others. And even the factory and other laborers had families and a degree of privacy. Except perhaps for the Gloucester doryman, virtually no mariner worked alone at sea; the success of his efforts and indeed his very life depended on the skill and cooperation of others. This principle of interdependence was also reflected in the joint ownership of vessels and their cargoes, and in the public's awareness of their coming and going. In short, mariners were and remain rather special people among Americans because they constantly risk their lives to bridge the dreaded moat.

The sea voyage has always been an extremely popular theme in American literature and to a slightly lesser extent in American art as well. By reading about those who went down to the sea, landbound Americans could themselves vicariously bridge the moat. That basic ingredient of all good stories—conflict—is a dominant theme at sea and compels the reader to put himself to the test, alongside the story's main characters. Furthermore, the sea is mysterious as well as dangerous, and the reader is transported into an environment totally different from the familiar land. "How I spurned that turnpike earth!" said Ishmael as he sailed for Nantucket, "that common highway all over dented with the marks of slavish heels and hoofs; and turned me to admire the magnanimity of the sea which will permit no records."[22]

The Atlantic, of course, is but one of the several seas upon which American mariners have sailed. While the Pacific and Indian oceans are more remote and are ringed by perhaps more exotic cultures, the Atlantic has borne the great majority of American coastal, fishing, and deepwater voyages. It remains the ocean that has most profoundly affected the history of America, both as a barrier separating us from our European past and as a bridge to that older world.

Benjamin W. Labaree

CHAPTER NINE

The Writings of Robert G. Albion

I. BOOKS

A. REFERENCE WORKS

Naval and Maritime History: An Annotated Bibliography. 1st edition, privately duplicated, 1951; 4th edition, Mystic Seaport, Conn., The Marine Historical Association, Incorporated, 1972.

B. GENERAL HISTORY

History of England and the Empire-Commonwealth (with J. B. Pope and W. P. Hall). 1st edition, New York, Ginn and Company, 1938; 5th edition, 1971.

Philip Vickers Fithian: Journal on the Virginia-Pennsylvania Frontier and in the Army Around New York, 1775-1776 (with L. Dodson). Princeton, N. J., Princeton University Press, 1938; Hamden, Conn., Archon Books, 1965.

C. MILITARY HISTORY

Introduction to Military History. New York, The Century Company, 1929.

D. NAVAL HISTORY

Forests and Sea Power, The Timber Problem of the Royal Navy, 1652-1862. (Harvard Economic Studies, No. 29.) Cambridge, Mass., Harvard University Press, 1926; Hamden, Conn., Archon Books, 1965.

The Development of Naval Districts, 1903-1945. Washington, United States Navy Department, 1945.

The Navy at Sea and Ashore, an Informal Account of the Organization and Workings of the Naval Establishment of the United States Today with Some Historical Notes on Its Development (with S. H. P. Reed). Washington, United States Navy Department, 1947.

Makers of Navy Policy, 1798-1947. Washington, D.C., 1950. (Manuscript available on microfilm at Harvard and Princeton libraries.)

Forrestal and the Navy (with R. H. Connery and J. B. Pope). New York, Columbia University Press, 1962.

E. MARITIME HISTORY

Square-Riggers on Schedule: The New York Sailing Packets to England, France, and the Cotton Ports. Princeton, N. J., Princeton University Press, 1938; Hamden, Conn., Archon Books, 1965.

The Rise of New York Port, 1815-1860 (with J. B. Pope). New York, Charles Scribner's Sons, 1939; Hamden, Conn., Archon Books, 1961. 2nd edition, Scribner's, 1972.

Sea Lanes in Wartime: The American Experience, 1775-1942 (with J. B. Pope). New York, W. W. Norton & Company, Inc., 1942; revised edition, (1775-1945), Hamden, Conn., Archon Books, 1968.

The National Shipping Authority, Its Origin and Early Development. 1951. (Manuscript copies available at the Department of Commerce and Harvard libraries.)

Seaports South of Sahara: The Achievements of an American Steamship Service. New York, Appleton-Century-Crofts, Inc., 1959.

Exploration and Discovery. New York, The Macmillan Company, 1965.

New England and the Sea (with W. A. Baker and B. W. Labaree). (American Maritime Library, V.) Middletown, Conn., Wesleyan University Press (for The Marine Historical Association, Incorporated), 1972.

II. CHAPTERS IN COOPERATIVE WORKS

"Primacy of the Port of New York," in A. C. Flick, ed., *History of the State of New York*. New York, Columbia University Press, 1935.

"Maritime Adventures of New York in the Napoleonic Era," in *Essays in Modern History Presented to Wilbur Cortez Abbott*. Cambridge, Mass., Harvard University Press, 1941.

"Sea Routes," in Critchell Rimington, ed., *Merchant Fleets*. New York, Dodd, Mead & Company, 1944.

"Colonial Commerce and Commercial Regulation," in H. F. Williamson, ed., *Growth of the American Economy*. New York, Prentice-Hall, Inc., 1944; 2nd edition, 1951.

"Foreign Trade in the Era of Wooden Ships," in Williamson, *Growth of the American Economy*.

"Sea Lure," in Robert W. Howard, ed., *This Is the South*. Chicago, Rand McNally & Company, 1959.

III. REFERENCE ARTICLES

A. DICTIONARY OF AMERICAN BIOGRAPHY

Josiah Barker
William Bayard
Jacob Bell
John Bertram
Thomas Boyle
Thomas Buchanan
James W. Chever
Elijah Cobb
Edward K. Collins
Josiah P. Creesy
George Crowninshield
Ralph Earle
Edmund Fanning
Preserved Fish
Robert B. Forbes
Caleb Gardner
Thomas Gibbons
William R. Grace
John C. Green
Nathan Green
John W. Griffiths
Samuel Hall
Gardiner G. Howland
Stephen Jumel
Edward C. Knight
Henry Laurens
George Law
Charles A. McAllister
Charles H. Marshall
William L. Merry
Robert B. Minturn
Charles Morgan
Walter D. Munson
Aaron Ogden
David B. Ogden
Charles S. Olden
Eugenius H. Outerbridge
Nathaniel B. Palmer
Josiah Peabody
John Pintard
Lewis P. Price
Rodman M. Price
George W. Quintard
Marshall O. Roberts
Samuel Samuels
Comfort Sands
William Scarborough
Nathaniel Scudder
Thomas L. Servoss
Arthur Sewall
Harold M. Sewall
William J. Sewell
Joshua Slocum
Junius Smith

Richard Smith
Robert A. C. Smith
Samuel L. Southard
John H. Starin
John L. Stephens
Thomas Tileston
Enoch Train
Charles Vaughan
William Vernon
James E. Ward
William H. Webb
Jacob A. Westervelt
William Wheelwright
Isaac H. Williamson

B. ENCYCLOPAEDIA BRITANNICA

Salem

C. ENCYCLOPEDIA INTERNATIONAL

Cargo
Columbus
Exploration
History of the Pacific Ocean
Inland Waterways
Merchant Marine Academies
Merchant Shipping
Titanic

D. COLLIER'S ENCYCLOPEDIA

Merchant Marine

E. ENCYCLOPEDIA AMERICANA

Merchant Marine
Warships

F. GROLIER'S ENCYCLOPEDIA

Flags of Convenience
Merchant Marine

G. AMERICAN NEPTUNE

"Recent Writings in Maritime History," 1952-1958.

IV. PERIODICAL ARTICLES

"Admiralty Prize Case Briefs," *American Historical Review,* XXXIII (April 1928), pp. 593-595.

"New York and Its Rivals," *Journal of Economic and Business History,* III (August 1931), pp. 602-629.

"The Communication Revolution," *American Historical Review,* XXXVII (July 1932), pp. 718-720.

"Yankee Domination of New York Port, 1820-65," *New England Quarterly,* V (October 1932), pp. 665-698.

"The Communications Revolution, 1760-1933," *Transactions of the Newcomen Society,* XIV (1933-1934), pp. 13-25.

"Commercial Fortunes in New York . . . About 1850," *New York History,* XVI (April 1935), pp. 158-168.

"Problems of Sea Power," *Princeton University Faculty-Alumni Forum,* 14 June 1935, pp. 17-31.

"New York Port in the New Republic, 1783-1793," *New York History,* XXI (October 1940), pp. 388-403.

"Inspection Comments on American Ships and Barks," *American Neptune,* I (January 1941), pp. 42-50.

"Early Nineteenth-Century Shipowning, a Chapter in Business Enterprise," *Journal of Economic History,* I (May 1941), pp. 1-11.

"Administration of the Navy, 1798-1945," *Public Administration Review,* V (Autumn 1945), pp. 293-302.

"The First Days of the Navy Department," *Military Affairs,* XIII (Spring 1948), pp. 1-11.

"State, War, and Navy—Under One Roof, 1882," *United States Naval Institute Proceedings,* LXXC (July 1949), pp. 792-795.

"Timber Problem of the Royal Navy, 1652-1852" (Maritime Miscellany Series, No. 5), *Mariners' Mirror,* XXXVIII (February 1952), pp. 1-22.

"Naval Affairs Committees, 1816-1947," *United States Naval Institute Proceedings,* LXXVIII (November 1952), pp. 1226-1237.

"Distant Stations," *United States Naval Institute Proceedings,* LXXX (March 1954), pp. 264-273.

"The Two Ports," *Ships and the Sea* (Fall 1954), pp. 22-23, 44-50.

"Communications and Remote Control," *United States Naval Institute Proceedings,* LXXXII (August 1956), pp. 832-835.

"Logistics in World War II: A Bibliographical Survey," *United States Naval Institute Proceedings,* LXXXIII (January 1957), pp. 97-102.

"From Sails to Spindles: Essex County in Transition," *Essex Institute Historical Collections,* XCV (April 1959), pp. 115-136.

JOAN BENTINCK-SMITH

Notes

CHAPTER FOUR

SEAFARING AND THE EMERGENCE OF AMERICAN SCIENCE

1. Contribution from the Woods Hole Oceanographic Institution No. 3546. This paper originated in a lecture given at the Munson Institute in 1964 and 1965; I am grateful to R. G. Albion and J. H. Kemble for their invitation. I wish also to acknowledge the support of my research by the National Science Foundation through a grant to W. H. O. I.

2. D. H. Fleming, "Science in Australia, Canada, and the United States: Some Comparative Remarks," *Proceedings of the Tenth International Congress of the History of Science,* 2 vols. (Paris, 1964), pp. 179-196.

3. N. Reingold, "Nathaniel Bowditch," *Dictionary of Scientific Biography, 2* (New York, 1970), pp. 368-369; H. L. Burstyn, *At the Sign of the Quadrant* (Mystic, 1957) and "The Salem Philosophical Library: Its History and Importance for American Science," *Essex Institute Historical Collections, 96* (1960), pp. 169-206.

4. D. C. North, *The Economic Growth of the United States* (New York, 1961), Part 1. In the text above I have followed North's interpretation that shipping prior to 1815 and cotton cultivation between 1815 and 1860 were the key growth sectors of the American economy. Though I do not wish to enter into the technical arguments of economic historians, it seems plausible that the cotton-trade figures, from which North deduces his conclusions about the period after 1815, conceal profits from the carrying of the cotton in American ships. That is, his argument that the *cultivation* of cotton alone powered American economic growth may not be conclusive. In either case, whether shipping was a key *growth* sector after 1815, or whether (as North claims) shipping furnished a small and declining portion of national income, it was a part of the American economy on which the key cotton sector depended for its carrying services.

5. G. A. Weber, *The Coast and Geodetic Survey* (Baltimore, 1923), Chapter 1.

6. A. H. Dupree, *Science in the Federal Government* (Cambridge, Mass., 1957), pp. 39-43; L. D. White, *The Jeffersonians* (New York, 1951), pp. 41-42.

7. W. F. Cannon, "History in Depth: The Early Victorian Period," *History of Science, 3* (1964), pp. 20-38.

8. E. I. Mendelsohn, "The Emergence of Science as a Profession in Nineteenth-Century Europe," in K. F. Hill, ed., *The Management of Scientists* (Boston, 1964), Chapter 1. For the American scene, see G. H. Daniels, "The Process of Professionalization in American Science: The Emergent

Period, 1820-1860," *Isis, 58* (1967), pp. 151-166, and A. H. Dupree, *Asa Gray, 1810-1888* (Cambridge, Mass., 1959), Chapters 2 and 3.

9. R. G. Albion, "Makers of Naval Policy, 1798-1947" (Manuscript, 1950), p. 215.

10. Thomas Jefferson wrote in 1813: "In our country, every man is engaged in some industrious pursuit, and science is but a secondary occupation, always subordinate to the main business of life." (Quoted in D. J. Boorstin, *The Americans: the Colonial Experience* [New York, 1958], p. 314.)

11. F. A. P. Barnard *et al.*, "Report on the History and Progress of the American Coast Survey," *Proceedings of the American Association for the Advancement of Science, 13* (1860), pp. 27-150, 48. On Southard, see White, *Jeffersonians,* pp. 281, 364.

12. *Dictionary of American Biography, s. v.* Charles W. and Louis M. Goldsborough; G. A. Weber, *The Hydrographic Office* (Baltimore, 1926), Chapter 1; White, *Jeffersonians,* pp. 281-282.

13. *Dictionary of American Biography, s. v.* James M. Gilliss.

14. N. Reingold, ed., *Science in Nineteenth-Century America* (New York, 1964), pp. 108-126; Dupree, *Science in the Federal Government,* pp. 56-61; "Centenary Celebration of the Wilkes Exploring Expedition of the United States Navy, 1838-1842," American Philosophical Society, *Proceedings, 82* (1940), pp. 519-800. William Stanton's definitive history of the Expedition, *The Great United States Exploring Expedition of 1838-1842,* is scheduled for publication in 1975.

15. D. E. Borthwick, "Outfitting the United States Exploring Expedition: Lieutenant Charles Wilkes' European Assignment, August-November 1836," American Philosophical Society, *Proceedings, 109* (1965), pp. 159-172.

16. Reingold, *Science in America,* p. 90.

17. W. C. Rufus, "Astronomical Observatories in the United States Prior to 1848," *Scientific Monthly, 19* (1924), pp. 120-139; D. F. Musto, "A Survey of the American Observatory Movement, 1800-1850," *Vistas in Astronomy, 9* (1968), pp. 87-92.

18. F. L. Williams, *Matthew Fontaine Maury* (New Brunswick, N. J., 1963), p. 141; L. D. White, *The Jacksonians* (New York, 1954), Chapter 12.

19. C. O. Paullin, "Naval Administration, 1842-1861," U. S. Naval Institute *Proceedings, 33* (1907), pp. 1435-1477, 1443, reprinted in *Paullin's History of Naval Administration, 1775-1911* (Annapolis, 1968); White, *Jacksonians,* Chapter 11.

20. Cannon, "History in Depth."

21. P. S. de Laplace, *Mécanique Céleste,* translated by N. Bowditch, 4 vols. (Boston, 1829-1839). Though Bowditch translated only the first four volumes (1799-1805), he incorporated much of the fifth volume (1825) from his own reworking and from Laplace's articles.

22. N. Reingold, "Alexander Dallas Bache," *Dictionary of Scientific*

Biography, 1 (New York, 1970), pp. 363-365. Davis' support became especially important after his election to the Senate in 1846.

23. G. R. Taylor, *The Transportation Revolution, 1815-1860* (New York, 1951), Chapter 6; North, *Economic Growth,* Part 2; D. C. North, "Ocean Freight Rates and Economic Development, 1750 to 1913," *Journal of Economic History, 18* (1958), pp. 537-555, and "The Role of Transportation in the Economic Development of North America," *Les Grandes Voies Maritimes dans le Monde, 15e-19e Siècles* (Paris, 1965), pp. 209-246.

24. P. Temin, *The Jacksonian Economy* (New York, 1969), pp. 155-165.

25. H. S. Miller, "Science and Private Agencies," in D. D. Van Tassel and M. G. Hall, eds., *Science and Society in the United States* (Homewood, 1966), pp. 191-221, 197.

26. S. Kohlstedt, "A Step Towards Scientific Self-Identity in the United States: The Failure of the National Institute, 1844," *Isis, 62* (1971), pp. 339-362.

27. Dupree, *Science in the Federal Government,* pp. 14-15, 39, 62-63.

28. B. A. Gould, "An Address in Commemoration of Sears Cook Walker," *Proceedings of the American Association for the Advancement of Science, 8* (1855), pp. 18-45.

29. See the *Annual Report of the Superintendent of the United States Coast Survey* for the years concerned. These reports are scattered through the House and Senate series of Congressional Documents in most libraries; that of the Marine Biological Laboratory, Woods Hole, has a consecutive series.

30. E. Lurie, *Louis Agassiz* (Chicago, 1960), p. 131.

31. C. H. Davis, Jr., *Life of Charles Henry Davis, Rear Admiral, 1807-1877* (Boston, 1899).

32. H. H. Hildebrandsson and L. Teisserenc de Bort, *Les Bases de la Méteorologie Dynamique,* 2 vols. (Paris, 1898-1905), I, p. 22.

33. M. Grosser, *The Discovery of Neptune* (Cambridge, Mass., 1962).

34. Williams, *Maury,* pp. 67-68; Gould, "Address in Commemoration of Walker," pp. 29-31.

35. Williams, *Maury,* pp. 168-172.

36. Reingold, *Science in America,* pp. 136, 140-143; Gould, "Address in Commemoration of Walker," pp. 30-31.

37. G. A. Weber, *The Naval Observatory* (Baltimore, 1926), p. 18; Williams, *Maury,* Chapter 10.

38. J. Lyman, "The Centennial of Pressure Pattern Navigation," U. S. Naval Institute *Proceedings, 74* (1948), pp. 309-314. Lyman claims (p. 311) that the relationship between the pressure gradient and the direction of the wind (i.e., the wind blows along the isobars at right angles to the gradient) was not known in Maury's day. In fact, this relationship, generally known as Buys Ballot's Law, after the Director of the Royal Netherlands Meteorological Service who announced it in 1857, was first

stated by an American, Professor James H. Coffin of Lafayette College, in "An Investigation of the Storm Curve," *Proceedings of the American Association for the Advancement of Science,* 7 (1856), pp. 83-101, 88.

39. 9 Statutes at Large 374-375. Slipping major enactments for science through the legislative process in this manner seems to have been a common practice; the act that established the National Academy of Sciences in 1863 is the most prominent example.

40. G. A. Weber, *Naval Observatory,* pp. 5-6.

41. *Ibid.,* p. 27.

42. B. Z. Jones and L. G. Boyd, *The Harvard College Observatory* (Cambridge, Mass., 1971), Chapter 2, gives an excellent account of the Observatory in this period with only scattered references to the Almanac Office; see the review by H. L. Burstyn, *Isis, 64* (1973), pp. 560-563.

43. *Dictionary of American Biography, s. v.* Benjamin Apthorp Gould.

44. Temin, *Jacksonian Economy;* Taylor, *Transportation Revolution,* pp. 354-360.

45. Albion, "Makers of Naval Policy," p. 215, conveniently summarizes the average annual expediture of the Navy during periods of peace and war respectively. The original data may be found in *Statement of Appropriations and Expenditures of the Navy Department* (Senate Executive Document 3, 45th Congress, 1st Session) (Washington, 1877).

46. The expeditions were as follows:

Dates	*Leader*	*Destination*	*Purpose*
1847-1849	Lt. William F. Lynch	Dead Sea	Geographical exploration
1849-1852	Lt. James M. Gilliss	Chile	Astronomical research
1850-1851	Lt. Edwin J. DeHaven	Arctic	Exploration and search for Franklin
1851-1852	Lt. William L. Herndon	Amazon basin	Geographical exploration
1853-1856	Lt. Thomas J. Page	La Plata estuary	Marine surveying
1853-1855	Dr. Elisha Kent Kane	Arctic	Exploration (search for Franklin and open polar sea)
1853-1855	Cdr. Cadwallader Ringgold; Lt. John Rodgers	North Pacific	Marine surveying

Their details are summarized in V. Ponko, Jr., *Ships, Seas, and Scientists* (Annapolis, 1974). The other major Navy expedition in this period was that of Commodore Matthew C. Perry to Japan (1852-1854); there were also minor expeditions to the Isthmus of Darien and to West Africa.

47. H. L. Burstyn, "British Science Goes to Sea," paper delivered to the American Association for the Advancement of Science, Washington, 1971.

48. E.g., Captain James Cook's voyage to the Pacific to observe the transit of Venus in 1769 was motivated primarily by the search for Terra Australis, the fabled fourth corner of the world.

49. H. N. Smith, *Virgin Land* (New York, 1957), pp. 175-176; E. Genovese, *The Political Economy of Slavery* (New York, 1967) pp. 27-28, 248-250.

50. Reingold, *Science in America,* pp. 136, 144-145.

51. North, "Ocean Freight Rates"; also *Economic Growth,* pp. 67-71.

52. Maury's claims to have shortened sailing passages are viewed with skepticism by D. C. North (personal communication), whose analysis of five thousand voyage records suggests that sailing passages were shortened more by improved ship design than by improved information about winds and currents.

53. Williams, *Maury,* pp. 189-192.

54. A. D. Bache, "Address," *Proceedings of the American Association for the Advancement of Science, 6* (1852), pp. xli-lx, xliv.

55. Williams, *Maury,* pp. 205-224; T. Coulson, *Joseph Henry* (Princeton, 1950), pp. 194-199; E. van Everdingen, *C. H. D. Buys Ballot* (The Hague, 1953), pp. 61-70.

56. J. Hall, "Presidential Address," *Proceedings of the American Association for the Advancement of Science, 10* (1857), p. 230 (Part 2).

57. Bache, "Address," p. xlv.

58. B. Peirce, "Address on Retiring from the Duties of President," *Ibid., 8* (1855), pp. 1-17, 1-2.

59. J. Leighly, "Introduction," M. F. Maury, *The Physical Geography of the Sea and its Meteorology,* (Cambridge, Mass., 1963), pp. ix-xxx.

60. *Proceedings of the American Association for the Advancement of Science, 1-13* (1849-1860), *passim.*

61. J. Leighly, "M. F. Maury in his Time," *Bulletin de l'Institut Océanographique,* Special Issue 2 (1968), pp. 147-161, 158. For further details, see H. L. Burstyn, "Matthew Fontaine Maury," *Dictionary of Scientific Biography, 9* (New York, 1974), pp. 195-197.

62. George W. Blunt (1862), as quoted by Leighly, "Maury in his Time," p. 157, from F. A. P. Barnard *et al.,* "Report of the Committee to Investigate Commander Maury's Publications," National Academy of Sciences, *Report for the Year 1863* (Washington, 1864), pp. 98-112.

63. A.de Tocqueville, *Democracy in America,* translated by G. Lawrence (Garden City, 1969), p. 461.

64. *Ibid.,* Vol. II, Part 1, Chapter 10.

65. The traditional historiography of American science has held otherwise: see R. H. Shryock, "American Indifference to Basic Research During the Nineteenth Century," *Archives Internationales d'Histoire des Sciences, 2* (1948), pp. 50-65, reprinted many times; see also I. B. Cohen,

Science and American Society in the First Century of the Republic (Columbus, 1961). To rebut this view is beyond the scope of the present paper; a beginning has been made by N. Reingold ("American Indifference to Basic Research: A Reappraisal," in G. H. Daniels, ed., *Nineteenth-Century American Science* [Evanston, 1972], pp. 38-62), but more remains to be said when the detailed history of the mathematical sciences in the nineteenth century has been written.

66. Benjamin Peirce made significant contributions to mathematics; Benjamin Apthorp Gould was offered in 1851 a professorship at Göttingen (Reingold, *Science in America,* p. 161). Donald Fleming's list of a dozen American scientists who gained European reputations before 1870 ("American Science and the World Scientific Community," *Cahiers d'Histoire Mondiale, 8* [1965], pp. 666-678, 673) is incomplete, since it omits Peirce and Gould among others.

67. J. van Mieghem, "International Co-operation in Meteorology: An Historical Review," *Proceedings of the 14th Assembly of the International Association of Meteorology and Atmospheric Physics* (Geneva, 1967), pp. 109-128.

CHAPTER FIVE

THE MACHINE AT SEA

1. Henry Adams, *The Education of Henry Adams* (Boston, 1918), p. 5; Douglas T. Miller, *The Birth of Modern America, 1820-1850* (New York, 1970), p. ix.

2. George Templeton Strong, *The Diary of George Templeton Strong,* edited by Allan Nevins and Milton Halsey Thomas, Vol. I, *Young Man in New York, 1835-1849* (New York, 1952), p. 84.

3. Philip Hone, *The Diary of Philip Hone, 1828-1851,* edited by Allan Nevins (New York, 1936), pp. 316, 317.

4. Vincent Nolte, *The Memoirs of Vincent Nolte* (New York, 1934 [original edition, 1854]), p. 424.

5. *British Almanac for 1839,* quoted in Howard Robinson, *Carrying British Mails Overseas* (New York, 1964), p. 128.

6. Grahame E. Farr, "The *Great Western,*" *The Mariner's Mirror,* XXIV (April 1938), pp. 148-149.

7. *Illustrated London News,* I (4 June 1842), p. 57.

8. Hone, *Diary,* pp. 318-319; Edgar C. Smith, *A Short History of Naval and Marine Engineering* (Cambridge, England, 1937), p. 133; W. S. Lindsay, *History of Merchant Shipping and Ancient Commerce,* IV (New York, 1965) [original edition, London, 1874]), pp. 575-576.

9. Smith, *Short History of Engineering,* pp. 129-132.

10. *Ibid.*, pp. 128-129.

11. Zachariah Allen, *Sketches of the State of the Useful Arts . . . in Great Britain, France, and Holland,* I (Hartford, 1835), p. 208.

12. T. Sheppard, "The *Sirius:* The First Steamer to Cross the Atlantic," *The Mariner's Mirror,* XXIII (January 1937), p. 88; Smith, *Short History of Engineering,* p. 130.

13. Arthur J. Maginnis, *The Atlantic Ferry, Its Ships, Men, and Working* (London, 1892), p. 173.

14. T. A. Bushell, *"Royal Mail:" A Centenary History of the Royal Mail Line, 1839-1939* (London, 1939), p. 34.

15. George Rogers Taylor, *The Transportation Revolution, 1818-1860* (New York, 1968 [original edition, New York, 1951]), p. 113; R. H. Thornton, *British Shipping,* second edition (Cambridge, England, 1959), pp. 26-27.

16. *Ibid.* For a particularly good discussion of these vessels, see H. Philip Spratt, *Transatlantic Paddle Steamers* (Glasgow, 1951).

17. Bushell, "*Royal Mail,*" p. 76.

18. Reminiscences of Mr. Brownrigg, quoted in John Kennedy, *The History of Steam Navigation* (Liverpool, 1903), p. 75.

19. Bushell, "*Royal Mail,*" p. 27.

20. Edouard A. Stackpole, comp., "The Wreck of the Steamer San Francisco: The Loss of the Steamship During the great Atlantic Hurricane of December, 1853, etc." Marine Historical Association, Incorporated Publications No. 27 (December, 1954), p. 4.

21. Instructions to Capt. Woodruff of the *Britannia* before first voyage in 1840, quoted in Capt. E. G. Diggle, *The Romance of a Modern Liner* (New York, 1930), pp. 59-60, 61.

22. R. B. Forbes, *Notes on Navigation* (Boston, 1884), pp. 21-22; F. Lawrence Babcock, *Spanning the Atlantic* (New York, 1931), p. 80; R. A. Fletcher, *Steam-Ships: The Story of Their Development to the Present Day* (Philadelphia, 1910), p. 169.

23. Harriet Beecher Stowe, *Sunny Memories of Foreign Lands,* I (Boston, 1854), pp. 1-2.

24. Martin Tupper, letter to his wife upon departure of Cunard steamer *Asia* from Liverpool in March 1851, quoted in Frank Staff, *The Transatlantic Mail* (London, 1956), p. 87; Charles Dickens, *American Notes and Pictures from Italy* (London, 1907 [original edition, 1842]), pp. 6-7.

25. *Ballou's Pictorial,* XVI (26 February 1859), p. 136.

26. Unidentified passenger on *Britannia,* writing to friend on eve of departure, 4 July 1840, Liverpool to Halifax and Boston, quoted in Lamont Buchanan, *Ships of Steam* (New York, 1956), p. 24.

27. John S. C. Abbott, "Ocean Life," *Harper's New Monthly Magazine,* V (June 1852), p. 61; William Makepeace Thackeray, *The Letters and Private Papers,* edited by Gordon N. Ray, III (Cambridge, Mass., 1946), pp. 118-119.

28. Richard Henry Dana, Jr., *To Cuba and Back: A Vacation Voyage* (Boston, 1859), pp. 9-10. A comparable if more humorous description of the confusion of a steamer's embarkation is Artemus Ward, (*His Travels*) *Among the Mormons,* Part I, Chapter 1, "On the Steamer," in *The Complete Works of Artemus Ward* (London, 1897), p. 190, describing an 1863 departure of the steamer *Ariel* from New York.

29. Fredrika Bremer, *The Homes of the New World: Impressions of America,* translated by Mary Howitt, I (New York, 1853), p. 1.

30. Charles Dickens to Frederick Dickens, 3 January 1842, and to Thomas Mitton, 3 January 1842, from Liverpool, in *The Letters of Charles Dickens* (The Pilgrim Edition), ed. by Madeline House, Graham Storey, and Kathleen Tillitson, Vol. III: *1842-1843* (Oxford, 1974), pp. 7, 10; Dickens, *American Notes,* pp. 1, 2.

31. Dickens, describing the departure of a channel steamer from Admiralty Pier, Dover, in "Calais Night Mail," *The Uncommercial Traveller* (London, 1909 [original edition, ca. 1860]), pp. 179-180; Dickens, *American Notes,* p. 9. For a comparable description of a steamer's departure, see Benjamin Silliman, *A Visit to Europe in 1851* (fifth edition), 2 vols. (New York, 1856), I, p. 8.

32. Alex. Mackay, *The Western World; or, Travels in the United States in 1846-47; etc.* I (Philadelphia, 1849), p. 13. Also remarking on the smooth and virtually silent operation of the machinery was William Cullen Bryant on an 1849 departure of the steamer *Tennessee* from New York to Savannah, in *Letters of a Traveller; or, Notes of Things Seen in Europe and America,* fourth edition (New York, 1855), p. 336.

33. Dana, *To Cuba and Back,* p. 11.

34. Frederick Augustus Delano, quoted in Hall Roosevelt, *Odyssey of an American Family: An Account of the Roosevelts and Their Kin as Travelers, from 1613 to 1938* (New York, 1939), p. 249.

35. *Ibid.*

36. *Ballou's Pictorial,* XVI (February 26, 1859), p. 136, describing the departure of the Cunard steamer *Arabia,* Boston to Halifax and Liverpool.

37. Julian Hawthorne, *Nathaniel Hawthorne and His Wife,* (Boston, 1895) Vol. II, p. 17, quoting from Sophia Hawthorne's notebook entry of 8 July 1853, on the S. S. *Niagara,* Halifax to Liverpool.

38. Dana, *To Cuba and Back,* p. 19.

39. Stowe, *Sunny Memories,* I, p. 3.

40. *Ballou's Pictorial,* XVI (26 February 1859), p. 136.

41. Stowe, *Sunny Memories,* I, pp. 2-3.

42. Dickens, "Calais Night Mail," *The Uncommercial Traveller,* p. 180.

43. F. A. Delano, quoted in Roosevelt, *Odyssey,* p. 258.

44. Rachel Henning, on the steamer *Great Britain* in mid-March, 1861, quoted in Basil Greenhill and Ann Gifford, *Women Under Sail: Letters and Journals concerning eight women travelling or working in*

sailing vessels between 1829 and 1949 (Newton Abbot, Eng., 1971), p. 142.

45. Dickens, *American Notes,* pp. 217, 219.

46. Mrs. L. H. Sigourney, *Pleasant Memories of Pleasant Lands* (Boston, 1842), pp. 355-356.

47. Stowe, *Sunny Memories,* I, p. 8.

48. Mackay, *The Western World,* I, p. 15.

49. Henry W. Bellows, *The Old World in Its New Face: Impressions of Europe in 1867-1868,* I (New York, 1868), p. 16.

50. *Gleason's Pictorial,* VII (19 August 1854), p. 112, describing the Cunard steamer *Arabia;* Silliman, *Visit to Europe in 1851,* I, p. 13.

51. Boston *Mercantile Journal* describing the steamer *Britannia* in the early 1840's, quoted in Babcock, *Spanning the Atlantic,* p. 69; Silliman, *Visit to Europe in 1851,* I, p. 12.

52. Rachel Henning, quoted in Greenhill and Gifford, *Women Under Sail,* p. 141.

53. William McFee, *Watch Below: A Reconstruction in Narrative Form of the Golden Age of Steam* (New York, 1940), p. 74.

54. James H. Lanman, "American Steam Navigation," *Hunt's Merchants' Magazine,* IV (February 1841), p. 120.

55. Richard Henry Dana, Jr., *The Journal,* Robert F. Lucid, ed., 3 vols. (Cambridge, Mass., 1968), II, pp. 696, 817; describing the engine room of the S. S. *Persia,* 1856. Dana noted that a trip on this "new and splendid steamer" was so desirable that ticket holders were being offered £25 extra for their tickets. *Ibid.,* p. 816.

56. Dana, *Journal,* III, p. 1077; 26 June 1860 entry on board S. S. *Madras,* a "large screw steamer" in the Indian Ocean on the way to Bombay.

57. Smith, *Short History of Engineering,* p. 137.

58. Grahame Farr, *The Steamship Great Western: The First Atlantic Liner* (Bristol, England, 1963), p. 9, quoting the Engineer's log for 17 and 19 April 1838.

59. McFee, *Watch Below,* p. 74.

60. R. Taylor, "Manning the Royal Navy: The Reform of the Recruiting System, 1852-1862," *The Mariner's Mirror,* XLIV (November 1958), p. 305.

61. Dickens, *American Notes,* p. 15.

62. John Forster, *The Life of Charles Dickens,* 3 vols. Tenth edition (London, 1872), I, pp. 307-308, quoting a 24 February 1842 letter from Dickens to Forster.

63. Dickens, "Aboard Ship," *Uncommercial Traveller,* p. 307.

64. Stowe, *Sunny Memories,* I, pp. 7-8.

65. Captain Lauchlan B. Mackinnon, R. N., "English and American Ocean Steamers," *Harper's New Monthly Magazine,* VII (July 1853), p. 206, comparing his crossing the Atlantic from New York to Liverpool, November 1852, in the Collins steamer *Baltic* with his return voyage in

July 1853 in the Cunard steamer *America*. For a similarly enthusiastic impression of the *Baltic's* behavior, see Silliman, *Visit to Europe in 1851*, I, p. 12.

66. *Ibid.*

67. Pliny Miles, *The Advantages of Ocean Steam Navigation, Foreign and Coastwise, to the Commerce of Boston, and the Manufactures of New England* (Boston, 1857), p. 44; G. W. Buckwell, "The Early History of Steam Navigation," *The Steamship: A Scientific Journal of Marine Engineering, Shipbuilding, and Shipping,* II (1 September 1890), p. 88; Thomas Rainey, *Ocean Steam Navigation and the Ocean Post,* second edition (New York, 1858), pp. 112-113.

68. Captain W. N. Glascock, R. N., *The Naval Officer's Manual, for Every Grade in Her Majesty's Ships, etc.*, second edition (London, 1848), p. 406.

69. Henry Morford, quoted in John Malcolm Brinnin, *The Sway of the Grand Saloon: A Social History of the North Atlantic* (New York, 1971), p. 214.

70. Anthony Trollope, quoted in Robinson, *Carrying British Mails Overseas,* pp. 156, 157.

71. Bellows, *Old World,* I, p. 18.

72. Edward A. Mueller, "Great Britain," *Nautical Research Journal* XV (Spring 1968), p. 4; *Illustrated London News* (6 and 20 September 1845), pp. 157, 187; *The Nautical Magazine and Naval Chronicle for 1845* (London, 1845), pp. 713-714.

73. Smith, *Short History of Engineering,* pp. 77-79.

74. C. S. Graham, "The Transition from Paddle-Wheel to Screw Propeller," *The Mariner's Mirror,* XLIV (February 1958), pp. 45-46; Arthur J. Maginnis, *The Atlantic Ferry, Its Ships, Men, and Working* (London, 1892), pp. 175, 177.

75. Rachel Henning, on the steamer *Calcutta* in 1854, quoted in Greenhill and Gifford, *Women Under Sail,* p. 126.

76. Dickens, "Aboard Ship," *Uncommercial Traveller,* pp. 308-313.

77. Samuel S. Cox, *A Buckeye Abroad; or, Wanderings in Europe, and in the Orient,* seventh edition (Columbus, Ohio, 1860), pp. 11, 12, 14; describing a May 1851 Atlantic crossing on the Cunard steamer *Asia;* Rachel Henning, on the steamer *Calcutta* in 1854, quoted in Greenhill and Gifford, *Women Under Sail,* p. 128; Eliot Warburton, *Hochelaga; or, England in the New World,* 2 vols., second edition, revised (London, 1846), II, pp. 354-355, 357; Sigourney, *Pleasant Memories,* pp. 11-13.

78. Warren Tute, *Atlantic Conquest: The Men and Ships of the Glorious Age of Steam* (Boston, 1962), pp. 53-54.

79. Sir Charles Lyell, *A Second Visit to the United States of North America,* 2 vols. (New York, 1849), I, p. 15.

80. Farr, *Steamship Great Western,* p. 11.

81. *Ibid.,* pp. 8-10.

82. Grahame Farr, "The *Great Britain,*" *The Mariner's Mirror,* XXXVI (January 1950), pp. 47-48; *Illustrated London News* (22 November 1845), p. 322; Mueller, "Great Britain," *Nautical Research Journal,* XIV (Autumn-Winter 1967), pp. 110-111.

83. Robert Woolward ["Old Woolward"], *Nigh on Sixty Years at Sea,* second edition (London, 1894), pp. 48-50; Bushell, "*Royal Mail,*" p. 21.

84. Lyell, *Second Visit,* II, pp. 273-274.

85. Alexander Crosby Brown, *Women and Children Last: The Loss of the Steamship Arctic* (New York, 1961), *passim.*

86. Dickens, "Aboard Ship," *Uncommercial Traveller,* p. 311.

87. John Henry Vessey, *Mr. Vessey of England: Being the Incidents and Reminiscences of Travel in a Twelve Weeks' Tour through the United States and Canada in the Year 1859,* edited by Brian Waters (New York, 1956), pp. 21, 24-25.

88. Robert C. Leslie, *A Waterbiography* (London, 1894), p. 118. Benjamin Silliman received the same impression during his return to New York from Liverpool on the Collins liner *Pacific* in September 1851; *Visit to Europe in 1851,* II, p. 461.

89. Dana, *Journal,* II, pp. 695, 696, 698.

90. Hone, *Diary,* pp. 924-925; Abbot, "Ocean Life," p. 62.

91. Heinrich Schliemann, *Schliemann's First Visit to America, 1850-1851,* Shirley H. Weber, ed. (Cambridge, Mass., 1942), pp. 17-18; *Illustrated London News* (1 February 1854), pp. 75, 76.

92. Strong, *Diary,* II, pp. 35, 37, 38; his diary entries for 21, 23, and 28 January, 4 and 14 February 1851.

93. *Harper's New Monthly Magazine,* X (December 1854), p. 119; "Editor's Easy Chair" column, contrasting loss of *Arctic* with news of the safety of the *Atlantic,* "three or four years since." When still quite young, the novelist Henry James recalled, he had been with his parents at the theatre when the news of the *Atlantic's* safe arrival was breathlessly announced. "The house broke into such plaudits, so huge and prolonged a roar of relief," James wrote, "as I had never heard the like of and which gave me my first measure of a great immediate public emotion." *A Small Boy and Others* (London, 1913), pp. 289-290.

94. Schliemann, *First Visit,* pp. 21-22.

95. Strong, *Diary,* II, p. 38.

96. F. A. Delano, quoted in Roosevelt, *Odyssey,* pp. 251, 256, 259, 261.

97. Dickens, *American Notes,* p. 222.

98. Miles, *Ocean Steam Navigation,* p. 29. Appreciation of a steamer's unprecedented regularity is apparent in the concluding remarks of James F. W. Johnston, *Notes on North America: Agricultural, Economical, and Social,* 2 vols. (Edinburgh and London, 1851), II, p. 512. Johnston sailed from Boston on 3 April 1850 "by the regular Cunard Steamer." Despite a rough passage, the steamer made Liverpool in thirteen days. "The evening of the same day which brought us into Liverpool saw me safe

at home in Durham, being the very evening I had fixed for my arrival four weeks before, in my letters from Boston. Such certainty of calculation do we now owe, even in the uncertain weather of spring, to the conjoined triumphs of mechanism and steam!"

99. Mackinnon, *Harper's New Monthly Magazine,* VII, p. 205.

100. Cox, *Buckeye,* p. 20.

101. *Gleason's Pictorial Drawing-Room Companion,* I (6 September 1851), p. 293, commenting on the Philadelphia-to-Liverpool steamer *City of Glasgow.*

102. A "jingle recited at a Cunard festival," quoted in Babcock, *Spanning the Atlantic,* p. 50.

103. Rainey, *Ocean Steam Navigation,* pp. 79, 49.

104. Hone, *Diary,* pp. 239, 240.

105. Lt. J. D. Jerrold Kelley, USN, "The Ship's Company," in F. E. Chadwick *et al., Ocean Steamships: A Popular Account of Their Construction, Development, Management, and Appliances* (New York, 1891), pp. 149-150, 152.

106. Michael Lewis, *The Navy in Transition, 1814-1864: A Social History* (London, 1965), p. 194; Francis Steinitz, *The Ship, Its Origin and Progress* (London, 1849), pp. 606-607.

107. Bremer, *Homes of the New World,* I, p. 531.

CHAPTER SIX

THE AMERICAN MERCHANT MARINE AS AN EXPRESSION OF FOREIGN POLICY,

1. "The Merchant Marine: Step-Child of the Economy," Bentley address, New York City, 12 May 1970, as contained in *Vital Speeches of the Day,* XXXV, No. 18 (1 July 1970), pp. 569-572.

2. Woodrow Wilson, *A History of the American People* (five vols., Baltimore, 1902), V, pp. 292, 294-296; "Democracy and Efficiency," *Atlantic Monthly,* LXXXVII (March 1901), pp. 289-299; "The Ideals of America," *ibid.,* XC (December 1902), pp. 721-734; Harley Notter, *The Origins of the Foreign Policy of Woodrow Wilson* (Baltimore, 1937), p. 144.

3. Wilson's attitudes are best developed in William Appleman Williams, "The Frontier Thesis and American Foreign Policy," *Pacific Historical Review,* XXIV (February 1955), pp. 379-395; in Williams, *The Tragedy of American Diplomacy* (New York, 1962), pp. 61-83; and in N. Gordon Levin, Jr., *Woodrow Wilson and World Politics: America's Response to War and Revolution* (New York, 1968), pp. 13-21.

4. John Wells Davidson, ed., *A Cross-roads of Freedom: The 1912 Campaign Speeches of Woodrow Wilson* (New Haven, Conn., 1956), pp. 33-34.

5. See, for example, William Appleman Williams, *The Roots of the Modern American Empire: A Study of the Growth and Shaping of Social Consciousness in a Marketplace Society* (New York, 1969); Howard R. Schonberger, *Transportation to the Seaboard: The "Communications Revolution" and American Foreign Policy, 1860-1900* (Westport, Conn., 1971); Edward P. Crapol and Howard Schonberger, "The Shift to Global Expansion, 1865-1900," in W. A. Williams, ed., *From Colony to Empire: Essays in the History of American Foreign Relations* (New York, 1972), pp. 135-202.

6. William C. Redfield to Philip T. Dodge, 5 June 1915, Woodrow Wilson Papers, Manuscript Division, Library of Congress.

7. McAdoo, "The Pan American Financial Conference," *World's Work,* XXX (August 1915), pp. 393-396. See also McAdoo to William Jennings Bryan, 31 July 1916, William G. McAdoo Papers, Manuscript Division, Library of Congress; McAdoo address, 18 April 1916, as contained in Senate Document No. 437, 64th Congress, 1st Sess.

8. Ray Stannard Baker and William E. Dodd, eds., *The Public Papers of Woodrow Wilson* (six volumes, New York, 1926-1927), II, Part I, pp. 406-428, Annual Message of 7 December 1915.

9. Levin, *Woodrow Wilson and World Politics,* p. 7.

10. Remarks before the House Committee on the Merchant Marine and Fisheries, 17 February 1916, *Hearings on Creating a Shipping Board,* 64th Cong., 1st Sess., p. 275.

11. "Three Kinds of Preparedness," Stone address in the Senate, *Cong. Rec.,* 64th Cong., 1st Sess., 13 April 1916, pp. 6025-6026.

12. House to Wilson, 14 May 1916, Private Papers of E. M. House, Yale University Library.

13. "Arthur J. Balfour's Draft Reply to Colonel House," 24 May 1916, in John Milton Cooper, Jr., "The British Response to the House-Grey Memorandum: New Evidence and New Questions," *Journal of American History,* LIX, No. 4 (March 1973), pp. 958-971.

14. Carl P. Parrini, *Heir to Empire: United States Economic Diplomacy, 1916-1923* (Pittsburgh, 1969), Ch. 2.

15. William S. Culbertson, *Commercial Policy in War Times and After: A Study of the Application of Democratic Ideas to International Commercial Relations* (New York, 1919), p. 348.

16. Lansing to Wilson, 23 June 1916, *Papers Relating to the Foreign Relations of the United States: The Lansing Papers, 1914-1920* (two vols., Washington, D. C., 1939), I, p. 312.

17. For agricultural expression, see House Committee on the Merchant Marine and Fisheries, *Hearings on Creating a Shipping Board,* 64th Cong., 1st Sess., pp. 672-698. For industrial expression see, for example, National Foreign Trade Council, *European Economic Alliances: A Compilation of Information on International Commercial Policies After the European War and Their Effect upon the Foreign Trade of the United States* (New York, 1916), p. 10.

18. McAdoo to Lawrence F. Abbott, 10 June 1916, McAdoo Papers; Darrell Hevenor Smith and Paul V. Betters, *The United States Shipping Board: Its History, Activities and Organization* (Washington, D. C., 1931), pp. 6-8; Paul M. Zeis, *American Shipping Policy* (Princeton, N. J., 1938), pp. 92-94.

19. United States Shipping Board, *Sixth Annual Report, 1922* (Washington, D. C., 1922), p. 47; Edward N. Hurley, *The Bridge to France* (Philadelphia, 1927), pp. 32, 39-41, 110-111; Hurley, *The New Merchant Marine* (New York, 1920), pp. 38-40; Thomas A. Bailey, *The Policy of the United States Towards the Neutrals, 1917-1918* (Baltimore, 1942), p. 201.

20. See Jeffrey J. Safford, "Edward Hurley and American Shipping Policy: An Elaboration on Wilsonian Diplomacy, 1918-1919," *The Historian,* XXXV, No. 4 (August 1973), pp. 568-586.

21. Hurley to Bernard Baruch, 21 May 1918, Wilson Papers; Hurley, *Diary,* entry of 14 August 1918, Edward Hurley Papers, University of Notre Dame Library.

22. Hurley, *Diary,* entry of 9 December 1918, Hurley Papers.

23. Hurley to Wilson, 9 November 1918, Wilson Papers.

24. Hurley to Wilson, 12 December 1918, Hurley Papers.

25. See, for example, Assistant Secretary of State William Phillips to L. P. Sheldon, "Summary of the Effect of the Armistice on Shipping," 24 November 1918, Papers of the Supreme Economic Council, Hoover Institution on War, Revolution, and Peace, Stanford University; John H. Rosseter (Director of Operations, USSB) to Hurley, ca. 4 December 1918, United States Shipping Board Papers, National Archives, Record Group No. 32, Subject Classified General Files, 1916-1936, Operations File. [Hereafter cited as RG 32, plus file number, NA.] For the feelings of the Southern Commercial Congress and the Council of Foreign Relations, see *The New York Times,* 2 and 10 December 1918.

26. Hurley cable to Baker, Colby, Lord, Rosseter, Franklin, and McCormick, 13 December 1918, RG 32/618-3, NA.

27. Hurley to Wilson, 20 December 1918, Wilson Papers.

28. Hurley, *Diary,* entries of 23 December 1918 and 1 January 1919, Hurley Papers.

29. Benson memorandum, 16 May 1921, Naval Records Collection of the Office of Naval Records and Library, National Archives, Record Group No. 45, Subject File, 1911-1927, Case File UB (Admiral Benson's Personal Correspondence); Josephus Daniels to Captain Dudley W. Knox, 29 January 1937, *ibid.;* "Memorandum for Chief of Naval Operations," 30 January 1919, *ibid.* [Hereafter cited as RG 45, plus file number, NA.]

30. Wilson to Hurley and Newton D. Baker, 24 March 1919, as printed in Herbert Hoover, *An American Epic* (two vols., Chicago, 1960), II, pp. 398-399; Levin, *Woodrow Wilson and World Politics,* pp. 139-140, 190-196.

31. Hurley to Wilson, 3 March 1919, Wilson Papers.

32. United States Shipping Board, *Second Annual Report, 1919*

(Washington, D. C., 1919), pp. 10-11, 15, 18-19; "Report of the War Trade Board," 30 June 1919 (Washington, D. C., 1920), p. 182; Department of Commerce, *Merchant Marine Statistics, 1933* (Washington, D. C., 1933), p. 30.

33. Benson to Wilson, 28 April 1919, Josephus Daniels Papers, Manuscript Division, Library of Congress; Benson to Daniels, 6 May 1919, *ibid.*

34. For the clearest expression of Payne's justification, see Payne to Sir Joseph Maclay, 14 October 1919, RG 32/555-8, NA. For background and the State Department's view, see John Foster Dulles memorandum for Lansing, "In Re German Ships," undated [ca. 1-2 October 1919], *ibid.*

35. Polk to Lansing, 30 September 1919, Department of State, File 862.85/109C, National Archives. [Hereafter cited as SD, plus file number, NA.] A pro rata distribution would have given Great Britain 86 per cent of all German vessels confiscated during or after the war.

36. Lansing to Polk, 16 October 1919, SD 862.85/126, NA.

37. E. David Cronin, ed., *The Cabinet Diaries of Josephus Daniels, 1913-1920* (Lincoln, Nebraska, 1963), entry of 21 October 1919, p. 451.

38. Lansing to Polk, 19 November 1919, SD 862.85/146, 3809, NA; "Notes of a Meeting of the Heads of Delegations of the Five Great Powers held in Paris," 17 November 1919, SD 180.03501/94, NA.

39. Payne to Donald, Scott, Rosseter, and Cushing, 17 November 1919, RG 32/555-8, NA; RG 32/Minutes of Proceedings of the USSB, 20 November 1919, NA.

40. R. C. Lindsay to Lansing, 19 December 1919, RG 32/555-8, NA.

41. Lansing to Payne, undated and transferred to Payne on 21 December 1919, *ibid.;* Payne to Lansing, 21 December 1919, *ibid.;* Edith Bolling Wilson to Payne, 23 December [probably should be 21 December], 1919, *ibid.*

42. Remarks before the Senate Committee on Commerce, 21 January 1920, "The Establishment of an American Merchant Marine" (Washington, D. C., 1920), 64th Cong., 2nd Sess., pp. 323, 397-409.

43. Wilson to Polk, 4 March 1920, Wilson Papers.

44. Benson to W. T. Christensen, 21 July 1920, RG 32/618-4, NA.

45. C. J. France to Benson, 19 August 1920, *ibid.*

46. Benson to Wilson, 5 June 1920, RG 32/Benson, NA.

47. *New York Times,* 25 September 1920.

48. *Ibid.,* 30 September 1920. The clause extending the coastal monopoly was also never applied.

49. *Papers Relating to the Foreign Relations of the United States, 1920,* Vol I, vii-xii. This was Wilson's Annual Message, 7 December 1920.

50. Samuel A. Lawrence, *United States Merchant Shipping: Policies and Politics* (Washington, D. C., 1966), p. 41.

51. *New York Times,* 30 September 1920.

52. Benson memorandum, 16 May 1921, RG 45/UB/Benson, NA.

CHAPTER SEVEN

THE BRITISH STRATEGIC INHERITANCE IN AMERICAN NAVAL POLICY, 1775-1975

1. Most standard American diplomatic history textbooks stress Anglo-American differences, particularly throughout the nineteenth century. Intellectual histories, however, show quite strong ideological bonds. See, for example, Robert Kelley, *The Transatlantic Persuasion: The Liberal-Democratic Mind in the Age of Gladstone* (New York, 1969), which stresses a common political philosophy found in Britain, the United States, and Canada, namely that to "foster a sense of international community . . . [and] the protection of international law and morality," a view shared by Thomas Jefferson and Adam Smith, Grover Cleveland and W. E. Gladstone, p. 416 and *passim*. For the colonial period, see Carl Bridenbaugh, *Mitre and Sceptre: Transatlantic Faiths, Ideas, Personalities, and Politics, 1689-1775* (New York, 1962). For the overt development of a widespread American Anglophilia during the late nineteenth century, see Cushing Strout, *The American Image of the Old World* (New York, 1963), pp. 132ff.

2. Among the most important post-World War II studies on the causes of the two Anglo-American wars are Bernhard Knollenberg, *Origin of the American Revolution: 1759-1766* (New York, 1960); Edmund S. and Helen M. Morgan, *The Stamp Act Crisis: Prologue to Revolution* (Chapel Hill, 1953); Benjamin W. Labaree, *The Boston Tea Party* (New York, 1964); Bernard Bailyn, *The Ideological Origins of the American Revolution* (Cambridge, Mass., 1967); Jack M. Sosin, *Agents and Merchants: British Colonial Policy and the Origins of the American Revolution, 1763-1775* (Lincoln, 1965); Bradford Perkins, *Prologue to War: England and the United States, 1805-1812* (Berkeley, 1961); and Reginald Horsman, *The Causes of the War of 1812* (Philadelphia, 1962).

3. John U. Nef, *War and Human Progress* (1950; New York, 1963), p. 328.

4. Alfred Thayer Mahan, *The Influence of Sea Power upon History, 1660-1783* (Boston, 1890), pp. 38-39, 58. For a criticism of this view, see my "The Thalassocratic Determinism of Captain Mahan," in Reynolds and William J. McAndrew, eds., *University of Maine 1971 Seminar in Maritime and Regional Studies* (Orono, Me., 1972), pp. 77-85.

5. In strategic terms, both Great Britain and the United States may be regarded as maritime, blue-water states. See my *Command of the Sea: The History and Strategy of Maritime Empires* (New York, 1974), pp. 3ff, 323, 356ff.

6. Naval officers from David Porter to Ernest J. King at most resented or at least mistrusted the British. See, for example, David F. Long, *Nothing Too Daring: A Biography of Commodore David Porter, 1780-1843*

(Annapolis, 1970), p. 61; see also Ernest J. King and Walter Muir Whitehill, *Fleet Admiral King: A Naval Record* (New York, 1952), pp. 569-570.

7. Russell F. Weigley, *The American Way of War: A History of United States Military Strategy and Policy* (New York, 1973), pp. 77ff; Thomas E. Griess, "Dennis Hart Mahan: West Point Professor and Advocate of Military Professionalism, 1830-1871" (Ph.D. dissertation, Duke University, 1968), p. 290 and *passim.*

8. See, for the French, E. H. Jenkins, *A History of the French Navy* (London, 1973), pp. 38ff, 304-305, and *passim;* see especially Theodore Ropp, "The Development of a Modern Navy: French Naval Policy 1871-1914" (Ph.D. dissertation, Harvard University, 1937), pp. 258ff. Henri Martin's *History of France* greatly influenced Mahan, recalled in the latter's *From Sail to Steam: Recollections of Naval Life* (New York, 1907), pp. 280-282.

9. Reynolds, *Command of the Sea,* pp. 106ff, 214ff, 325ff, 440ff.

10. "Blood is thicker than water," Albion has often remarked. See *Maine Proceedings,* p. 15, in which he attributes the remark to Flag Officer Josiah Tattnall, USN, during the Arrow War in China.

11. Charles Oscar Paullin, *Paullin's History of Naval Administration, 1775-1911* (Annapolis, 1968), pp. 15, 30, 167, 209, 260, 312, 330-331, 420, 432, 434-435; Robert Greenhalgh Albion, "Makers of Naval Policy, 1798-1947," two vols. (unpublished ms., Washington, Office of Naval History, 1950), pp. 750, 753, and *passim.* For the British, see Leslie Gardiner, *The British Admiralty* (London, 1968).

12. J. Wade Caruthers, "The Influence of Maritime Trade in Early American Development: 1750-1830," *The American Neptune,* XXIX, no. 3 (July 1969), p. 204. "By the time of the Revolution New England [colonial] hostility towards the Royal Navy does not appear to have been remarkable in community action or thought, with the possible exception of Rhode Island." Phillip S. Haffenden, "Community and Conflict: New England and the Royal Navy, 1689-1775," unpublished paper delivered at the Twelfth Conference of the International Commission for Maritime History, Greenwich, England (July 1974), p. 6. Also Neil R. Stout, *The Royal Navy in America, 1760-1775: A Study of Enforcement of British Colonial Policy in the Era of the American Revolution* (Annapolis, 1973). Resentment began with the British naval reduction of Falmouth, Maine, in 1775. See Donald A. Yerxa, "Admiral Samuel Graves and the Falmouth Affair: A Case Study in British Imperial Pacification, 1775" (M.A. thesis, University of Maine, 1974), and Ira D. Gruber, *The Howe Brothers and the American Revolution* (New York, 1972).

13. Benjamin W. Labaree, "The Roots of a Maritime Heritage," in Robert G. Albion, William A. Baker, and Labaree, *New England and the Sea* (Middletown, Conn., 1973), p. 43.

14. Adams to the Dutch States General, 8 March 1781, quoted in John J. Kelly, Jr., "The Struggle for American Seaborne Independence as

Viewed by John Adams," (Ph.D. disseration, University of Maine, 1973), p. 148. See also Caruthers, "Influence of Maritime Trade," pp. 199-201, and Arthur Meier Schlesinger, *The Colonial Merchants and the American Revolution, 1763-1776* (New York, 1939), pp. 30-32, 50ff, 91ff, and *passim*.

15. Kelly, "American Seaborne Independence," pp. 190, 281.

16. *Ibid.*, pp. 85, 211-212, 217, 254ff, 265-266, 317, 320, 357; Frederic H. Hayes, "John Adams and American Sea Power," *The American Neptune*, XXV (January 1965), p. 41; Harold and Margaret Sprout, *The Rise of American Naval Power, 1775-1918* (Princeton, 1967), pp. 21, 37; Edward Handler, *America and Europe in the Political Thought of John Adams* (Cambridge, Mass., 1964), pp. 159ff. For the American treatment of the Barbary pirates, see Robert Greenhalgh Albion with Jennie Barnes Pope, *Sea Lanes in Wartime: The American Experience, 1775-1945*, 2nd enl. ed. (Hamden, Conn., 1968), pp. 126ff.

17. Kelly, "American Seaborne Independence," pp. 256-273, 276, 314, 362; Sprouts, *American Naval Power*, pp. 17, 21, 26-27, 37, 53, 56-59, 71; H. A. Washington, ed., *The Writings of Thomas Jefferson*, 9 vols. (Washington, 1853-1854), VIII, pp. 413-414; Caruthers, "Influence of Maritime Trade," p. 204.

18. Letter of 11 March 1812, quoted in Kelly, "American Seaborne Independence," p. 343. See also pp. 150-151.

19. Kelly, "American Seaborne Independence," pp. 275, 280, 284, 321, 351-352.

20. See Richard Glover, "The French Fleet, 1807-1814; Britain's Problems; and Madison's Opportunity," *Journal of Modern History*, 39 (September 1967), pp. 233-252.

21. Albion, *Sea Lanes*, p. 125.

22. Kelly, "American Seaborne Independence," pp. 194, 212.

23. George Selement, "Impressment and the American Merchant Marine, 1782-1812: an American View," *The Mariner's Mirror*, 59, no. 4 (November 1973), p. 415; Albion, *Sea Lanes*, pp. 116-118.

24. Caruthers, "Influence of Maritime Trade," p. 203.

25. Walter Millis, *Arms and Men* (New York, 1956, 1967), p. 49; Sprouts, *American Naval Power*, pp. 43-44, 69.

26. Albion, *Sea Lanes*, p. 34; Labaree in *New England and the Sea*, p. 64.

27. Hayes, "John Adams," pp. 36, 40; Adams to Lafayette, 21 February 1779, cited in Kelly, "American Seaborne Independence," pp. 109-110, also 153. On American naval efforts in the Revolutionary War, see Nathan Miller, *Sea of Glory* (New York, 1974).

28. Dudley W. Knox, *The Naval Genius of George Washington* (Boston, 1932).

29. Kelly, "American Seaborne Independence," pp. 304, 308.

30. Howard I. Chapelle, *The History of the American Sailing Navy* (New York, 1949), pp. 38-39, 120-121, 126, 177-178, 194, 234-235.

31. Albion, "The Golden Age, 1815-1865," in *New England and the Sea,* pp.97-99; Albion, *The Rise of New York Port* [1815-1860] (New York, 1939); Caruthers, "Influence of Maritime Trade," pp. 205-206.

32. See, for example, Van Wyck Brooks, *The Flowering of New England, 1815-1865* (New York, 1940).

33. Millis, *Arms and Men,* p. 71.

34. C. J. Bartlett, *Great Britain and Sea Power, 1815-1853* (Oxford, 1963), pp. 71-73.

35. "The American international position . . . really rested upon the acquiescence, if not the benevolent neutrality, of the Royal Navy."—Millis, *Arms and Men,* p. 99. See also Albion, "Golden Age," pp. 118ff.; Sprouts, pp. 90-91; Kenneth Bourne, *Britain and the Balance of Power in North America, 1815-1908* (Berkeley, 1967), and Barry M. Gough, *The Royal Navy and the Northwest Coast of North America, 1810-1914* (Vancouver, 1971).

36. Sprouts, *American Naval Power,* pp. 95-96; Bartlett, *Great Britain,* pp. 63-64, 77-80, 88-95; James A. Field, Jr., *America and the Mediterranean World, 1776-1882* (Princeton, 1969), pp. 58ff, 104ff, 207ff, 245ff.

37. Bartlett, *Great Britain,* pp. 103ff; Jill Lisk, *The Struggle for Supremacy in the Baltic, 1600-1725* (London, 1967), p. 32.

38. See William A. Morgan, "Sea Power in the Gulf of Mexico and the Caribbean during the Mexican and Colombian Wars of Independence, 1815-1830" (Ph.D. dissertation, University of Southern California, 1969); Maury Davison Baker, Jr., "The United States and Piracy During the Spanish-American Wars of Independence" (Ph.D. dissertation, Duke University, 1946); Albion, "Golden Age," p. 122; Caruthers, "Influence of Maritime Trade," pp. 206-208; Bartlett, *Great Britain,* pp. 65-74; Albion, *Sea Lanes,* pp. 139-146; Edward Warner Billingsley, *In Defense of Neutral Rights: The United States Navy and the Wars of Independence in Chile and Peru* (Chapel Hill, 1967); Richard Carl Froelich, "The United States Navy and Diplomatic Relations with Brazil, 1822-1871" (Ph.D. dissertation, Kent State University, 1971). On antislaving patrols, see Christopher Lloyd, *The Navy and the Slave Trade* (New York, 1949); W. E. F. Ward, *The Royal Navy and the Slavers* (London, 1969); and Earl E. McNeilly, "The United States and the Supression of the West African Slave Trade, 1819-1862" (Ph.D. dissertation, Case Western Reserve University, 1973).

39. Grace Fox, *British Admirals and Chinese Pirates, 1832-1869* (London, 1940); Robert Erwin Johnson, *Thence Round Cape Horn: The Story of United States Naval Forces on Pacific Station, 1818-1923* (Annapolis, 1963); Caruthers, "Influence of Maritime Trade," pp. 208-210; Curtis Talmon Henson, Jr., "The United States Navy and China, 1839-1861" (Ph.D. dissertation, Tulane University, 1965), which dates Anglo-American naval cooperation there from 1853 (p. 187).

40. Quoted in Sprouts, *American Naval Power,* p. 102.

41. Paullin, *Naval Administration,* p. 205. Sprouts, *American Naval*

Power, pp. 139-140, 144-147, attribute part of the reason for Southern interest in the Navy to fear of a possible war in the Gulf of Mexico with Spain, France, and/or Britain.

42. See K. Jack Bauer, *Surfboats and Horse Marines: U.S. Naval Operations in the Mexican War, 1846-48* (Annapolis, 1969) and George E. Buker, *Swamp Sailors: Riverine Warfare in the Everglades, 1835-1842* (Gainesville, Fla., 1975). Jackson, like Jefferson before him, realized the folly of his anti-Navy stance at the end of his administration and admitted it. Sprouts, *American Naval Power,* pp. 106-107, 116, 121ff, and *passim,* a major theme of this classic work being the sectional differences over naval expansion.

43. British diplomacy also accommodated American expansion overland, notably on the Oregon and Texas questions. Rather than develop "experimental squadrons" of their own new warships on the British example, "the British activities were watched with interest" by the Americans. Chapelle, *American Sailing Navy,* pp. 368-370, 405-406.

44. See note 7 above.

45. John B. Heffernan, "The Blockade of the Southern Confederacy: 1861-1865," *The Smithsonian Journal of History,* II, no. 4 (Winter 1967-1968), p. 37; also Theodore Ropp, "Anacondas Anyone?" *Military Affairs,* XXVII, no. 2 (Summer 1963), pp. 71-76.

46. John Lenthall and B. F. Isherwood to the Secretary of the Navy, 17 March 1862, quoted in Sprouts, *American Naval Power,* pp. 159-160.

47. Samuel R. Bright, Jr., "Confederate Coast Defense" (Ph.D. dissertation, Duke University, 1961); see also John D. Hayes, "Sea Power in the Civil War," *U.S. Naval Institute Proceedings,* 87, no. 11 (November 1961), pp. 60-69.

48. Stuart L. Bernath, *Squall Across the Atlantic: American Civil War Prize Cases and Diplomacy* (Berkeley, 1970); Frank J. Merli, *Great Britain and the Confederate Navy* (Bloomington, Ind., 1970); Benjamin Franklin Gilbert, "Naval Operations in the Pacific, 1861-1866" (Ph.D. dissertation, University of California, 1951).

49. Albion, "Golden Age," pp. 105-118, 160; Albion, *Sea Lanes,* pp. 153-173. In the late 1840's Congress briefly subsidized the shipping companies for the dubious strategic reason that new steamers could be converted to warships in emergencies. Sprouts, *American Naval Power,* pp. 133-135. See also William A. Baker, "The Dark Age," in *New England and the Sea,* pp. 161-164, 225-226; and, for a good case study, John E. Chapin, "Impact of the Civil War on Maine Shipping and Shipbuilding" (Unpublished M.A. thesis, University of Maine, 1970).

50. Stanley Sandler, "A Navy in Decay: Some Strategic Technological Results of Disarmament, 1865-69 in the U.S. Navy," *Military Affairs,* XXXV, no. 4 (December 1971), pp. 138-142; Lance C. Buhl, "The Smooth Water Navy: American Naval Policy and Politics, 1865-1876" (Ph.D. dissertation, Harvard University, 1968).

51. Samuel P. Huntington, *The Soldier and the State* (New York,

1957), pp. 222ff. American commerce "could flourish as long as Europe, which usually meant Great Britain, was interested more in markets than in territory."—Kenneth J. Hagan, *American Gunboat Diplomacy and the Old Navy, 1877-1889* (Westport, Conn., 1973), p. 10.

52. To list but a few such incidents, the "*Alabama* claims," the Fenian raids from Canada, the border dispute over the San Juan Islands, the Samoan and Hawaiian ventures, the new American naval base at Bremerton, the Venezuela boundary dispute, and the constant Canadian fears of possible American annexation.

53. French galleys and gunboats were copied from 1798. Chapelle, *American Sailing Navy,* pp. 151-154, 189. In the 1870's the underwater ram preceded the torpedo as a panacea in American naval thought. Sprouts, *American Naval Power,* pp. 173, 174n, and *passim.* Millis, *Arms and Men,* p. 148: "Given both the financial and technological limitations and actual political context of the times, [the naval policy of the 1880's] was by no means so backward or as illogical as it has been represented" by most historians of the period.

54. Nef, *War and Human Progress,* p. 368.

55. See D. M. Schurman, *The Education of a Navy: The Development of British Naval Strategic Thought, 1867-1914* (Chicago, 1965); Arthur J. Marder, *The Anatomy of British Sea Power; A History of Naval Policy in the Pre-Dreadnought Era, 1880-1905* (New York, 1940).

56. Sprouts, *American Naval Power,* p. vii, 182ff, 202ff; Hagan, *American Gunboat Diplomacy,* pp. 5-10, 188, and *passim;* Millis, *Arms and Men,* pp. 147, 158. See also Richard Wellington Turk, "Strategy and Foreign Policy: The United States Navy in the Caribbean, 1865-1913" (Ph.D. dissertation, Fletcher School of Law and Diplomacy, 1968) and Ronald Harvey Spector," 'Professors of War': The Naval War College and the Modern American Navy" (Ph.D. dissertation, Yale University, 1967). For African waters, see Thomas J. Noer, "Commodore Robert W. Shufeldt and America's South African Strategy," *The American Neptune,* XXXIV, no. 2 (April 1974), pp. 81-88.

57. Sprouts, *American Naval Power,* pp. 188, 213; Robert Seager, II, "Ten Years before Mahan: The Unofficial Case for the New Navy, 1880-1890," *Mississippi Valley Historical Review,* 40 (1953-1954), pp. 491-512.

58. Kenneth Bourne and Carl Boyd, "Captain Mahan's 'War' with Great Britain," *U.S. Naval Institute Proceedings,* 94, no. 7 (July 1968), pp. 71-78.

59. John A. S. Grenville and George Berkeley Young, *Politics, Strategy and American Diplomacy: Studies in Foreign Policy, 1873-1917* (New Haven, 1966), p. 307.

60. *Ibid.,* pp. 270ff.

61. Richard D. Challener, *Admirals, Generals, and American Foreign Policy, 1898-1914* (Princeton, 1973), pp. 26, 409, and *passim;* Sprouts, *American Naval Power,* pp. 241-247.

62. Quoted in Challener, *Admirals and Generals,* p. 26.

63. Challener, *Admirals and Generals,* pp. 26-30, 227, 260. For Britain's part, Challener, p. 28, quotes *Brassey's Naval Annual, 1903:* "We do not mean to fight with America, nor she with us; and if war should break out between the two branches of the race, it will be in the nature of a civil war, and against civil wars it is impossible to prepare." See also William Reynolds Braisted, *The United States Navy in the Pacific, 1909-1922* (Austin, 1971), pp. 17-18.

64. An exceptionally good recent account of the origins of this rivalry, 1916-1922, may be found in Braisted, *Navy in the Pacific, 1909-1922,* pp. 171ff.

65. See Basil Collier, *The Lion and the Eagle: British and Anglo-American Strategy, 1900-1950* (New York, 1972). It may be argued that inasmuch as the Royal Navy served as the general model for the Imperial German and Imperial Japanese navies, the constitution and size of the latter two bore on the essential characteristics of the United States Navy as their potential enemy—an indirect but important British influence on American naval policy. See, for example, Patrick James Kelly, "The Naval Policy of Imperial Germany, 1900-1914" (Ph.D. dissertation, Georgetown University, 1970) and John Curtis Perry, "Great Britain and the Imperial Japanese Navy, 1858-1905" (Ph.D. dissertation, Harvard University, 1961).

66. See Baker, "The Twentieth Century," in *New England and the Sea,* pp. 227ff.

67. Arthur J. Marder, *From the Dreadnought to Scapa Flow: The Royal Navy in the Fisher Era, 1904-1914,* 5 vols., I: *The Road to War, 1904-1914* (London, 1961), pp. 40-42; Colonel Roger Willock, USMCR, *Bulwark of Empire: Bermuda's Fortified Naval Base, 1860-1920* (Princeton, 1962) and his "Gunboat Diplomacy: Operations of the North American and West Indies Squadron, 1875-1915," *American Neptune,* XXVIII, no. 1 (January 1968), pp. 5-30, and XXVIII, no. 2 (April 1968), pp. 85-112.

68. Says Albion: "Gradually in both wars, the United States assumed England's role in past Continental conflicts of 'Paymaster of the Allies.' "—*Sea Lanes,* p. 211. See also Nef, *War and Human Progress,* pp. 376-377.

69. Seward W. Livermore, "The American Navy as a Factor in World Politics, 1903-1913," *American Historical Review,* LXIII, no. 4 (July 1958), p. 879. Also, p. 865: "American naval authorities, obsessed by fears of German aggression, made little attempt to conceal their partiality for the Anglo-French combination [Entente of 1903]."

70. See Samuel R. Williamson, Jr., *The Politics of Grand Strategy: Britain and France Prepare for War, 1904-1914* (Cambridge, Mass., 1969); H. I. Lee, "Mediterranean Strategy and Anglo-French Relations, 1908-1912," *Mariner's Mirror,* 57, no. 3 (August 1971), pp. 267-285.

71. Livermore, "World Politics," p. 873.

72. Warner R. Schilling, "Admirals and Foreign Policy, 1913-1919" (Ph.D. dissertation, Yale University, 1953), pp. 30, 68, 84, and *passim;*

Sprouts, *American Naval Power,* pp. 313, 316, 325, 331-334.

73. Sprouts, *American Naval Power,* pp. 259-285.

74. Challener, *Admirals and Generals,* pp. 34ff, 81ff; Grenville and Young, *Politics and Strategy,* pp. 301-304. For United States naval activities in South America beyond the Caribbean, see Seward W. Livermore's two articles, "American Strategy Diplomacy in the South [eastern] Pacific, 1890-1914," *Pacific Historical Review,* XII, no. 1 (March 1943), pp. 33-51, and "Battleship Diplomacy in South America: 1905-1925," *Journal of Modern History,* XVI, no. 1 (March 1944), pp. 31-48.

75. Challener, *Admirals and Generals,* pp. 288-315, 323ff., 379ff.; Schilling, "Admirals and Foreign Policy," *passim;* Sprouts, *American Naval Power,* pp. 251-253; Grenville and Young, *Politics and Strategy,* pp. 304-306, which includes a discussion of initial German war plans against the United States during 1899-1903 (pp. 309-310). See also Marder, *Dreadnought to Scapa Flow,* I, pp. 124-125, 183-184.

76. Challener, *op. cit.,* pp. 288-315, 323ff, 379ff.

77. Schilling, "Admirals and Foreign Policy." pp. 47, 67, 94. The Naval Act of 1916 called for essentially that standard but for the postwar world; Sprouts, *American Naval Power,* pp. 344-347, 359ff.

78. David F. Trask, *Captains and Cabinets: Anglo-American Naval Relations, 1917-1918* (Columbia, Mo., 1972), p. 364.

79. *Ibid.,* p. 361.

80. See Gerald E. Wheeler, "William Veazie Pratt, U.S. Navy: A Silhouette of an Admiral," *Naval War College Review,* XXI, no. 9 (May 1969), pp. 36-61 and Wheeler, *Admiral William Veazie Pratt, U.S. Navy: A Sailor's Life* (Washington, 1974), pp. 89ff.

81. Trask, *Captains and Cabinets,* pp. 360-365 and *passim;* Schilling, "Admirals and Foreign Policy," pp. 97-101; Arthur J. Marder, *From the Dreadnought to Scapa Flow,* V: *1918-1919: Victory and Aftermath* (Oxford, 1970), pp. 121-127. See also Elting E. Morison, *Admiral Sims and the Modern American Navy* (Boston, 1942).

82. Challener, *Admirals and Generals,* pp. 17-18, 30-32. For its history, see Kemp Tolley, *Yangtze Patrol: The U.S. Navy in China* (Annapolis, 1971).

83. William Reynolds Braisted, *The United States Navy in the Pacific, 1897-1909* (Austin, 1958; New York, 1969), p. 244 and *passim.* See also Grenville and Young, *Politics and Strategy,* pp. 311-314; Sprouts, *American Naval Power,* pp. 250ff.

84. This theme constitutes much of Braisted's work, *Navy in the Pacific, 1909-1922,* pp. 3-340. See also Challener, *Admirals and Generals,* pp. 40-41, 179ff, 243ff, 270-288, 367ff; Schilling, "Admirals and Foreign Policy," pp. 70ff; Grenville and Young, *Politics and Strategy,* pp. 314ff; Sprouts, *American Naval Power,* pp. 286ff, 304ff.

85. Braisted, *Navy in the Pacific, 1909-1922,* pp. 343ff. The Benson school continued its suspicions of Britain, while the Sims-Pratt group "held that world peace should be based on a firm understanding between

the two greatest naval powers, Britain and the United States." —p. 410. See also Marder, *Dreadnought to Scapa Flow,* V, pp. 224ff.

86. Stephen Roskill, *Naval Policy Between the Wars: The Period of Anglo-American Antagonisms, 1919-1929* (London, 1968), p. 20. See also George V. Fagan, "Anglo-American Naval Relations, 1927-1937" (Ph.D. dissertation, University of Pennsylvania, 1954).

87. Harold and Margaret Sprout, *Toward a New Order of Sea Power: American Naval Policy and the World Scene, 1918-1922* (Princeton, 1943; New York, 1969), p. 296.

88. Arthur J. Marder, "The Royal Navy and the Ethiopian Crisis of 1935-36," *American Historical Review,* LXXV (June 1970), 1327-1356.

89. Ernest Andrade, "U.S. Naval Policy in the Disarmament Era, 1921-1937" (Ph.D. dissertation, Michigan State University, 1966); Meredith William Berg, "The United States and the Breakdown of Naval Limitation, 1934-1939" (Ph.D. dissertation, Tulane University, 1966), pp. 33-34, 101, and *passim;* John C. Walter, "The Navy Department and the Campaign for Expanded Appropriations, 1933-1938," (Ph.D. dissertation, University of Maine, 1972).

90. Roskill, *Naval Policy,* p. 20. Winston Churchill did not accept the idea of naval parity with the United States until 1939—Albion, "Makers of Naval Policy, 1798-1947," II, 744. From that year American naval participation in World War II grew. See Patrick Abbrazia, "Mr. Roosevelt's Navy: The Little War of the U.S. Atlantic Fleet, 1939-1942" (Ph.D. dissertation, Columbia University, 1972).

91. In the vast literature on Anglo-American strategy during World War II, with particular emphasis on the naval aspects, see all or parts of Samuel Eliot Morison, *History of United States Naval Operations in World War II,* 15 vols. (Boston, 1947-1962); Stephen Roskill, *The War at Sea, 1939-1945,* 3 vols. (London, 1954-1962); Sir James Butler, ed., *History of the Second World War,* 20 vols.: *Grand Strategy,* 6 vols. (London, 1952-1969): King and Whitehill, *Fleet Admiral King;* Fleet Admiral William D. Leahy, USN, *I Was There* (New York, 1950); Robert Beitzell, *The Uneasy Alliance: America, Britain and Russia, 1941-1943* (New York, 1972); Maurice Matloff, *Strategic Planning for Coalition Warfare, 1943-1944* (Washington, 1959); Forrest C. Pogue, *George C. Marshall,* Vols. 2, 3 (New York, 1966, 1973); Winston L. S. Churchill, *The Second World War,* 6 vols. (Boston, 1948-1956); Sir Arthur Bryant, *A History of the War Years Based on the Diaries of Field-Marshal Lord Alanbrooke,* 2 vols. (Garden City, N.Y., 1957-1959).

92. In addition to the above, Albion, "Makers of Naval Policy, 1798-1947," II, 743.

93. See especially Captains Harold Hopkins, RN, *Nice to Have You Aboard* (London, 1964); E. M. Evans-Lombe, "The Royal Navy in the Pacific, *Journal* of the Royal United Service Institute, 92 (August 1947), pp. 333-347; Clark G. Reynolds, *The Fast Carriers: The Forging of an Air Navy* (New York, 1968), pp. 301ff.

94. Vincent Davis, *Postwar Defense Policy and the U.S. Navy, 1943-1946* (Chapel Hill, N.C., 1966), pp. 29-30, 91-92, and *passim*.

95. See Stephen George Xydis, "The American Naval Visits to Greece and the Eastern Mediterranean in 1946—Their Impact on American-Soviet Relations" (Ph.D. dissertation, Columbia University, 1956). During 1945-1947 both nations "thought in terms of an operative Anglo-American accord in any future military crisis. Neither conceived of fighting a major conflict without the assistance of the other."—R. N. Rosecrance, *Defense of the Realm: British Strategy in the Nuclear Epoch* (New York, 1968), p. 50.

96. Sprouts, *Toward a New Order of Sea Power,* pp. 288-289.

97. Rosecrance, *Defense of the Realm,* pp. 1-11, 39-42, 68ff, 233: "It was largely British urging that brought the United States to Western support in 1948 and 1949." See also Admiral J. J. Clark, USN, with Clark G. Reynolds, *Carrier Admiral* (New York, 1967), pp. 258-261.

98. Vice-Admiral B. B. Schofield, RN (Ret.), *British Sea Power: Naval Policy in the Twentieth Century* (London, 1967), pp. 219-220.

99. L. W. Martin, *The Sea in Modern Strategy* (New York, 1967), pp. 55-56. See also Rear Admiral John D. Hayes, USN (Ret.), "*Sine Qua Non* of U.S. Seapower: The Merchant Ship," *U.S. Naval Institute Proceedings,* 91, no. 3 (March 1965), pp. 26-33, and "Patterns of American Sea Power, 1945-1956: Their Portents for the Seventies," *USNI Proceedings,* 96, no. 5 (May 1970), pp. 337-352.

100. Martin, *Sea in Modern Strategy,* p. 171.

101. Schofield, *British Sea Power,* p. 228, quoting himself from an earlier article in *Brassey's*. Rosecrance, *Defense of the Realm,* pp. 15-16, 36-37, 116-119, 151, 250ff.

102. Rosecrance, *Defense of the Realm,* pp. 176-177, 186, 209-213; Michael Howard, "The Classical Strategists," in The Institute for Strategic Studies, *Problems of Modern Strategy* (London, 1970), pp. 54ff; William James Crowe, Jr., "The Policy Roots of the Modern Royal Navy, 1946-1963" (Ph.D. dissertation, Princeton University, 1965), pp. 71ff, 101ff, 147ff, 161ff. For details of these busy years, see Reynolds, *Command of the Sea,* pp. 545ff.

103. Rosecrance, *Defense of the Realm,* pp. 223-224.

104. *Ibid.,* pp. 264-266; Crowe, "Policy Roots of the RN," pp. 161, 180, 199, 202, 222, 230.

105. Rosecrance, *Defense of the Realm,* pp. 266-268.

106. *Ibid.,* pp. 13-14.

107. See Lieutenant Commander Thomas C. Bird, USN, "British East of Suez Policy: A Victim of Economic Necessity," *Naval War College Review,* XXII, no. 8 (April 1970), pp. 54-70; Lieutenant Commander Beth F. Coye, USN, *et al,* "An Evaluation of U.S. Naval Presence on the Indian Ocean," *Naval War College Review,* XXXIII, no. 2 (October 1970), pp. 35-52; Lieutenant Commander R. Kaul, IN (Ret.), "The Indo-Pakistani War and the Changing Balance of Power on the Indian Ocean," *USNI*

Proceedings, 99, no. 5 (May 1973), pp. 172-195.

108. See Hayes, "Patterns of American Sea Power" and his "Sea Power and Sea Law," *USNI Proceedings,* 90, no. 5 (May 1964), pp. 60-67; see also Carl Q. Christol and Charles R. Davis (with Quincy Wright), "Maritime Quarantine: The Naval Interdiction of Offensive Weapons . . . to Cuba, 1962," *American Journal of International Law,* 57 (July 1963), pp. 525-565.

109. James Cable, *Gunboat Diplomacy: Political Applications of Limited Naval Force* (London, 1971), p. 169.

CHAPTER EIGHT

THE ATLANTIC PARADOX

1. *Genesis,* I, 9; VII, IX, 11-17.

2. Edmundo O'Gorman, *The Invention of America* (Bloomington, Ind., 1961), pp. 9-47.

3. Alfred W. Crosby, *The Columbian Exchange* (Westport, Conn., 1972), pp. 4, 20-21.

4. *Ibid.,* p. 22.

5. Peter N. Carroll, *Puritanism and the Wilderness: The Intellectual Significance of the New England Frontier, 1629-1700* (New York, 1969), pp. 28-29.

6. Carroll, *Puritanism,* pp. 38-42.

7. Peter Force, ed., *American Archives* (Washington, D. C., 1837-1853), 4th ser., V, pp. 1275-1276.

8. Oscar Handlin, *The Uprooted,* 2nd edition, (Boston, 1973), p. 48.

9. Robert Louis Stevenson, *The Amateur Emigrant* (New York, 1895), p. 26.

10. Richard M. Dorson, *American Folklore and the Historian* (Chicago, 1971), p. 36.

11. Edmund Burke, *Works,* Little Brown edition (Boston, 1866), II, pp. 125-126.

12. Thomas Paine, *Common Sense* (Philadelphia, 1776), Doubleday Dolphin edition, p. 31.

13. Thomas Paine, *The Pennsylvania Magazine,* January 1775, in Philip S. Foner, ed., *The Complete Writings of Thomas Paine* (New York, 1945), p. 1110.

14. Stanislaus M. Hamilton, ed., *The Writings of James Monroe* (New York, 1902), VI, pp. 339-340.

15. Henry Clay, "Speech on Increase in the Naval Establishment"

(22 January 1812), in James F. Hopkins, ed., *The Papers of Henry Clay* (Lexington, Ky., 1959-), I, p. 619.

16. Bernard Bailyn, "Communications and Trade: The Atlantic in the Seventeenth Century," *Journal of Economic History,* XIII (1953), pp. 378-387.

17. Bailyn, "Communications and Trade," *passim;* also *The New England Merchants in the Seventeenth Century* (Cambridge, Mass., 1955).

18. Benjamin W. Labaree, *Patriots and Partisans: The Merchants of Newburyport, 1764-1815* (Cambridge, Mass., 1962), pp. 207-208.

19. Robert F. Dalzell, "The Rise of the Waltham-Lowell System: Some Thoughts on the Political Economy of Modernization in Ante-Bellum Massachusetts," (mimeographed draft, 1974).

20. Lewis Namier, *England in the Age of the American Revolution* (London, 1930), p. 13.

21. James B. Connolly, *Port of Gloucester* (New York, 1940), p. 332.

22. Herman Melville, *Moby-Dick,* Hendricks House edition, (New York, 1952), p. 59.

Index

(NOTE: Mr. Albion's writings named in this index include only those mentioned in the text. For complete list, see pp. 218-222.)